MUQTADA AL-SADR AND THE FALL OF IRAQ

Muqtada al-Sadr
and the Fall of Iraq

PATRICK COCKBURN

faber and faber

First published in 2008
by Faber and Faber Limited
3 Queen Square London WC1N 3AU

Typeset by Palindrome
Printed in England by Mackays of Chatham, plc

A CIP record for this book
is available from the British Library

ISBN 0–571–23974–0

10 9 8 7 6 5 4 3 2 1

To Janet, Henry and Alexander

Contents

Acknowledgements

When the publisher first asked me to write a book about Muqtada al-Sadr and the Shia of Iraq I regretfully turned him down. I believed the topic he had in mind was extraordinarily interesting, but I feared it would be far too dangerous to carry out research. I wanted to rely wholly on Iraqi eyewitnesses, but I knew that many of them lived in districts of Baghdad or provincial cities that I dared not visit. It was entirely due to the publisher's persistence that I came back to the project, after deciding that I could get the information I needed if I proceeded very carefully and relied on Iraqi intermediaries to contact people I needed to talk to and to carry out many of the interviews. I first went to Iraq in 1977 and over the following thirty years I witnessed a large number of the crises and battles described. In other cases I have relied on Iraqis to ask questions; without their assistance this book could not have been written. I am very grateful to these anonymous helpers whose identities must be concealed for reasons of personal safety.

Thanks are also due to my agent David Miller of Rogers, Coleridge and White and Melanie Jackson in New York. I am also grateful for the assistance of Simon Blundell, the librarian of the Reform Club in London, who has a magical ability to make obscure publications and books appear moments after I asked for them.

Maps

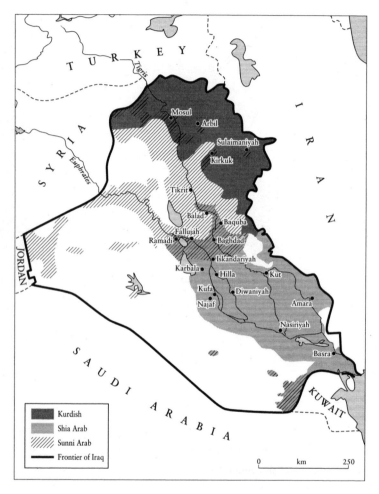

Map of Iraq showing principal ethnic divisions

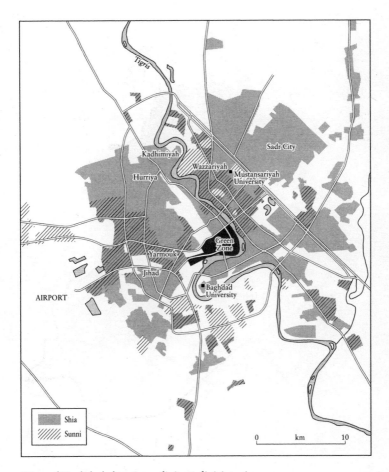

Map of Baghdad showing religious divisions in 2007

CHAPTER ONE

The Road To Kufa

'He's an American spy!' shouted the Mehdi Army militiaman as he leaned in the window of my car and grabbed the red-and-white *keffiyeh*, the Arab headdress I was wearing as a disguise. It was 19 April 2004 and I was trying to get to the holy city of Najaf where Muqtada al-Sadr, the mysterious Shia cleric whose men had seized much of southern Iraq earlier in the month, was under siege by American and Spanish troops. A US general had said he would be killed or captured. I was wearing the *keffiyeh* because the 63-mile long road from Baghdad to Najaf passes through a string of very militant and very dangerous Sunni towns where foreigners had been attacked. I have fair skin and light brown hair but I hoped that the headdress might convince anybody glancing at the car that I was an Iraqi. It was not intended for close inspection.

I should have been more wary. I was travelling in a white Mercedes Benz car of a type not very familiar in Iraq which might easily have attracted attention. I sat in the back to be less conspicuous. In the front passenger seat was Haider al-Safi, a highly intelligent and cool-headed man in his early thirties who was my translator and guide. An electrical engineer by training, he had run a small company fixing photocopying machines in the years before the fall of Saddam Hussein. He lived in the ancient Shia district of Kadhimiyah in Baghdad, site of one of the five great Shia shrines in Iraq. He neither drank nor smoked but was otherwise secular in outlook. My driver was Bassim Abdul-Rahman, a slightly older man with close-cropped hair. A Sunni from west Baghdad, he had shown he had good nerves ten days earlier when we were caught in the ambush of an American fuel convoy near Abu Ghraib on the road to Fallujah. All three of us had got out of the car and lain on the ground until there was a break in the firing when Bassim had driven us slowly and deliberately past bands of heavily armed villagers running to join the fight. I crouched down in the back of the car hoping they did not recognise me as a foreigner.

We had come across the Mehdi Army militiamen in their black shirts and trousers as we approached the city of Kufa on the west bank of the Euphrates river a few miles from Najaf. They were standing or sitting cross-legged in the dust beside the road where it turned off to Kufa before crossing the bridge over the river. They were well-armed young men, carrying Kalashnikov assault rifles and rocket-propelled grenade-launchers slung across their backs and pistols stuck in their belts. Many had ammunition belts filled with cartridges criss-crossed over their chests. There were too many of them for a normal checkpoint. They were edgy because they expected the US troops to attack them at any minute. In the distance I could hear the distant pop-pop of gunfire to the north along the Euphrates.

Checkpoints in Iraq did not at this time have the reputation they later gained of being places of terror, often run by death squads in or out of uniform, looking for somebody to torture and kill. Probably we were too relaxed because the worst danger seemed to be behind us in the grim towns of Mahmoudiyah, Iskandariyah and Latafiyah where permanent traffic jams gave passers-by plenty of time to look us over. There was also a truce. It was the Prophet's birthday and Muqtada's spokesman in Najaf, Sheikh Qais al-Khazali, had declared that there would be no fighting with the Americans for two days in honour of the event and to protect the pilgrims flooding into the city to celebrate it. I had lived long enough in Lebanon during the civil war to have a deep suspicion of truces. When they were declared, as happened frequently, I used to tell friends jokingly: 'It's all over bar the shooting: so keep your head down.' True to form we could already hear the menacing crackle of machine-gun fire coming from somewhere in the date-palm groves around Kufa. But the sound was still intermittent and far away, and was not discouraging the thousands of enthusiastic Shia pilgrims I could see marching on both sides of the road, banging their drums and waving green and black flags as they walked to the shrine of Imam Ali in Najaf. One of the most surprising and attractive aspects of the new Iraq was the popularity among the Shia of pilgrimages that had been banned or limited in number by Saddam Hussein.

Haider told Bassim to stop so we could ask the militiamen if we were on the right road to Kufa – they would know if the Americans were firing on the road – and if they had heard anything about a press conference being given by Qais al-Khazali. They were immediately suspicious. Some ran to the car and started staring at me. It was then that one of them started to yell: 'This is an American! This is a spy!' Things then got worse very fast. They dragged me out of the car and started handing around the *keffiyeh* to each other as evidence of guilt. Haider was trying to say I was Irish and a journalist. It did no good. Other militiamen took up the shout: 'He is an American! He is an American!' Two of the militiamen turned on Haider and said: 'How dare you bring him to the shrine of Imam Ali!' Haider protested he came from a family of sayyids, descendants of the Prophet Muhammad, and furthermore his family originally came from Najaf.

The Mehdi Army men started to go through my brown shoulder bag. I had bought it in Peru three years earlier because it was exactly the right size for carrying the small number of items necessary for a journalist. They found the contents very incriminating as they took out a notebook, a Thuraya satellite phone, which looked like a large black mobile, and a camera. For some reason cameras have always been regarded with deep suspicion by Iraqis as evidence of espionage. The militiamen waved it around saying that I wanted to photograph them and send the photos to the Americans who would then arrest them. They started to push me around and one of them kicked me. I thought they were working themselves up to kill us. Bassim thought so too. 'I believe that if Patrick had an American or English passport they would have killed us all immediately,' he said later.

One of the militiamen was peering at me suspiciously and suddenly sniffed. He pointed at me and said: 'He is drunk; he drank alcohol before coming here.' A second Mehdi Army man turned on Haider and accused him of drinking alcohol with foreigners. Bridling at this, Haider, who was losing no chance to stress his Shia credentials, shot back: 'How dare you accuse me of coming to the Holy City drunk when I don't drink and come from a sayyid's family? If I was drunk you would smell the alcohol.'

While this curious argument was going on – the militiamen probably had no idea what alcohol smelled like – two of the angriest men were trying to hustle me into a separate car. I thought if they did succeed in driving me away they would in all likelihood shoot me. I put my hand flat on the chest of one of them and pushed him back firmly but I was also very eager to avoid a fight. Nobody seemed to be in charge of this Mehdi Army detachment and there was no reason why one of them should not decide to end the argument there and then with his pistol or Kalashnikov. They looked like men who killed very easily.

They asked, reasonably enough, why I was wearing a *keffiyeh*. Haider explained that it was 'to avoid kidnappers in Latafiyah'.

'Are you scared for your money?' asked one of the Mehdi Army.

'It is for our life, not just our money,' Haider replied. He kept repeating that we had come to meet Qais al-Khazali, the one aide to Muqtada of whom we hoped they might have heard. Finally, to my intense relief, one of the militiamen said that they would take us to the main mosque in Kufa and 'the sheikh [a Shia cleric] will decide what to do with you'. There was a casualness about our reprieve just as there had been a chilling casualness about the way they had come close to killing us a few moments earlier. Bassim asked if he could drive our Mercedes to wherever they wanted us to go but the man said: 'No, you are hostages.' Three gunmen clutching their weapons and festooned with ammunition pouches crammed into our car. We followed a second car, also filled with fighters, which made for the green-domed mosque of Imam Ali in the centre of Kufa. Haider was crushed against the door of our car so he could hardly speak. Nevertheless he kept talking, he told me later, in order to make us appear less strange to our captors. There was no doubt about their commitment to Muqtada's cause. They were poor men. Most came, not from Kufa or Najaf, but the great Shia shantytown in east Baghdad that had once been called Thawra, then Saddam City and within the last year had been renamed Sadr City after Muqtada's revered father Muhammad Sadiq al-Sadr, assassinated with two of his sons in Najaf on the orders of Saddam Hussein in 1999. It was less a district than a twin-city to Baghdad and its two million impoverished people were the core of Muqtada's movement.

One man in the car explained fervently that joining the battle was the most the most important thing in his life. 'I left my wife who has just given birth to our daughter so I could come here and fight for Muqtada,' he said. 'I took up a collection from my friends so I could get transport here.' Turning to Haider he asked: 'If you are from a sayyid's family you are a cousin of Muqtada's so why don't you fight for him too? If either of us dies we will be martyrs.'

'Everybody must play his role in life,' replied Haider. 'You are fighting while I'm writing about your fight and tell the facts about American defeats and crimes.' Bassim was meanwhile berating them for threatening to kill a disabled man – myself – since they could see I walked with a severe limp (the result of catching polio as a child in 1956).

Our car stopped on a patch of open ground outside the Imam Ali mosque, named after the son-in-law and cousin of the Prophet. It was here that Muqtada, wearing a white shroud to show he was ready to die, had delivered a sermon two days earlier, defying the gathering US forces and saying: 'I am ready to face martyrdom.' The gunmen ordered Haider and Bassim out of the car and took them through a door into the mosque. I did not like us being split up but I was reassured by the fact that the militiamen were becoming less aggressive. One of them offered me a cigarette and, though I had given up smoking, this did not seem a good moment to reject a friendly gesture. I chain-smoked five cigarettes one after another. Another gunman discovered a copy of the *The New Yorker* I had been reading lying on the back seat and leafed through it. At the sight of a cartoon of a woman in a low-cut blouse he muttered '*haram*' (forbidden) and peered at it for a long time. Inside the mosque Haider was being interrogated politely by a well-educated man who called himself Sayyid Abbas. 'I don't know anything about a truce,' he told Haider, confirming my scepticism about the ceasefire we had heard about in Baghdad . 'You shouldn't have taken the risk of coming because there's fighting here and this is a battlefield.' Getting up he gave Haider some tea and brought me a glass of orange juice to drink in the car. Suddenly we were being smothered in politeness. 'We Iraqis don't want war,' Abbas told me, 'but the Americans want our oil and the Israelis want to rule the Middle East. As for you we want just to be sure that you are who say you are. Don't worry. We'll take you to Najaf.' My belongings were all returned aside from my satellite phone, which I saw a gunman in black Arab robes tucking into his belt. I thought of demanding it back but was so relieved that we had got away with our lives that I did not want to start a fresh dispute.

Sayyid Abbas got into his own car to drive ahead of us so we would not be stopped by other Mehdi Army militiamen. He was immediately proved wrong in saying our worries were over. We had only gone a few hundred yards and were

driving past the high white wall of another mosque called the
Muslim bin Qaleel on the outskirts of Kufa when there was a
staccato burst of gunfire. It seemed to come from a heavy
machine gun on the far bank of the Euphrates. I could see the
bullets smashing into the masonry of the wall above our
heads, sending little chips of plaster flying into the air. At the
sound of the first shots the marching pilgrims began to run
down the road in panic, clutching their flags and drums as
they looked desperately for cover. We had the same idea and
swerved off the road so we could shelter behind the far side
of the mosque. Above us black-clad gunmen raced along the
top of the walls to take up firing positions. A commander,
waving his pistol, was shouting orders to them. In the face of
this common threat to all of us the gunmen, who earlier in
the day had debated whether or not to kill us, appeared keen
to win us over to their point of view. There was one point
they kept on repeating as if it mattered a lot to them. 'It is
wrong,' they asserted, 'for people to call us a militia: we are
an army.' The distinction in their eyes was that they were not
just a Shia defence force but a real army in the service of
Islam and the most revered leader of the faithful on earth,
Muqtada al-Sadr.

Shielded by the mosque, we waited for the firefight to end.
I thought about Muqtada and why he was able to inspire
young men to borrow small sums of money to go to fight
and, if necessary, die for him. The Iraqi police and the army
the US was trying to rebuild were notorious for taking their
pay while making very clear they did so only in order to
support their families and without the intention of being
killed for anybody. President Bush and Tony Blair repeatedly
stated that American and British troops would leave when
Iraqis were ready to take over. They never seemed to
understand that the problem was not training or equipment
but legitimacy and loyalty. Few Iraqis outside Kurdistan felt
that the US-led occupation was legitimate and they therefore
did not give their loyalty to it or the Iraqi governments it
sponsored. Sayyid Abbas might be leading an undisciplined

and dangerous rabble, but they believed their cause was not only right but sanctioned by God, and they were willing to die for it.

The firing on the other side of the Muslim bin Qaleel mosque finally died away. We peered gingerly around the corner but could not see much because of the broad green leaves of the many date palms growing on the banks of the Euphrates. The pilgrims began to return to the road to resume their journey. Nobody had been killed or wounded and many were laughing with relief. Sayyid Abbas got back in his car and led us towards Najaf. He drove very fast. It was obvious that we would not have got through without his help. There were many other Mehdi Army checkpoints blocking the road and several times gunmen ran forward to stop us but waved us through as soon as Sayyid Abbas leaned out of the window of his car and they saw his face.

Najaf was not far away. In 661 AD Imam Ali, the son-in-law and first cousin of the Prophet Muhammad, whose followers became the first Shia, had been assassinated by a dissident Muslim called Ibn Muljam wielding a poisoned sword that struck him on his head as he entered the doorway of a mosque in Kufa to perform the morning prayer. The blade was partly deflected by the wooden frame of the door so Ali was only badly wounded and did not die for two days.[1] There was time for him to tell his followers that when he died his body was to be strapped to the back of a white camel, which was to be allowed to wander where it wanted. Where it finally stopped they were to dig his grave. The camel did not roam far. Six miles south of Kufa, on the edge of the desert, it stood still and Ali was buried on the spot. Over the centuries his tomb became a shrine and Najaf grew up around it, the true centre of Shia Islam, the home of its most revered leaders and the longed-for destination of millions of pilgrims.

I always found Najaf an entrancing city, one of the strangest in the world. It is a dusty place on the edge of the desert, always short of water in the past, unlike Kufa on the cool-looking banks of the Euphrates. The road linking the two small cities runs between tawdry modern villas and looks no better than depressing ribbon development in the rest of Iraq. But suddenly in the distance the visitor sees the golden dome and minarets of the great shrine where Ali lies buried. It springs into view like a burst of sunlight in the sky as it rises above the low buildings of brown brick that surround it. People, groping to explain the significance of Najaf, would sometimes describe it as 'the Vatican of the Shia', but this is true only in the loosest of senses. Unlike the Vatican in Rome the shrine of Ali is not surrounded by architectural marvels but by a *suq* or bazaar, its small shops and battered corrugated iron roofs shabby even by Iraqi provincial standards. The outside walls of the shrine are of brick and are pierced by gates adorned with mosaics portraying birds and flowers that lead into a wide stone-paved courtyard surrounding the shrine. It is often filled with pilgrims, most very poor, the women all dressed in black, sitting on the ground eating from packages of food they have brought with them. They queue quietly to enter the shrine itself, bright with neon lights reflecting from mirrors and mosaics.

I first visited Najaf in 1977, guided by an amiable young man from the Ministry of Information in Baghdad called Adnan Sabri. A Christian and a committed, if naïve, Baathist, he spoke sincerely of Saddam Hussein as the great secular moderniser and showed me around Najaf as if we were visiting Stonehenge or the Pyramids, picturesque survivals from earlier times but irrelevant to the development of the Iraq of tomorrow. Even so his confidence faltered at the doors of the shrine and he said that, since both us were non-Muslims, it would perhaps be best not to enter. Adnan turned out to be wrong about the place of both Saddam and Najaf in Iraqi history. Within three years the great leader, by now president of Iraq, had started a long and bloody war with Iran that left little money for developing anything else in the country. When Saddam was hanged in Baghdad at the end of December 2006 it was the Shia religious leaders in their modest houses in Najaf who held the future of the country in their hands. Some of the witnesses to Saddam's execution chanted 'Muqtada! Muqtada!' as he went to his death.[2]

I had other memories of the shrine. During the bombing of the Iraqi army in Kuwait by the US-led coalition in 1991 I would go there to look at sad processions carrying the cheap wooden coffins, draped with the Iraqi flag, containing the bodies of dead soldiers. Desperate to conceal its military losses, the regime insisted that mourning be kept to a minimum, but it did not dare prevent families carrying their dead sons into the shrine before they were buried in Wadi al-Salaam, Najaf's vast cemetery which stretches over twelve square miles. The largely Sunni regime in Baghdad always distrusted the Shia masses and their religious leaders, but was wary of provoking them. Its suspicion of their loyalty was correct. A few months later I was back in Najaf, permitted to go there by an Iraqi government eager to tell the world it had crushed the Shia uprising which, in March 1991, had followed Saddam's shattering defeat in Kuwait. The pale stone flags of the courtyard were pitted where mortar rounds or rocket-propelled grenades had landed and the blasts had torn off some of the tiles around the shrine. The only people there were tough-looking soldiers in their camouflage uniforms. At this time the Iraqi army was showing how far it had advanced by putting up pictures of Saddam. On a chair on a pile of rubble at the entrance to the shrine soldiers had placed a ludicrously inappropriate picture of the leader. It showed him in tweeds climbing a mountain slope in what looked like Austria, the whole scene reminiscent of a scene from *The Sound of Music* with Saddam about to burst into song.

Najaf's buildings are not the sole reason it is such an extraordinary place. The great shrine does not have the splendour of the Taj Mahal or the Dome of the Rock in

Jerusalem. Kufa, Najaf and Kerbala, another shrine city 50 miles to the north, make such a strong impression because it was here, in a small area west of the Euphrates, that so many of the dramas and tragedies of early Islam were played out 1,400 years ago. It is not just that Ali was murdered and buried here. In Kerbala are the tombs of his sons Imam Hussein and Abbas who died, betrayed by their friends and hopelessly trapped by their enemies, in their last battle in 680 AD. The great festivals and rituals of the Shia revolve around commemorating the tragedy of their deaths much as Christians commemorate the crucifixion of Christ.

What makes Najaf so different from Jerusalem and Rome is that the martyrdoms here have never ended. The Shia religious leaders who congregated in the city lived on the edge of the torture and death under Saddam. Many of them were killed with hideous cruelty in his prisons. Others had disappeared, taken out into the desert to be shot, or else they endured a living death in one of his dungeons. Ayatollah Muhammad Baqir al-Sadr, a leading thinker of Shia Islam and a resolute opponent of the Baath party, had been tortured and executed by Saddam along with his sister in 1980. He became known as 'The First Martyr' or Sadr I. Muqtada, a cousin of the Ayatollah, went on to marry his daughter in 1994. The father of Muqtada, Muhammad Sadiq al-Sadr, had received their mutilated bodies and buried them in Najaf in 1980. Sadiq then built up the Sadrist movement in the 1990s until he in turn was assassinated with two of his sons and became known as 'The Second Martyr' or Sadr II. The semi-divine attributes of his father and father-in-law were crucial to the rise of Muqtada and to the awe with which he was regarded by his followers.

In the wake of the uprising in April 1991 I was brought by Ministry of Information officials to see the Grand Ayatollah Abu al-Qasim al-Khoei, the leading figure in the Shia hierarchy, in his home beside the Euphrates in Kufa. A white-bearded man in his nineties he had played little part in the rebellion but was under house arrest. Twelve years later, soon after the US invasion, I was back in Najaf looking at the room pockmarked with bullet holes where the Grand Ayatollah's son, Sayyid Majid al-Khoei, whom I had come to know and esteem in London, had been trapped by an armed and angry mob reportedly led by followers of Muqtada. When he gave himself up he was hacked to death in a street outside the shrine.

The blood of the martyrs is famously the seed of the church. The Shia religious leaders had shed blood in torrents under Saddam and were to go on doing so. This helped give them an authority in their community which Shia politicians, exiled after fleeing Iraq and deemed by many Iraqis, sometimes unfairly, to have spent their years abroad cavorting in five-star hotels, could never match. In the summer of 2003 I had gone to a narrow alleyway in Najaf, halfway along which was the house of Grand Ayatollah Ali al-Sistani. There was a long line of people waiting outside the door to hand in petitions or seeking an interview. The leader of the Shia community since the death of al-Khoei, al-Sistani was the most influential figure in Iraq. American officials in Baghdad knew of his importance though he refused to meet them. At the same time these arrogant men could never quite take on board that this ageing cleric in his seventies, sitting on a frayed carpet, was going to play a far more important role than themselves in determining the future of Iraq.

On the day in April 2004 when Haider, Bassim and myself entered Najaf after our nasty experience with the Mehdi Army, the mood was a peculiar mixture of religious celebration and warlike preparations. Thousands of pilgrims were happily sitting on the ground in front of the Imam Ali shrine watching ritual dances of mourning by a troop of men striking their backs with symbolic metal flails to the beat of an enormous drum and the chanting of prayers. But there were also fighters with their machine guns and bulging ammunition pouches wandering through the knots of pilgrims. At the end of one street we heard cheering. The skirmish by the Muslim bin Qaleel mosque in Kufa that had forced us to take cover earlier in the day turned out to have been with American and not Spanish troops as we had supposed. The 200-strong Spanish contingent was being withdrawn by the new government in Madrid that opposed involvement in Iraq. It was a newly arrived American unit that had been doing the shooting. Some of its men had advanced too far towards the Mehdi Army positions and had been forced to abandon an armoured vehicle. Its burned out remains were now being displayed as a trophy in the streets of Najaf to delighted applause from gunmen and pilgrims.

We finally located the press conference with Sheikh Qais al-Khazali, Muqtada's spokesman, which was taking place in the open courtyard of a dilapidated building near the shrine that could only be reached by clambering up broken brick steps. I spoke to al-Khazali, a tall unsmiling man in grey robes, and asked him if he expected the Americans to launch an offensive into the heart of Najaf. 'I think the Americans understand about Iraq's holy places,' he said. 'I don't think they are so stupid as to attack us.' Having seen Paul Bremer, the US viceroy in Iraq, in action over the previous year I was by no means so confident about relying on his wisdom or restraint. Most American military and political leaders in Baghdad underestimated the capacity of Iraqis, both Shia and Sunni, to cause them trouble. During his year in power as virtual dictator of Iraq Bremer showed a peculiarly bovine inability to learn from his mistakes. On this occasion, however, with the Sunni insurrection escalating by the day, even he and his advisers hesitated to storm Najaf and provoke a wider rebellion by the Shia community.

I have given an account in some detail of what happened to us on the road to Najaf on a single day in April 2004 because it was an ominous foretaste of what was to come.[3] In the following years thousands of Iraqis were to die because they were stopped at checkpoints just like the one that we had encountered. By the end of 2006, the UN, employing Iraqi government figures from the Health Ministry and the

Baghdad morgue, reported that some 3,000 civilians were being killed every month. Iraqis began to carry two sets of identity papers, one showing that they were Sunni and the other that they were Shia. Faked papers avoided identifiably Sunni names like 'Omar' or 'Othman'. Shia checkpoints started carrying out theological examinations to see if a person with Shia papers was truly familiar with Shia ritual and history and was not a Sunni in disguise. Many of the dangerous young men manning these checkpoints came from Sadr City and belonged, or claimed to belong to, the Mehdi Army just like the detachment we had met. It was true, if Haider had been less persuasive or I had been carrying an American or British passport they would certainly have killed us.

There is a final reason for dwelling on our brief abduction by the Mehdi Army. Complicated though Iraq is, both as a country and a society, it is possible to set out the main themes of its politics before and after the invasion in a way that is comprehensible to those who have not experienced Iraq at first hand during this time. It is far more difficult to convey the atmosphere of permanent fear in which Iraqis lived. 'Can a man who is warm understand a man who is freezing?' asks Alexander Solzhenitsyn in *One Day in the Life of Ivan Denisovitch*. A similarly deep emotional chasm separates those who are afraid from those who are not. The divide is not only between different individuals. Seconds after the few occasions I thought my life truly in danger in Iraq I found it impossible to recapture the emotion of terror I had felt at the time. Nor did I try very hard to do so, because I wanted to forget such grim moments as quickly as possible. But it is worth remembering that Iraq was full of people who had every reason to be terrified both before and after Saddam Hussein was overthrown. The Mehdi Army militiamen we met outside Kufa were trigger-happy and suspicious because they knew they would soon have to fight better-armed and better-trained American and Spanish troops. They feared, rightly, that many of them would be killed.

In Baghdad I would see parents become frantic with fear if they could not immediately find their children at the school near my hotel because they instantly suspected they had been kidnapped. Once I watched police commandos terribly wounded by a suicide bomb being carried on stretchers into Yarmouk hospital in west Baghdad. Their faces were hidden by black masks and they were more worried that these would be removed while they were under anaesthetic, revealing their identity, than they were by the thought that their mangled legs or arms might be amputated. Over the coming years the number of Iraqis killed and wounded each month came to be seen as a barometer of the gravity of the war in Iraq, but these raw casualty figures did not begin to convey the sense of misery and fear that was engulfing the country. By June 2007 the UN High Commission for Refugees was announcing bleakly: 'The situation in Iraq continues to worsen with more than two million Iraqis believed to be displaced inside Iraq and another 2.2 million sheltering in neighbouring states.'[4] By then the Mongol invasion of 1258 was the only cataclysm in the last one thousand years of Iraq's history comparable to the disasters that have followed the invasion of 2003.

I hoped but did not really expect to see Muqtada in Najaf. I had heard he was moving from house to house. This was scarcely surprising since US generals had spoken glibly of killing him and evidently believed that, if he disappeared, so would many of their problems in dealing with the Iraqi Shia. It was already evident that Paul Bremer, the US army and the Iraqi politicians in Baghdad had grossly underestimated the strength of Muqtada and the Sadrist movement which he led.

Muqtada was a figure of mystery in April 2004 and has largely remained so until the present day. The foreign media had commonly called him a 'maverick' though his main policies, such as his hostility to the US occupation, have been unwavering. Another journalistic cliché frequently used to describe him is 'firebrand cleric', but in practice he has proved a cautious and skilful politician, knowing when to advance and when to retreat. Commentary on Muqtada has come to admit his importance though it usually demonises or belittles him, veering between presenting him as a clerical gangster or as a successful demagogue of limited intelligence and ability who somehow leads the only mass movement in Iraqi politics.

Part of the mystery about Muqtada has its origin in simple ignorance. Few non-Iraqis have much idea of the rich and complex history of Shiism in Iraq. 'The Americans seem to think,' a Shia friend once snapped at me, 'that the history of Iraq started when they invaded in 2003.' This is not quite fair, but it is true that very few people outside the Iraqi Shia community understood the religious, political and social forces that produced the Sadrist movement. The sudden emergence of Muqtada as a powerful figure at the time of the fall of Saddam is only astonishing if one does not know this background and above all the bloody and dramatic story of resistance to Saddam Hussein by the Iraqi Shia as a whole and the al-Sadr family in particular. Readers may be surprised that in a biography of Muqtada al-Sadr the chief protagonist should only take centre stage in chapter nine. But the delay in his appearance is wholly necessary. Muqtada and his followers are intensely religious and see themselves as following in the tradition of martyrdom in opposition to tyranny established when Hussein and Abbas were killed by the Umayyads on the plains of Kerbala 1,400 years ago. Little about the Sadrists or modern Iraq will be explicable without an understanding of the Shia faith. Moreover, the heroic resistance of the Shia to Saddam is little known because so many of the protagonists were killed or, if they survived, never related what had happened to them. I was in Iraq just before and just after the great Shia intifada, or uprising, of 1991 and wrote what I could about it. I thought that in the coming years others would gather more information about the rebellion in which some 150,000 Shia Iraqis were killed. To my surprise few detailed accounts of the fighting, so important to the more recent history of Iraq, have been published hitherto, which is why I have described the uprising in some detail.

Biographies of individuals normally include an account of their family background and some reflections on how far this influenced their character. There is no doubt that Muqtada wholly identifies with his father, Sadr II, and father-in-law, Sadr I, to the point that his own personality and beliefs become shadowy. Muqtada and his advisers are acutely conscious of the reasons behind their political appeal. Posters pasted on every wall in Kufa and Najaf on the day we were there in 2004 illustrated the sources of Muqtada's popularity. The red, white and black Iraqi flag formed the background, in front of which stood the figures of three men in dark clerical robes: Muqtada himself, his father and father-in-law. The power of this blend of religion and patriotism among the Iraqi Shia was to be demonstrated many times in the years to come but it first displayed its strength in April 2004.

The mystery surrounding Muqtada's personality has another source. Shia sages and leaders have traditionally been old men. He needed to cultivate the gravitas of a man who stood close to God though he was born on 12 August, 1973 and was only thirty years old when he first confronted the US army in Najaf. His father could tell jokes to his followers, but there are no accounts of Muqtada doing the same. His opponents later claimed that his father ignored him, but in fact he played a central role in his father's political and religious organisation during the 1990s. Few people in Iraq had more on-the-ground experience of organising the Shia masses. After the assassination of his father and two brothers in 1999, he only survived by persuading Saddam Hussein that he was too simple-minded to present a threat. Stories of his incapacity may well have been spread, and certainly not denied, by his own family to keep him alive. Few people can have lived so long knowing that each day could end with their death. The picture that emerges is of a man who is highly intelligent though moody and suspicious. It is notable that no rivals to him have emerged within his inner circle. And there was another aspect to his character that was not obvious during his first armed clashes with the Americans in April 2004: he was a man who learned from his mistakes. He might wear the white martyr's shroud, but after the battles for Najaf he always sought to avoid struggles he did not control and could not win.

The energy with which US officials and their Iraqi allies demonised Muqtada was perhaps because he personified the broader dilemma facing the US occupation from the moment it began. The stated US objective in the war was to overthrow Saddam Hussein. But if he was to be replaced by a democratically elected government then this was inevitably going to be dominated by the Shia, since they make up 60 per cent of the population. They believed their day had come. And not only was the government going to be Shia, but it would be led by religious parties with links to Iran. Muqtada represented the ultimate American nightmare in Iraq. They had not got rid of Saddam only to see him replaced by a black-turbaned virulently anti-American Shia cleric. What-ever reason the US had invaded Iraq for, it was not for this.

CHAPTER TWO

The Shia of Iraq

In April 2003, the US troops who had just captured Baghdad and overthrown Saddam Hussein saw a strange sight that they did not understand. All over central and southern Iraq more than a million Iraqis had taken to the roads and started walking towards the holy city of Kerbala. The journey took them between three and five days and they often slept in the fields at night. Many of the pilgrims carried green flags as the symbol of Imam Ali or black flags as a sign of mourning. Others bore once-green palm fronds that were turning yellow as they dried in the intense heat of the Iraqi plain. Young men poured out of the great Shia stronghold, now called Sadr City (a fortnight earlier it had been Saddam City) in Baghdad and headed for Kerbala 60 miles away. Straggling along the roads from other parts of Iraq were knots of people representing every Shia city, town and village in the country. Often the pilgrims were accompanied by an elderly vehicle, usually a battered white pick-up van, carrying their food and a few people too old or sick to walk. The mood was buoyant and confident but they were not celebrating the fall of the Baathist regime, though if it had still been in power the giant assembly could scarcely have taken place. The pilgrimage was in fact the first demonstration of the ability of Muqtada al-Sadr to mobilise great masses of pious Shia. In his first Friday sermon in his martyred father's mosque in Kufa on 11 April Muqtada, liberally quoting his father's words, had called for people to walk on foot to Kerbala as a sign of their faith.[1]

The American troops who sped past the walkers in their trucks would have been surprised to learn that the people walking beside the road were commemorating a battle. It was not one that had just been fought as the American army advanced north, but a battle that had taken place 1,400 years earlier at Kerbala. In military terms it was no more than a skirmish that ended in a massacre. But it was here, nor far from the Euphrates, that the great Shia martyr Imam Hussein and his warrior half-brother, Abbas, had been killed in 680 AD. The grandson of the Prophet Muhammad and the son of Ali, assassinated in Kufa nineteen years earlier, Hussein was overwhelmed with his small caravan of solders and family members by the greatly superior forces sent against them by their arch-enemy Yazid, the devilish ruler of Damascus and Hussein's rival to be ruler of the Muslim world. It is this battle at Kerbala which is at the centre of the Shia faith. The story of what happened so long ago on the banks of the Euphrates has become a symbol, like the crucifixion in Jerusalem for Christians, of the eternal conflict between good and evil. The legend of the death of Hussein, Abbas and their followers tells of courage, martyrdom and redemption through sacrifice on one side; and betrayal, cruelty and violence on the other. It is the tale, too, of a righteous minority against a powerful but evil government authority.

The pilgrimage I saw on the roads around Baghdad in the days following its capture was the Arba'in, which marks the fortieth day of mourning after Imam Hussein's martyrdom. In any country of the world at any time so many pilgrims on the roads at once would have been a striking event. The processions and marches dwarfed in size the Roman Catholic religious processions in Mexico. They were hundreds of times larger than those that I had seen as a child in Ireland where the columns of carefully ordered marchers belonging to religious organisations blocked the main street of Youghal, the small town where I was born in county Cork. But what made this pilgrimage unique was not only its size but its timing: it was taking place within days of the end of a war.

The roads were not safe. Burned-out Iraqi tanks had only just stopped smouldering beside the road. Well-armed looters were still active, their trucks piled high with stolen property. Edgy American soldiers were beginning to earn a grim reputation among Iraqis for opening a torrent of fire at anything that made them feel nervous.

Astonishing though the Arba'in may have been, it passed almost unnoticed in the US and Western Europe. This was a pity because what we were seeing was of great significance for the future of Iraq. The throngs of people answering Muqtada's call and making their way to Kerbala were the first open display of the strength of the Shia of Iraq, who made up 16 million out of the country's total population of 27 million. The giant pilgrimage showed their religious commitment, their solidarity as a community, and their ability to mobilise vast numbers. The US, supremely confident after its easy initial victory, was about to try to fill the power vacuum left by the fall of the old regime itself. Pre-war plans for an Iraqi provisional government were cast aside. 'Occupiers always call themselves liberators,' said my friend the Kurdish leader Sami Abdul-Rahman disgustedly when told just before the war that America's plans for democracy in Iraq had been put on hold. Nobody in Washington paid any attention to the pilgrims, numerous though they were, or foresaw that they were serious competitors to the US for control of Iraq.

Perplexity among American soldiers over the religious rituals of Iraqis did not diminish over the coming years. The next Arba'in came in April 2004. A year into the occupation, the mood was angrier in the Shia community. On 2 March Sunni insurgents had planted five bombs in Kerbala and Kadhimiyah that killed 270 worshippers and injured 570. The confrontation between the Mehdi Army and the US military was escalating by the day. The American forces were having great difficulty in distinguishing between the Mehdi Army and pilgrims marching across Iraq waving green flags to commemorate Arba'in. One day in early April I was driving on the main road on the northern outskirts of

Baghdad when I saw that a heavily armed US patrol had herded about a hundred Iraqis into a field and forced them to sit down. The American soldiers were eyeing their captives with suspicion and demanding to know why they were carrying green banners. It turned out the pilgrims came from the town of Dujail, one of the few Shia centres north of Baghdad. It was famous as the place where Shia fighters had tried to assassinate Saddam Hussein in 1982 and 147 townspeople had subsequently been executed or tortured to death in retaliation. It was for this crime that Saddam Hussein was hanged on 31 December 2006.

We came across a group of six men carrying a green flag walking beside a date-palm grove near a main road. They turned out to come from Sadr City and were very willing to talk. A slightly built man wearing black clothes, who seemed to be their leader, said his name was Hamid al-Ugily and that he and his friends were spending two or three days walking to Kerbala. Surprisingly, he said he had made the pilgrimage under Saddam but had had to do so secretly, walking mainly at night. He showed no gratitude to the Americans for overthrowing the old dictator. 'The Americans are just as bad as Saddam Hussein,' he said. 'We think they will attack Muqtada in Najaf. We will defend our religious leaders.' These opinions were not unexpected. The occupation was becoming ever more unpopular among the Shia. I asked the pilgrims what jobs they held and the answers they gave underlined the fragility of the Americans' hold on Iraq. All six men said they were soldiers in the Iraqi Civil Defence Corps (ICDC). This paramilitary body, created by the Coalition Provisional Authority, was supposed to take over duties currently being carried out by American soldiers. Abbas, one of the marchers, said: 'I have been in the ICDC one year and the Americans didn't do anything for Iraq.' The ICDC was just the first of a series of Iraqi military and paramilitary organisations created by the US on whose loyalty it found it could not rely.

*

I had visited Kerbala, the site of the golden-domed shrines to Hussein and Abbas, a few weeks after it was recaptured by the Iraqi army in March 1991 after the Shia had risen up in the wake of Saddam Hussein's defeat in Kuwait. The desperation of the Shia rebels besieged by Saddam Hussein's Republican Guard cannot have been so different from that of the outnumbered followers of Hussein and Abbas trapped in the same place in 680 AD. The original martyrs of the Shia faith likewise knew that they could expect no mercy from their murderous enemy. In both cases defeat was inevitable. Iraq is full of the ghosts of terrible tragedies, both recent and buried in the distant past, but nowhere do they jostle one so closely as in Kerbala, Najaf and Kufa. Here, just to the west of the Euphrates, the death by assassination or in battle of the progenitors of the Shia faith was mirrored by the persecution and massacre of their followers during the thirty-five-year rule of Saddam Hussein.

The Mesopotamian plain is the birthplace of civilisation where writing was discovered, but few Iraqis identify with Ur of the Chaldees, the Babylonians or Nebuchadnezzar and the Assyrian empire. (An exception was Saddam Hussein who portrayed himself as being in the tradition of Iraq's ancient rulers and had ugly yellow bricks inscribed with his name used to rebuild parts of Babylon.) It is what is believed to have happened after the first Islamic army burst out of the desert into the lush Euphrates valley in 633 AD that Iraqis, and above all the Shia, see as belonging to a past which they feel is truly theirs. Saddam attempted to create a nationalist anti-Iranian counter-myth surrounding the battle of al-Qadisiyya, when the Islamic Arab army decisively defeated the Persians (Iranians) in 637 AD. As a propaganda ploy it never quite took wing. Saddam's dismal lack of success on the battlefield also belied his attempts to present himself as being a successor to the great Arab conquerors. The only positive outcome of this self-regarding myth was to give employment to Iraqi artists adept at painting battle scenes showing the triumph of the Arabs. The lobby of the al-

Hamra Hotel where I stay in Baghdad is to this day dominated by an enormous picture of the battle of al-Qadisiyya in which Arabs and Persians swirl around each other as they wield their swords and spears while in the centre of the picture towers a stricken Persian war elephant with an arrow stuck in its eye.

The central drama of the Shia faith begins with the departure of a small expedition from Medina nearly 1,400 years ago. In 680 AD the seventy-seven-year-old caliph Mu'awiyah, whose rule over the newly conquered Islamic world had been secured by the assassination of Ali, had died in Damascus. An astute and determined empire-builder he was the founder of the Umayyad dynasty. The claim of Ali to the caliphate had been based on being the first cousin of Muhammad, the husband of the Prophet's favourite daughter Fatima (Muhammad left no sons) as well as the father of Muhammad's best-loved grandsons Hussein and Hasan. When Ali was killed in 661 AD his followers – the Shiat Ali – were simply those who had supported his right to the caliphate. But this became transmuted over the centuries into a more revolutionary belief that Ali's piety and virtue – as well as his claim as a member of the Prophet's family – should have counted for more than the wealth and power of the Umayyads, the new dynasty based in Damascus, in selecting the leader of the Islamic world. Shiism was starting on its way to being the faith of the dispossessed and opponents of the powers-that-be.

On the death of Mu'awiyah he was succeeded as caliph in Damascus by his son Yazid, deemed by Shia to be a licentious drunk and the epitome of evil. Messengers hurried from leaders in Kufa to Medina pleading with Hussein to cross the desert to their city where they would join him in raising his banner as the true leader of Islam. Hussein and his brother Abbas, urged on by their supporters in Medina, responded to the call. In the event, like so many so many exiles and would-be revolutionaries, Hussein found his friends more prudent and his enemies more proactive than he had hoped. His cousin, Muslim, who had ridden ahead to Kufa to scout out the ground, found his presence in a safe house betrayed and he was captured and killed. The ruthless governor of Kufa and Basra, Ubaydullah, had secured both cities for Yazid long before Hussein began to approach. He had left Medina with only thirty cavalry and forty foot soldiers, expecting to recruit an army from enthusiastic supporters when he reached the Euphrates valley. Bedouin tribes along his route kept their distance from what they saw as a doomed venture. A poet called Farazdaq rode out from Kufa bearing the news of betrayal 'for though the heart of the City is with thee, its sword is against thee'.[2]

Unable to advance or retreat Hussein pitched his tents to the north of Kufa on the edge of the desert close to the west bank of the Euphrates. At first the little band was shadowed by a small cavalry detachment sent by Ubaydullah and then by a larger force of 4,000 cavalry and archers from Kufa. At the campsite where the city of Kerbala now stands Hussein dug a ditch behind his men, filled it with brushwood and prepared to set fire to it to make sure he was not attacked from the rear and to show he would not retreat. His followers were very thirsty because they were already cut off from the river. On the day before the final battle Hussein told his close family to give themselves up to the enemy but they refused. Abbas, seeing the women and children in the camp crying out for water, stole to the riverbank and filled his water skin. On his way back to the camp he was detected and fought a lonely battle with enemy soldiers until first his right arm and then his left were cut off. Propping his body against the trunk of a date palm he tried to resist until Ubaydullah's men bludgeoned him to death with sticks and clubs.

In the face of hopeless odds Hussein's followers made a valiant charge, but fell one by one pierced by a rain of arrows. Hussein, standing at their head, the Koran in one hand and a sword in the other, died with thirty-three lance and sword wounds. The survivors were ridden down and their heads chopped off by the triumphant Umayyad horsemen. By evening the heads were being rolled out of leather sacks to show the completeness of the victory to Ubaydullah in Kufa and, days later, to the caliph Yazid in his palace in Damascus. It is the anniversary of this great defeat on the tenth day – Ashura – of Moharram that is commemorated by Shia across the world as a day of penitence and mourning equivalent to the Christian celebration of Easter. Hussein's last battle and death is presented not as a failed bid for power, but as an intentional martyrdom, deliberately sought to expose the sinfulness of the worldly Umayyads as persecutors of the pious and the good.[3]

Shia religious leaders today are highly conscious of parallels between what happened in the seventh century and what is happening now. When Muqtada al-Sadr was trapped in Kufa in April 2004 he denounced President Bush as a modern Yazid. The significance of the reference may have eluded political operatives in the White House. I was perplexed to notice on the website of Grand Ayatollah Ali al-Sistani, where the most detailed questions from the faithful are answered, that the game of chess is strictly forbidden. One questioner who asked if he could play chess on his computer was firmly told: 'Playing chess is *haram mutlaqan* (prohibited absolutely or under any circumstances) even though betting is not used.'[4] I asked an Iraqi friend why al-Sistani objected so strongly to chess. He explained impatiently, as if it was something that everybody should know, that 'the reason al-Sistani condemns the game is that Yazid was playing chess in his palace in Damascus when the head of Imam Hussein was brought to him'.

The legacy of the grim circumstances in which Shiism was born has had a profound effect on the beliefs and actions of its followers. It is a faith conceived in defeat and subjection. It contrasts with Sunni Islam which is a doctrine of victory and power. The details of the bloody skirmish at Kerbala provided the building blocks out of which was created a religious faith of high sophistication as well as a folk-religion of great intensity and appeal. Shiism with its emphasis on the endurance of suffering under an oppressive state was peculiarly well suited to the psychological needs of a community living under the rule of a leader as cruel as Saddam Hussein.

The Shia believed that the descendants of the Prophet should exercise leadership over the Islamic community. The Imams, starting with Ali, were the true heirs of Muhammad who, when the time was right, would overthrow tyrannous governments and establish justice in the world. Predictably, the time was never quite right for the establishment of this new order. Those Shia sects that did succeed soon abandoned their Messianic pretensions once they were in power, while those that did not were extirpated as perpetual rebels. The branch that triumphed in Iran and Iraq – the great majority of Shia today – was known as the 'Twelvers' because its followers believe there have been twelve Imams in succession. The Twelfth Imam, al-Mahdi, disappeared in Samarra north of Baghdad in the ninth century, but did not die and will one day return to purify the world of evil. The Imams – most lived and died obscurely after the death of Hussein – did not bid for political power, but the Shia developed a distinction between spiritual and temporal leadership that is similar to the Christian distinction between church and state. In contrast to Sunni Muslims, Shia obedience to the government of the day is qualified and conditional. The Shia were never Islamic Bolsheviki, underground dissidents permanently plotting the destruction of the status quo, but the doctrines and institutions of their faith provided a fertile breeding ground for dissent.

Popular Shia religious culture in Iraq remained vibrant despite persecution by Saddam's regime. State-sponsored secular nationalism was discredited by the disastrous Iran–Iraq war, in which half a million Iraqis were killed, wounded or taken prisoner, the defeat in Kuwait, the

uprising of 1991, and the economic disaster of sanctions. The
government tried, at different times, guardedly to tolerate or
covertly restrain prayer meetings and processions. They were
always suspicious that they might be used by opponents of
the regime. When they went ahead they were carefully
monitored and video film was taken so participants could be
identified.[5] Despite this constant persecution secular
Baathism failed to erode the popularity of such expressions
of Shia identity. It was an important failure. The Shia clergy
focused on sacred texts and canonical traditions and the Shia
middle class in the cities was partly secularised. But the
political punching power of the Shia community came from
the religious solidarity of millions of people that at times
made even Saddam Hussein hesitate to confront them
directly.

Shia religious culture is expressed in many forms. In contrast to the Sunni it is highly pictorial. Folk art, using highly
coloured paintings or elaborate embroidery, recalls dramatic
incidents in the battle of Kerbala such as Hussein's riderless
but noble white horse returning to camp with blood dripping
from the saddle. An oft-repeated motif is the severed arm of
Abbas whose fierce bravery has always had a strong appeal
to the Iraqi tribesmen. The Shia tribes in the marshes north
of Basra consider swearing by the name of Abbas is a far
stronger oath than swearing by the name of Hussein.[6]

The elaborate ten-day-long rituals of Ashura and the
Arba'in pilgrimage that follows it are central to the Shia
sense of identity and solidarity. The form of these religious
ceremonies varies markedly in different parts of Iraq. In the
market town of Twaireej on the Euphrates 15 miles from
Kerbala, the birthplace of the Iraqi prime minister Nouri al-
Maliki, the Ashura ritual is spread over ten days, starting
with green, black and red flags being raised over the roofs of
houses. The green represents the sayyids, the religious
succession leading back to the Prophet, the black symbolises
sorrow and grief over the battle of Kerbala and the red the
blood of the murdered Imam Hussein. Men of the town wear

long black shirts to show grief. There are other more exotic symbols. Water pots and water tanks are displayed covered with black cloth and drinking water is offered from them for free in memory of the searing thirst of Imam Hussein's besieged followers. In the burning heat of the plains of Mesopotamia every Iraqi can visualise the suffering of those trapped without water to drink. It is a symbol of life itself.

Over ten days the faithful in Twaireej gather for two or three hours every evening for recitations, the chanting of hymns, young men beating their chests, whipping themselves or slightly cutting their scalps with a sword so as to draw blood. Passion plays and recitations retell stories from the days leading up to the last hopeless fight. 'The stories are known to every individual taking part in the ritual, whether as performer or spectator,' writes Faleh Jabar, the great expert on the Shia of Iraq. 'It is the journey of Hussein to Kerbala to regain his deserved caliphate. He is betrayed by supporters; outflanked and outnumbered by a brutal enemy; cut off from water; left almost alone with a few loyal supporters, a stranger in a foreign land with his children and his sister.' Stories are woven out of the individual fates of the martyrs, touching not only violence and death but love and marriage. The sacred and the mundane are combined in a way that is closer to the luxuriant displays of medieval Christianity than to more puritanical strains of Islam.[7]

It is important not to read history backwards: The successful political activism of the Shia in the Middle East only developed over the last half-century. Few paid much attention to the radical potential of Shiism before the Iranian revolution of 1978–9, the rise of Hezbollah in Lebanon following the Israeli invasion of 1982 or the Shia uprising in Iraq in 1991 which was followed by their gradual takeover of power after the US invasion of 2003. Shiism may have had its birth in schism and dissent but for most of its history it was an apolitical faith. It might be the religion of the underdog but it primarily taught resignation and endurance in the face of oppression, not revolt. The Abbasid dynasty replaced the Umayyads in 750 and established Baghdad as the centre of the Muslim world. It was during the Abbasid period that Shiism took its present form and its doctrinal differences from the Sunni took root. But the Shia believers were still a minority community that did not appeal to the masses. The last Shia dynasty to hold power in the Arab world was the Fatimids in Cairo who were overthrown by Saladin – a Sunni Kurd from Tikrit in northern Iraq – in 1171. When Ibrahim al-Jaafari became prime minister leading a Shia-dominated government in Baghdad in 2005, a Shia official proudly remarked to me: 'It is the first time we Shia have held power in the Arab world since the Fatimids.'

The position of the Shia in Iraq was changed by three events that have a fundamental impact to this day: the enforced conversion of Iran to Shiism by the Safavid dynasty in the sixteenth century, the rise of a powerful Shia clergy and the conversion of the southern Iraqi tribes to Shiism in the eighteenth and nineteenth centuries. The first Safavid Shah, Isma'il, a Turkish-speaking warrior who established his capital in Tabriz, seized power in Iran in 1501. He used 'Twelver' Shiism as the ideological glue to bind his disparate new realm to his dynasty through forced conversion. Shiite clergy were imported from Lebanon and Bahrain to indoctrinate Iranians. The first three Caliphs – Abu Bakr, Omar and Othman – who had displaced Ali were formally cursed during Friday sermons. The Safavid Shahs claimed to be descended from Ali through the seventh Imam. The Shia identity of Safavid Iran was further enhanced because it was continually at war with the Ottoman Empire as the supreme Sunni power. Baghdad changed hands a number of times but the Ottomans were able to maintain their grip and with a Sunni elite ruling in power locally the Iraqi Shia became permanently subordinate. Sharing a common religion with Iran they were suspected as possible traitors. 'Safawi' – Safavid – has become a derogatory term used by Sunni to imply that Iraqi Shia are Iranian pawns. Saddam Hussein spat out the words at his tormentors just before he went to the gallows.

A second development significant for the Shia was the rise of the power of their clergy or *ulema*. More specifically it was the *mujtahids*, the qualified interpreters of the sharia law, who became central to the organisation of the Shia religion. The clerical hierarchy was chosen because of its scholastic learning but members were willing to advise on all aspects of life. The most learned and highly regarded of the *mujtahids* were the *marji'iya* and the supreme religious figure was the paramount *marji' al-taqlid*. Pious Shia chose one of the senior clergy to emulate as a source of inspiration. All this took time to evolve but it introduced a further difference between the Shia and the Sunni that was pregnant with consequences for the future of Iran and Iraq. Unlike the Sunni community the Shia now possessed a clergy and a religious organisation that was separate from the state. Potentially it could provide an alternative leadership for the Shia.

This was an important development because for the first time the majority of Iraqis belonged to the Shia faith as a result of the conversion to Shiism of the Sunni tribes of southern Iraq. The clergy in Najaf and Kerbala needed the loyalty of the newly converted tribes. The shrine cities were wide open to attacks across the desert to the west. Najaf was twice besieged by anti-Shia Wahhabi from the Arabian peninsula and Kerbala was sacked in 1801. The Shia leaders of the shrine cities had every motive to convert the Sunni tribes surrounding them in order to gain protection. The tribes may also have converted to Shiism because they needed a new focus for their identity as they abandoned nomadic herding and adopted settled agriculture. This in turn bound them more closely to Najaf, Kerbala and other urban centres.[8] This conversion of the tribes had a political consequence that was to dominate the country's politics in the twentieth century: Iraq became a country with a Shia majority but was ruled by the Sunni. The rough British census of 1919 showed that the Shia were 53 per cent of the population[9]; a fuller census in 1947 showed the Shia Arabs as making up 51.4 per cent of Iraqis, Sunni Arabs 19.7 per cent and Sunni Kurds 18 per cent.[10]

Iraq differed from most other Middle Eastern states in another significant way. The first urban civilisations grew up along the fertile banks of the Tigris and Euphrates 5,000 years ago. But Iraq has an equally long history as a frontier zone squeezed between civilisations centred on the Iranian plateau, Anatolia, Arabia and the eastern Mediterranean. It was not only a frontier but a battlefield: Alexander the Great died in Babylon, the Romans were never able to hold the Mesopotamian plain and Ottoman rule was tenuous for much of their long rule. From the destruction of Baghdad by Hulagu the Mongol leader in 1258 until the monarchy was established under British auspices in 1921 central government control was always limited and often non-existent. This helps explain the continuing strength of non-state agencies such as tribe, clan and extended family in Iraqi life and also, perhaps, the extreme violence of its politics. There is a violent anarchic strain in Iraqi life. Commenting on this just after the fall of Baghdad an Iraqi neurosurgeon, who had only narrowly dissuaded looters from ransacking his hospital, warned me: 'Remember, even Saddam had difficulty ruling this country.'

CHAPTER THREE

Muhammad Baqir al-Sadr: The First Martyr

'If my little finger was Baathist, I would cut it off,' was the defiant retort of Muhammad Baqir al-Sadr, the Shia revolutionary thinker and leader, when he was asked to submit to the Baathist government in Baghdad.[1] His uncompromising words became a catchphrase for the Shia resistance to Saddam Hussein. Baqir was the progenitor of the politically activist Shia religious movement whose followers became known as the 'Sadrists'. He was executed by Saddam in 1980. In death Baqir's reputation was enough to make his cousin and student Muhammad Sadiq al-Sadr the Iraqi regime's most dangerous opponent until its gunmen in turn assassinated him with two of his sons in 1999. After the US invasion in 2003 it was the al-Sadr family name, by now twice sanctified by martyrdom, that promoted with astonishing speed Sadiq's little-known son Muqtada al-Sadr to be one of the most powerful men in Iraq, to the horror of the US and its Iraqi allies.

Baqir became known as the 'First Martyr' or Sadr I, and Sadiq the 'Second Martyr' or Sadr II. Baqir was the only Grand Ayatollah to be executed in modern history. His followers hoped, and the government in Baghdad feared, he would be 'the Khomeini of Iraq'. He openly supported the Iranian revolution in 1978-9. Saddam Hussein was determined not to share the fate of the Shah, forced to flee Iran as the Shia revolution triumphed in the streets of Tehran. Repression of Shia militants in Iraq was savage and carefully planned. On 4 April 1980 Baqir was arrested in Najaf and four days later was executed, together with his sister Amina Sadr Bint al-Huda, in a prison in Baghdad. Stories were whispered – and widely believed in Iraq – that his torturers had hammered an iron nail into his head and raped his sister before they were both killed. The cruelty of their deaths explains why hatred for the Baathists persisted so long after the overthrow of Saddam Hussein. 'Many Shia believe that they raped Huda in front of her brother before they executed them,' a Shia journalist in Baghdad told me in 2007. 'That is why the thirst among the Shia for revenge against the Baathists is so strong and why they get so angry when the Americans want to reverse de-Baathification.'[2]

Baqir suffered the same dire fate as many revolutionary leaders in history who hoped to emulate successful revolutions elsewhere. Throughout the twentieth century Islamic parties sought to overthrow secular states. All had failed. Now in Iran, to the amazement and bewilderment of the world, Ayatollah Khomeini had succeeded in over-throwing what had appeared to be a powerful government, flush with oil money, protected by ferocious security services and supported by the West. Euphoria gripped Islamic parties in the region. If it could be done in Iran why not in Iraq where the Shia were also a majority?

Baqir was not entirely swept away by religious enthusi-asm. He and many of his followers knew all too well that they faced a strong and ruthless security apparatus. Their own resources were limited. The Shia religious hierarchy was not united behind them and rightly feared a confrontation with the Baath. In Tehran the Iranian leaders were making the same mistake as successful socialist revolutionaries in Moscow, Beijing and Havana had made in the course of the twentieth century. They thought that their own recipe for a successful revolution could be successfully exported to other countries. From Bolivia to Indonesia socialist supporters paid a price in blood for this over-confidence. A revolution needs an element of surprise if it is to win. The powers-that-be must be caught napping. In Iraq the reverse was true. The government was prepared and the revolutionaries were not. In the summer of 1979 Shia militants hopefully chanted: 'In the name of Khomeini and al-Sadr, Islam will always be victorious.' Baqir himself sensed that such open defiance of the regime would lead to his death.[3]

Baqir was a member of one of the great religious families of the Middle East. Born in 1935 in the Kadhimiyah district of Baghdad he was one of the al-Sadrs, part of the clerical aristo-cracy. 'The family lineage,' says his son Jafar al-Sadr, 'goes back to the Prophet Muhammad through the Seventh Shia Imam, Musa al-Kazim. Our forefathers were living in the Jabal Amel [in Lebanon] from the twelfth century to the eighteenth century when the family's grandfather Sayyid Saleh bin Ibrahim Sharaf al-Dun emigrated to Iraq in 1785.'[4] Established in Kadhimiyah they were prominent in the affairs of their community. During the last years of Ottoman rule Sayyid Hussain al-Sadr was a revered *mujtahid*. His son Sayyid Muhammad al-Sadr took a leading part in the 1920 uprising against the British, preaching jihad against the occupation of Iraq; later he became a long-term president of the senate, briefly prime minister in 1948 and was known as 'the Rasputin of Iraq' because of his influence in court circles.[5]

Baqir's father, Haydar, died young and his elder brother Ismail, who was to be a religious leader in Kadhimiyah, played an important role in his upbringing. His mother came from the al-Yassin family that was also well connected to the Shia clerical leaders. Her brother Sheikh Murtada al-Yassin was a highly regarded religious activist in Kadhimiyah. It was an advantage, from the point of view of Baqir's future clerical career, that he came from Kadhimiyah, one of the four shrine cities of Iraq, the other three being Najaf, Kerbala and Samarra. It had originally been a separate township in a loop of the Tigris river, just north of Baghdad, until the capital grew round it. Baqir, as a child, would have seen the shrine's golden dome and four slender minarets outlined against the sky whenever he looked across the city. Devout pilgrims, many from Iran, poured into its spacious courtyard; they bought golden necklaces for weddings in the jewellers' shops that lined the ancient streets around the shrine. Originally built in 799 AD, it houses the double tomb of the seventh and ninth Imams, Musa, the ancestor of the al-Sadrs, who died in 799 AD, and his grandson Muhammad Jawad, who died in 835 AD. Destroyed by the Mongols in the thirteenth century it was rebuilt by the Turkish Ottomans and the Persian Safavids when each in turn occupied Baghdad in the sixteenth and seventeenth centuries. Both vied for Shia support by rebuilding and adorning the shrine.

At the age of eleven Baqir moved to Najaf with his family to study at the religious schools where he was, by all accounts, a highly talented student. His subsequent martyr-dom makes it difficult to discover the real character of the young religious student whose personality now lies hidden beneath layers of hagiography. 'In his eleventh year he studied the science of logic and genealogy in the study of which he showed himself a uniquely brilliant student,' says Hussein al-Shami who later became one of his students.[6] He joined a *hawza* (a Shia seminary similar to an academic college, but also used to describe the Shia clerical community as a whole) of leading *mujtahids* such as Ayatollah Muhammad Rouhani and later of the Grand Ayatollah Abu al-Qasim al-Khoei, who was to be his political and ideo-logical competitor in future years. Al-Khoei is said to have altered several of his judgements after discussion with his young student.

Baqir was joining a very hierarchical and introverted, but also comatose and beleaguered, world. The *marji'iya*, the most senior members of the Shia clergy, were somewhat akin in status to cardinals in the Roman Catholic Church, though they are less numerous (there are at present nine) and there is no Shia pope. They are traditionally not only venerated but emulated by the Shia who will choose one of them as his 'model' though go to a lower ranking cleric for rulings and advice. The *marji'iya* themselves were not very approachable and sat in their houses with their students. 'They all thought they were superior to each other in learning and wisdom so they would seldom deign to visit another member of the hierarchy,' comments Ghanim Jawad, a well-informed observer of Shia clerical politics.[7] 'So sometimes they didn't see each other for years, but would communicate by sending messengers carrying pieces of paper.' Authority was fragmented. There were divisions between Arab and Iranian Ayatollahs. The grand *marji' al-taqlid* (the Shia highest religious authority) when Baqir was in his twenties was Muhsin al-Hakim, whose family was to play a critical role in opposition to Saddam Hussein and who had been selected with the support of the Shah of Iran. The Shah wanted the position to go to an Arab rather than Iranian cleric because the Arab had fewer followers in Iran and would thus be less of a menace to the Shah's regime. One of the strengths of the Shia hierarchy was that those clerics critical of the Iraqi regime could live in Qom and those hostile to the Iranian government could live in Najaf.

The strange world of the Shia clerical class was under ever-growing threat in the 1950s. Secularism was undermining Islam, both Shia and Sunni, across the Middle East. Religion seemed to limp behind socialism and nationalism in devising an effective response to the political, cultural and economic impact of the West. The Shia clergy saw their grip on education weakening. Their income from *khums* – donations – was inadequate. The Shia community was split: there were the very wealthy Shia business elite in Baghdad, disaffected peasants on the great estates of southern Iraq, the workers in the cities increasingly under the influence of the Iraqi Communist Party, and a secular highly educated professional middle class. Many of the problems facing Iraqis were common to all Islamic countries seeking to throw off imperial control, direct or indirect, and to modernise. Iraq was different because its problems were more acute. Neither socialists nor nationalists turned out to have workable solutions to them. With the overthrow of the monarchy in the bloody coup by General Abd al-Karim Qasim in July 1958, the country was entering a period of turmoil that has lasted fifty years and shows no sign of stabilising to this day.

At first sight the Shia clergy looked peculiarly ill-equipped to cope with the coming challenges. The fall of the Hashemite monarchy opened the door to mass politics. Religious rituals suffered. In 1959 the numbers taking part in the pilgrimages to Najaf and Kerbala fell to an all-time low. 'The Communists and the nationalists were powerful in the government and on the streets,' recalls one Najaf cleric. 'They got a tremendous boost from the support they were getting from Egyptian president Gamal Abdel Nasser.'[8] In the face of these menacing developments, the way was open for Baqir and some of the younger clergy to try to make reforms aimed at protecting the *hawza* and the collective of senior clerics. They took the obvious course which was to set up a political party, called *al-Da'wa* (the Call), the first meeting of which took place in Najaf in 1957. Its aim was to defend Islam and its institutions. The traditionalists in the clerical leadership were briefly frightened enough to accept change even if the foundation of a party potentially challenged their authority. They could see they needed to emulate the Iraqi Communist Party with a cell structure, discipline and chain of command. Alarmed by the swift growth of Communism among the Shia masses Grand Ayatollah Muhsin al-Hakim assented to its creation.

A safeguard against the new party competing against the clerical hierarchy was that its founding members were almost all young men from families in the inner circle of Iraqi Shiism. There were representatives from many of the noble clerical families including Baqir himself. Almost all were young men, 90 per cent of them under thirty-five. Baqir al-Hakim, later the founder of the Supreme Council for Islamic Revolution in Iraq, was only fourteen when he joined. Many of the founder members were to be executed, assassinated or tortured to death, but half a century later the Iraqi government was dominated by the relatives and descendants of the men who had established the Dawa party.

Baqir himself was only twenty-five years old in 1958 which, in normal times, would have been too young to play a prominent role in a clerical elite where authority only came with age and prolonged training. He had the advantage of his family background but he also needed the patronage of senior and well-established religious figures. The way this was done – Iraqi clerical politics have some similarities, notably in the venom with which they are conducted, with university politics in the West, with Najaf playing the role of Oxbridge or Harvard – was to write a laudatory book on the work of a senior cleric, the recently selected Grand Ayatollah Muhsin al-Hakim. Khomeini had a similar sort of book. Moderniser he might be but Baqir could not hope to accomplish anything without the support of well-established elders. Despite his intelligence, ability, energy, popularity, family connections and powerful patrons, he still had a long way to go before he could join the *marji'iya*. General Qasim's coup gave Baqir and his new party their chance. Iraq was entering revolutionary times. Ageing and conservative Shia clerics might be uncomfortable with the innovations Baqir proposed, but they could scarcely do without him.

The extent to which Iraq had always been divided between Shia and Sunni became a matter of furious dispute in the years after the US-led invasion of 2003. The arguments were so bitter because several of the protagonists were in search of an alibi. If it could be shown that Iraq was always a mosaic of competing communities that hated each other, then the US and its allies could not be blamed for provoking a sectarian and ethnic civil war. The Sunni for their part were reluctant to admit that as a minority they had wielded power over the Shia who were three times more numerous than themselves.

It is true that there was no apartheid between Sunni and

Shia. They occasionally intermarried. Some Shia rose high in the Baath party and the government. Religion was not the only means through which Shia Iraqis established their identity. But in the exercise of power Iraq was a Sunni-dominated state and became more so during Saddam Hussein's long rule.

At first the 1958 coup opened doors to the Shia. The leaders of the powerful Iraqi Communist Party were Shia and swiftly radicalised the urban and rural poor. President Qasim was himself partly Shia. In east Baghdad he started building basic housing for impoverished Shia immigrants from the countryside. Fifty years later the area had become a political and military bastion of Muqtada al-Sadr, and called Sadr City. Containing one third of the capital's population, it was less of a district than a densely populated twin city to the rest of Baghdad.

The military coup in February 1963 in which the Baath party took a leading role was seen as an 'anti-Shia' action because the Iraqi army and security services were Sunni-dominated. The slaughter of Communists was also a massacre of the Shia. The sectarian balance began shifting decisively against them. The Baath party was ousted from power later in 1963 by its former allies, but most of the security police still came from Dulaim (later Anbar) province which, then as now, was almost entirely Sunni. Shia members of the Baath party found they were far more ruthlessly treated by the security police than its Sunni members. Saddam Hussein, beginning to emerge as an important Baathist leader, recorded how in 1966 he escaped from imprisonment. His account, given to a sympathetic biographer, shows how well-connected Sunni from the provinces were treated with kid gloves. He was appearing before the Higher Security Court charged with plotting to storm the Presidential palace and machine-gun members of the government attending a meeting. Despite the seriousness of the offence, on his way back to jail Saddam persuaded his prison guards to stop and let him eat a meal at a restaurant in Abu Nawas Street beside the Tigris. During the meal he and six companions simply walked out through the back of the restaurant.[9]

Arab nationalism could be a mask for sectarianism in a way not immediately obvious to non-Iraqis. In 1964, for instance, many banks, commercial and industrial companies were nationalised. The ostensible reason for this was to bring the Iraqi economy in line with state socialist Egypt, with which Iraq was supposedly to combine in the name of Arab unity. But the reality was that the majority of Iraqi business-men were Shia and the state officials who took over the nationalised companies were mostly Sunni. Sectarian divisions between Sunni and Shia in Iraq in the 1960s were not as deep as those dividing Arab from Kurd but, if they were not always dominant, they were also never absent.

The divisions were also about to get worse. The Baath party returned to power in a military coup in 1968 and did not intend to share power with anybody. It soon disposed of most of its military allies. It showed an exceptional capacity for using violence against its opponents. Authority was concentrated in the hands of President Hassan al-Bakr and his cousin Saddam Hussein, vice chairman of the Revolution Command Council. Saddam wielded power primarily through different agencies of the security police and the intelligence services. The most important posts went to his half-brothers and cousins, members of the Bejat clan of the Albu Nasir tribe from Tikrit. 'If you want to know how we rule Iraq,' reflected one of Saddam's relatives in later years, 'we do it just the same way as we used to run Tikrit.'[10] Military, police, tribal and party allegiances were adeptly combined to make the regime coup-proof. Most important, the jump in oil prices after 1973 provided the Baathists with vast funds, sufficient to raise the living standards of all Iraqis and quell popular discontent. Should the Shiite clerics or the politically active Shiites in the Dawa party choose to confront such a powerful and violent state machine their chances of success looked remote.

*

While these dramatic events were happening in Baghdad, Baqir was living a modest but energetic life in Najaf. 'He did not own a house but rented one and he did not drive a car,' says his student from those days Hussein al-Shami. 'He used to say that "while I am in this position, the leader of a Shia congregation, I must live at the same level as my students".' He was ascetic but did not see asceticism as being at the heart of religion. On the contrary he was eager to attract the younger Iraqi intelligentsia into the *hawza* by finding well-qualified teachers and he believed the students should be properly rewarded. 'He guaranteed them the same socio-economic status that they might have gained from government jobs.' He sought to get the *marji'iya* to pay for religious instructors sent to poorer areas. Previously these had been paid for by people in the districts into which they were sent, which inevitably meant that the richer parts of Iraq were over-supplied with religious teachers and poorer parts like Thawra were poorly provided for.[11]

It was in the three years after the fall of the monarchy that Baqir sought to lay the ideological basis for an Islamic counter-attack on Western capitalism and communism. He wrote two books *Falsafatuna* (*Our Philosophy*) and *Iqtisaduna* (*Our Economics*) which appeared in 1959 and 1960. His first ideas about how to save the Islamic *ummah* (community), though couched in abstract language, appeared in a periodical he had helped set up called *Adhwa*. At this stage it was still surprising that the Shia clergy, living in an essentially medieval world, should even have contemplated allowing a magazine to function. Baqir's contributions almost immediately caused him trouble. In 1960 he was forced to stop writing for the magazine and to sever his open connection with the Dawa party. For the next twenty years of his life, up to his execution, his political activism had to be masked or, at least, diluted in public, though in times of crisis the mask would slip.

During this whole period Baqir felt squeezed between the Baath and its brutal security agencies on the one hand, and those in the *marji'iya* who saw him as a dangerous radical on the other. Hussein al-Shami recalls that this lack of understanding and continual criticism by Baqir's clerical colleagues 'made him feel so lonely that he wished for death sometimes though he tried to be patient and carefully conceal this'. Clerical jealousies ran deep. 'He was so harshly criticised when he established the Islamic Dawa party that he used to say: "It is very strange that some religious people allow their sons to join the Baath party but they attack me for establishing the Dawa party." ' He felt his promotion within the ranks of the clergy was being blocked by unfair allegations from critics that he was too emotional as a personality and was a divisive figure. Some of his opponents within the *hawza* allegedly made use of his bad relations with the Baath party to further isolate him. 'They used to terrify anybody going to see him by saying that, if they did so, they were likely to be arrested by state security.'[12]

The Baath party's merciless security organisations always had the strength to crush the traditional Shia leadership. Saddam Hussein's real skill, though he enjoyed playing the role of military commander, was as a secret policeman. He and his lieutenants had seized power through a military putsch. They were determined that nobody should do the same to them. For all their revolutionary rhetoric they thought of politics in terms of plots devised by a small number of people probably backed by a foreign power. For this reason they wholly failed to foresee the success of the Iranian revolution, based on mass street protests, until the last moment. Saddam prided himself at his skill in smelling out his enemies. 'We used to be able to sense a conspiracy with our hearts before we even gathered the evidence,' he had once boasted to Baath party leaders.[13] The Dawa party had little chance against such well-organised ferocity. The *marji'iya* could also be intimidated. The real vulnerability of the regime, however, became evident when political dissent combined with popular piety as the Shia masses carried out the age-old rituals of Ashura and

Arba'in. These self-organised demonstrations and pilgrimages, which had no real leaders, were to pose the greatest
threat to the Baath in the 1970s.

Skirmishes between the Shia leaders and the Baath party
started early. In 1969 came a decision to deport all Iranian
nationals in Iraq. The regime claimed they totalled half a
million though this was an exaggeration. Whole groups such
as the Faili Kurds (Shia Kurds) were to be targeted in coming
years. There was a drumbeat of propaganda, similar to that
emanating from Washington during the US-led occupation
after 2003, insisting that Shia militants were pawns manipulated by Iran. At times there was enough substance in this
to give the claims some credibility. In January 1970 the
government alleged that it had discovered a plot to overthrow it which included Shia figures close to the Dawa party
such as the Grand Ayatollah's son Mahdi al-Hakim who was
forced to flee abroad. When the grand *marji'* Muhsin al-
Hakim himself died in June 1970 the enormous numbers
attending his funeral chanted verses against the Baath (there
are in fact several Grand Ayatollahs who collectively form
the *marji'iya,* but one is usually identified as the leading
figure). His successor, Grand Ayatollah Abu al-Qasim al-
Khoei, took a more pacifist and apolitical line than his
predecessor which led the politicised Shia laity to turn to
Baqir. He had a further advantage: his family, though it
might have had links with Iran in the distant past, was
identifiably Arab while al-Khoei had been born in Iran.

Repression increased. The General Directorate of Security
Services was still circumspect in dealing with senior clergy
but not with the laity. In 1972 Baqir was arrested but was
detained in Kufa hospital because he was ill. In 1974 five of
the most important Dawa party leaders from Najaf, Kerbala
and Basra were executed. The party leader for Baghdad,
Sahib al-Dakhil, had disappeared in 1971 and was never seen
again.[14] The executions and heavy sentences for other
militants led to a mass flight of party supporters. Baqir issued
an edict in the same year severing any connection between

the *hawza* and political work. This was partly a defensive measure. He feared that if the *hawza* and the Dawa party were too closely linked then 'the demolition of the political organisation by the Baath government would have a devastating effect on the Hawza'.[15] A second motive, according to a former student of Baqir, was recognition that the *hawza* was meant to be linked to all the Shia community and not a single group. Too close an association with the Dawa party would alienate some of the faithful.

Distancing himself publicly from a party opposed to the Baath was a matter of common sense but Baqir maintained covert links. He appointed one of his students to liaise with the Dawa party and channelled money to it whenever possible.[16] He may have had deep differences over the extent to which the Shia clergy should become involved in active politics with the Grand Ayatollah al-Khoei but he was highly conscious of the vulnerability of the Shia institutions to state action. The Baath government could, for instance, simply deny residency to the many Iranian students studying in Najaf, or it could call up Iraqi Arab students for military service. It targeted funds controlled by the clergy. Baqir may have advocated political activism but he was not without caution. Asked by the head of the Directorate for General Security, Fadhil al-Barak, to omit a passage criticising socialism from one of his books – because the Baath party was itself socialist – he complied on the grounds that government agents would probably change the passage anyway.

The government in Baghdad made intermittent attempts to cultivate him. Remarkably, he was asked to ghost a book on religion that would appear under the name of President Hassan al-Bakr. He refused without hesitation. On another occasion Fadhil al-Barak said he was prepared to ignore all the critical reports about Baqir made by the security directorate in Najaf. Unfortunately, he added spitefully, he could 'do nothing about reports that had been delivered direct to the leadership by members of the Hawza'. In other words some of Baqir's clerical colleagues would not have been sorry to see him disappear to prison. Over the coming years it was to be a constant and angry complaint of what was to become the 'Sadrist' movement that their rivals for leadership of the Shia community betrayed them in their hour of need.

The greatest challenge to the Baath came by surprise and came from below. It happened spontaneously in 1977 during the Arba'in pilgrimage. This was a year before the beginning of the revolution in Iran, indicating that many Iraqi Shia were in a militant mood even before the emergence of Ayatollah Khomeini. There were many reasons for their discontent. Anti-Baath feeling among the Shia peasantry was exacerbated by a drought caused by low water in the Euphrates, the result of a new dam built upriver in Syria. Some 15,000 soldiers, mostly Shia, had been killed in the war with the Kurds in 1974–5. Many of their coffins had been brought to the great Wadi al-Salaam (Valley of Peace) cemetery in Najaf. The government banned the pilgrimage in 1977 claiming it had discovered a Syrian plot to plant a bomb in the shrine in Kerbala.

The march went ahead anyway organised by villages and city quarters. Marchers from Najaf to Kerbala were in a militant mood: they chanted 'Noble Najafis/Hoist Aloft Your Banners'. On the second day of the march a crowd of some 30,000 neared a place called Khan al-Nus, halfway between Najaf and Kerbala. The police and security forces opened fire. In retaliation the pilgrims, many of them farmers who carried guns, stormed and sacked the local police station. Meanwhile in Najaf, Baqir, who had played no role in organising the march, was worried enough to send an emissary, Muhammad Baqir al-Hakim, to warn the marchers not to shout slogans against President Ahmad Hassan al-Bakr and Saddam Hussein. The pilgrims ignored the advice: they chanted:

Saddam take your hands off
Neither our army nor our people want you.

The outcome of such defiance was inevitable. Attack helicopters and armoured units commanded by Saddam Hussein's cousin Khairallah Tulfah were rushed to the spot and opened fire. Some sixteen demonstrators were killed and 2,000 arrested. Eight members of a spontaneously formed organising committee were executed and two died under torture. Muhammad Baqir al-Hakim and fourteen others were given life sentences. True to his character, Saddam Hussein regarded the sentences passed by the special court as far too lenient and had two of the judges responsible for them expelled from the Baath party.[17]

The critical moment in the twentieth century for the Iraqi Shia was the Iranian revolution of 1978–9. Baqir became its advocate and an open supporter of Ayatollah Khomeini. But Shiism in Iran and Iraq have very different histories. In the former it has been the state religion since 1501 and is followed by 90 per cent of the population; in the latter it was the religion of only 60 per cent and they were without political power. The revolution would not necessarily have spread to Iraq but Saddam Hussein was taking no chances. In 1979 he seized absolute power, massively repressed the Dawa party and, in the following year, launched a military attack on Iran. He thought he would win a quick and easy victory but in reality he had started a series of hot and cold wars that ultimately destroyed not only the Baath party rule but the centuries-old Sunni predominance in Iraq.

Baqir knew Khomeini during the latter's long exile in Najaf between 1964 and 1978, though there are differing accounts of the degree of intimacy. He encouraged his students to attend Khomeini's seminars on genealogy and other topics even though these were conducted in Farsi. In an extraordinary miscalculation the Shah asked Saddam Hussein to expel Khomeini from Najaf, where he had been forced to take refuge in 1964 and where he was largely isolated from the outside world. He left in October 1978 for Paris where he had instant access to the international media.

His every word was recorded and relayed to his millions of supporters in Iran. Vast crowds defied riot police, martial law and curfews to demonstrate in the streets of Tehran and other Iranian cities. Clerics united with liberals and the Marxist left in opposition to the regime. In February 1979 the Shah's nerve broke and he fled Iran to be replaced by Ayatollah Khomeini. Both the Baath party and the Iraqi opposition were astonished and uncertain how to respond.

Khomeini and Baqir were at one in their advocacy of political activism by the Shia clergy. They both opposed the tradition of quietism as represented by Grand Ayatollah al-Khoei. This concentrated on the morality and behaviour of the individual. Its supporters decried direct political involvement by the clergy as corrupting. Sadrists later quoted with approval Khomeini's jibe at Shia religious dignitaries: 'You busy yourself with Islamic laws concerning menstruation and giving birth; I am leading a revolution.'[18] For Khomeini, Islam is, and had always been, political. Accused of being 'a political cleric' he asked 'Was not the Prophet, God's prayers be upon him, a politician?'[19] During the lectures in Najaf that Baqir had advised his students to attend, Khomeini spelled out his belief in 'the guardianship of the jurist' under which the supreme leader is a jurist, an expert on Islamic law. Baqir agreed with Khomeini about the leading role of the *mujtahids*. But he gave the belief a critically democratic and less authoritarian twist. He proposed a division of powers between the nation and clerical class, retaining 'executive and legislative powers for the nation, while reserving judicial powers for the *mujtahids* – both accountable before the law and the constitution'. Baqir, unlike Khomeini, saw the traditional clerical leadership as fallible. He argued that the prophets and the Imams may be chosen by God but the selection of the *marji'iya* is 'determined by the nation'.[20] Elections were at the centre of his vision of an Islamic state.

Two months before the Shah fell lay leaders of the Dawa party visited Baqir in Najaf. They looked to him because he was a founder of their party, was of Arab lineage and, unlike al-Khoei, was a proponent of political activism. His response was cautious. He said he needed two or three years to enhance his religious standing. He did not get them. Events were beginning to build their own momentum. When Khomeini flew into Tehran to be greeted by millions, Baqir abandoned his earlier caution and began to force the pace. He declared a three-day holiday at the Najaf *hawza* on 11 February 1979 to celebrate Khomeini's coming to power. Demonstrators carried pictures of the Iranian leader. He sent his own disciple Sayyid Mahmoud al-Hashimi to Tehran. In messages he exchanged with Khomeini he was addressed as a subordinate. In street demonstrations Shia militants sought to repeat the tactics that had brought down the Shah. Iraqi security held its hand but collected detailed intelligence about Islamic militants. At 5 a.m. on 12 June 1979 some 200 security forces and policemen arrested Baqir and took him to General Security Directorate run by Fadhil al-Barak in Baghdad. There were demonstrations and protests on an unprecedented scale in Shia quarters of Baghdad and in Shia cities and towns across the country, as well as in Lebanon, United Arab Emirates, Britain and France.[21]

The government backed down and Baqir was released from prison. The threat was serious, and differences within the Baath leadership over the degree of violence to be used in combating it were enough to provoke a crisis within the ruling Revolution Command Council. This was the moment when Saddam Hussein seized total control of Iraq. The government changed its tactics; this time Baqir was held under house arrest but his disciples and members of the Dawa party were targeted. Some 4,000–5,000 were arrested and more than 200 were executed. Baqir's position in his house in Najaf was not comfortable. A supporter recalls that Iraqi security 'cut off electric power, the water supply and the telephone line . . . and even made it difficult for him to buy food'. This went on for months. 'Baqir's younger daughter suffered from a severe toothache, but he could not get medicine for her.' Baqir himself became physically weak and spent much of his time praying. His hopes for an Islamic revolution in Iraq were ebbing and his followers were being arrested, tortured and executed. He could see other members of the *marji'iya* were distancing themselves from him. Even so the government in Baghdad preferred to neutralise him rather than kill him. A presidential envoy came to his house to ask him to make a conciliatory gesture by publicly criticising the Islamic revolution in Iran or showing support for the Baathist government in Baghdad. The envoy said this could be done by public praise for some important government measure such as the nationalisation of oil, Kurdish self-government or the campaign against illiteracy. Baqir rejected the offer. 'Sayyid Muhammad Baqir chose death,' recalls his son Jafar al-Sadr, 'after he had seen that his friends abandoned him and Iran let him down despite his support for it.'[22]

As Islamic militants were eliminated, survivors began to turn in desperation to the idea of individual attacks to kill Baathist leaders. The Dawa party was shattered by arrests and executions even before the Baath Revolution Command Council issued a decree in March 1980 that made membership of the party punishable by death. It was no longer able to mobilise the Shia masses. Its efforts to do so had, as Baqir feared, made its activists too visible to the ever-watchful Iraqi intelligence services. If the Iranian recipe of ever-escalating street demonstrations was not feasible, what other means could be used to overthrow the government?

According to a student of Baqir in Najaf at the time, the Shiite leader covertly fell back on other means of confronting Saddam who, from the summer of 1979, was the sole ruler of Iraq. He looked to recruit anti-Baathist soldiers, hitherto the traditional means of staging a coup in Iraq. 'He worked on contacting critically placed officers in the armed forces. He knew of the crucial role the Iranian armed forces played in the victory of the Iranian Islamic Revolution.' By some accounts Baqir went further. A cleric close to the members of Baqir's entourage, who were with him in the last days of his life, says: 'He started building commando cells, connected indirectly with himself, whose primary goal was the assassination of Saddam Hussein. He put in charge Sheikh Abdul Ameer Muhsin al-Saidi and Jalil Mal Allah.' Their job was to find somebody who had enough access to Saddam to kill him and was willing to die doing so. A suitable candidate was found – a doctor who had joined the presidential medical staff – but he was unmasked and executed before he could carry out his mission.[23]

Baqir was not alone in thinking that single acts of terror were now the only way left to attack the regime. The Islamic Action Organization, a smaller Shia militant group founded in Kerbala in the 1970s, had been forced into exile in Beirut. It had been radicalised by contact with radical Palestinians in Yasser Arafat's Fatah movement and the Lebanese Shia Amal militia. It trained a number of cadres who, on their return to Iraq, remained undetected by Iraqi intelligence. On 1 April one of them called Samir Nuri Ali threw a hand grenade at the Iraqi Foreign Minister Tariq Aziz as he was visiting Mustansariyah, the ancient university in the heart of Baghdad. As it exploded Ali drew a gun and was killed, along with several students, in the shooting that followed. The next day, standing in the pouring rain, Saddam told a meeting of students: 'The Iraqi people is now a large and powerful mountain they cannot shake with all their bombs. By God, the innocent blood that was shed at Mustansariyah will not go unavenged.'[24] A few days later a second bomb was thrown at the funeral of those killed at Mustansariyah.

The riposte by the regime was immediate, savage and presumably prepared well in advance. Baqir was arrested. His sister Bint al-Huda was detained with him. She had long worked with him and led a women's religious study group. By one account she tied her dress to her wrists to try to avoid it being torn off when she was tortured. Both Baqir and Bint al-Huda were taken secretly to Baghdad. Did Saddam offer Baqir one last chance? Hussein al-Shahristani, the nuclear scientist and prison escapee, says that at the last moment the

Baathists offered Baqir a deal. 'They said they would release him in return for a promise of silence. Sadr said, "No, I have closed all doors, there is no escape for you now. Now you have to kill me so the people can rise up." '[25]

Baqir and his sister were hanged on 8 April. By one account Baqir's body, but not that of his sister, was returned to Najaf in a coffin the next day for burial in Wadi al-Salaam. Another more detailed account says that at about 9 or 10 p.m. that day the electricity suddenly went off in Najaf (presumably to get people off the streets). Security men went to the house of one of Sadr's relatives, Muhammad Sadiq al-Sadr, the father of the man who was to rebuild the Sadrist movement in the 1990s, and took him to a government building. There they handed over two coffins, one containing the body of Baqir and the other of Bint al-Huda. Marks on the faces of both showed they had been tortured. Iraqi security ordered Muhammad Sadiq to take the coffins, but not to tell anybody that Bint al-Huda had also been executed. If he spoke to anybody of her death he would be killed himself. It was only on his deathbed that Muhammad Sadiq spoke of what he had seen.

The government at first blacked out all information about the execution. But news leaked out through Baath party members in Najaf and was confirmed by Khomeini and in an announcement on the Arabic service of Iranian radio. As news spread there were sporadic demonstrations in Shia areas. They were bloodily repressed. Many were silent because the government was arresting and killing anybody who showed the slightest sign of dissent. Those who did demonstrate must have known they were going to their deaths. Even so there was an attempted protest march from Najaf to Kerbala led by the Abu al-Kalal family. It was dispersed in the Khan al-Nus area by the security forces who killed or arrested participants.[26] In Thawra in Baghdad 200 people took part in a demonstration. Surviving members of the Dawa party attended. The demonstration was led by Sayyid Qasim al-Mubarqaa who wore a white shroud to show that he knew he would be killed.[27] He was shot down along with other marchers. In the days after the execution of Baqir even distant relatives of members of the Dawa party were arrested and tortured. Women who were rounded up at this time had difficulty in getting married later because it was assumed they had been raped. Terrible stories were told of prisoners fed into wood-chipping machines or of acid being dripped into their open wounds. A wave of terror engulfed Shia districts. By executing Baqir and crushing his movement Saddam appeared to have won a total victory over the Shia radicals in Iraq, but he had also infuriated much of the Shia community. If his repression ever faltered they would confront him.

CHAPTER FOUR

The Iran–Iraq War

On 8 April 1980, the very day Muhammad Baqir al-Sadr was executed, an agent of the Defense Intelligence Agency, the intelligence arm of the Pentagon, sent a tantalising message from Baghdad warning that Saddam Hussein might invade Iran. The agent was evidently well informed and in contact with the Iraqi elite, though his name is blacked out in the declassified note. 'There is a 50 per cent chance that Iraq will attack Iran,' he reported. 'Iraq has moved large numbers of military personnel and equipment in anticipation of such an invasion.' Skirmishes had already started. An Iraqi commando unit had carried out a rocket attack on an Iranian oilfield two days earlier. The agent concluded by saying that Iraqi leaders were convinced that 'the Iranian military is now weak and can be easily defeated'.[1]

The likelihood of Iraq going to war with Iran increased with the passing days. The Iraqi security services understood that the attempt to assassinate Tariq Aziz at Mustansariyah showed that the militant Shia opposition was desperate and 'on its last legs'.[2] But they systematically exaggerated the gravity of the threat posed by a few sporadic bombings and shootings. They were a convenient excuse to portray the execution of Muhammad Baqir and the slaughter of anybody connected with the Dawa party as a defensive act directed against Iranian-orchestrated terrorism. (So convenient indeed that one Baathist ex-minister believed that the assassination attempt on Tariq Aziz was faked by Iraqi security.[3]) Saddam

Hussein made an angry speech on 5 April defining for the first time the conflict with Iran as one between 'the Arabs and the Persians' and denouncing Khomeini as 'a Shah in a turban'. He demanded that Iran restore Iraqi territorial rights on the Shatt al-Arab waterway, ceded by Iraq to end Iranian support for the Kurds in 1975, and sought to give the coming conflict a pan-Arab dimension by asking Iran to leave three small but strategically important islands, the Lesser and Greater Tumbs and Abu Musa at the entrance to the Gulf, that had been seized by the Shah in 1971. On 9 April Saddam deported 9,700 Iraqi Shias of supposedly Iranian origin and a further 16,000 were expelled in coming days. Some 400 businessmen were lured to the Ministry of Commerce in Baghdad for a meeting and were then stripped of their belongings, forced on to buses, driven to the Iranian border and dumped in no man's land.⁴ Houses, land and businesses were confiscated. The definition of who was an Iranian was haphazard and the relatives of many deportees found themselves conscripted into the Iraqi army as full-blooded Iraqis. In retaliation Iran escalated its rhetoric. On 22 April Khomeini revealed that Baqir and his sister had been executed and called for the overthrow of the Iraqi government. He asked Iraqi soldiers 'Leave your barracks and do not suffer this humiliating regime a minute longer: overthrow Saddam Hussein as we did the Shah.'⁵

On 22 September Saddam Hussein launched what he called the Whirlwind War, a classic misnomer since the bloody conflict that ensued was to last eight years. His main motive was that he believed, as the DIA agent had explained six months earlier, that he could win a swift and easy victory.

Saddam Hussein was at the peak of his power at home having ruthlessly crushed all his opponents, destroying the Dawa party as an organisation and intimidating the Shia clergy. The long-running Kurdish rebellion that had destabilised so many Iraqi governments had been defeated in 1975. For all Khomeini's bellicose calls to the Iraqi army to mutiny, Iran was in no position to launch a military attack on Iraq.

The Iraqi government had plenty of money because oil prices had soared, thanks in part to the revolution in Iran. Iraq was ruled by an all-powerful leviathan state machine and it was under Saddam's sole control. He ended the rivalries between the government administration, the security services, the Baath party and the armed forces and forced them to pursue common objectives. The loyalty of this formidable machine to Saddam was guaranteed by giving critical posts to members of his own kin. There were to be no more coups. The outlook for the anti-Baathist opposition looked very bleak.

Paradoxically, the weak point of the newly powerful Iraqi state was the very man who had created it. Adroit though Saddam had been in seizing and keeping power within Iraq, he consistently misjudged the balance of power in the Middle East as a whole. He was not a career military officer though he liked to present himself as a warlord. Though often compared to Stalin as an authoritarian ruler, he had a tendency to stumble into self-inflicted disasters that was more characteristic of Inspector Clouseau. He gathered intelligent and well-informed men around him but it was dangerous for them to counsel moderation. 'The other leaders understood that the only safe way to deal with Saddam was to be 10 per cent tougher than the boss,' reflected a senior Russian diplomat stationed in Baghdad for most of the Iran–Iraq war.[6] By starting a war with Iran, the Iraqi leader was taking a gamble that was likely to turn out badly. Powerful though the Iraqi state was in the summer of 1980, it was not strong enough to defeat Iran. Unless the rule of Ayatollah Khomeini collapsed in the face of the Iraqi army offensive, Saddam Hussein would find himself fighting a unified state with three times the population of Iraq. Khomeini had already proved during the Iranian revolution that he could mobilise millions of people for street demonstrations. He could certainly put the same number into uniform with guns in their hands.

True, Saddam Hussein had powerful allies. His war effort was backed by the US, the Soviet Union, the West European states and most of the Arab world with the important exception of Syria. But the Iraqi state was more fragile than it looked. The passivity of the Shia might be enough in peacetime but not in war. They were estimated to make up 20 per cent of the officer corps of the army but 80 per cent of the rank and file. Furthermore this predominantly Shia army would be fighting their co-religionists in Iran. The depth of soldiers' loyalties might not matter in a short victorious war. But the conflict in which Iran and Iraq were about to engage proved to be very drawn out. The struggle along the Iran–Iraq border – neither side was able to penetrate far inside each other's territory – came to resemble the static but lethal trench warfare on the Western Front in the First World War. Even if Iraq had been a country united by strong religious and ethnic bonds, the loyalty of its soldiers would have been under strain.

The failure of the mainly Shia Iraqi army to mutiny en masse between 1980 and 1988 was later used as evidence that the soldiers were Iraqis before they were Shia. This argument was somewhat specious, though it may have sounded convincing to Americans in the run-up to the invasion of 2003 when the Shia opposition to Saddam Hussein was eager to convince Washington that by over-throwing Saddam the US would not be doing Iran a favour. In reality the attitude of Shia soldiers was more nuanced and it changed over time. 'Early in the war I and other Shia soldiers used to shoot high in the air during battles,' recalled Jafar Ali, a Shia sergeant from Basra who fought throughout the war. 'We used to say it would be better for Saddam to fight the Israelis than kill Shia Muslims. But later on when we had seen our friends killed or wounded in the fighting we shot to kill at the Iranians. Soldiers who didn't believe in the war would still go on fighting because they knew they didn't have much choice.' By Jafar Ali's account Shia soldiers deserted at the beginning of the war because they did not approve of it, while eight years later they were deserting simply because they were war weary.[7] Iraqi government propaganda about Iranian atrocities had enough substance to

be effective. 'Initially I was against the war,' said Muhammad
Yassin, a Shia army captain from Kerbala who also fought
throughout the war, 'but later on we heard about the terrible
time our prisoners were having in Iranian prisons and the
way they were ill treated. After that we began hating the
Iranians and we fought very hard. We started to feel a sense
of Iraqi national unity, regardless of whether or not Saddam
was president.'[8]

It soon became clear to Iraqis that Saddam had made a
disastrous blunder in invading Iran. It was 5 October 1980
before Iraqi soldiers captured Khorramshahr despite its being
close to Basra, just on the other side of the Shatt al-Arab
waterway, and even longer before they took the nearby
Iranian oil terminal at Abadan. Iraq had a large superiority in
tanks, but Iranian light infantry fought to the death. Foreign
journalists invited by the Ministry of Information in Baghdad
to witness the easy triumph of the Iraqi army found that
shells from Iranian artillery were exploding around them
long before they had left Iraqi territory and entered Iran.
Local people in Basra had also noticed that Iranian shells
were falling in their midst despite self-glorifying claims on
Iraqi radio about the rapid advance of the Iraqi military.
They nervously asked the journalists what was really
happening at the front.

The war was fought in predominantly Shia and Kurdish
areas of Iraq. Shia civilians immediately felt its impact. In the
first days of the war my colleague Robert Fisk visited the salt-
marsh peninsula of Fao facing Iran across the Shatt al-Arab.
'Fao was almost deserted,' he discovered. 'I watched many of
its inhabitants – part of the constant flow of millions of
refugees which are part of Middle East history – driving
north-west to Basra in a convoy of old Chevrolet taxis,
bedding piled on the roofs and chador-clad mothers and wives
on the back seats, scarcely bothering to glance at the burning
refineries of Abadan. They were Iraqi Shia Muslims and now
they were under fire from their fellow Shias in Iran, another
gift from Saddam.'[9] Much of the war was fought in the

marshes where the Tigris and Euphrates meet, where a few years earlier I had watched graceful canoes gliding between villages of reed houses built on artificial islands on the shores of shallow lakes. Within fifteen years the impact of war and Iraqi government repression would end the 5,000-year-long history of the marsh people. Ominously for a country as wholly dependent on oil revenue as Iraq, the Iranians began firing ground-to-ground missiles at the Iraqi oil terminals Khor al-Amaya and Mina al-Bakr twenty miles offshore, the vital outlets through which much of Iraq's crude was exported. Idling at anchor in Basra port were ninety freighters trapped by the war that was closing the Shatt al-Arab, their only exit to the sea. Over the next eight years the vessels slowly rotted as they waited in vain for the conflict to end.

The Iranians held the Iraqi advance and then counter-attacked. In 1981 they won their first big victory at Dezful, capturing 15,000 prisoners. On several occasions whole battalions of Shia soldiers surrendered without firing a shot. In May 1982 Iranian forces recaptured Khorramshahr and in June Iraq offered a truce, declaring a voluntary withdrawal from the few pockets of Iranian territory it still held. Iran turned down the ceasefire and demanded the removal of Saddam Hussein as the price of peace. By the end of 1982, American intelligence estimated that Iraq had lost 45,000 prisoners and the same number dead. By then Khomeini had taken the critical decision to carry the revolution west on the bayonets of the Iranian army. Iran now exaggerated its strength just as Iraq had done two years earlier. Mass surrenders by Iraqi Shia units ceased. In July 1982 nine Iranian infantry divisions hurled themselves at the Iraqi lines defending Basra but failed to break through. This was to be the pattern for the next four years. Then in 1986 the Iranian army suddenly captured the Fao peninsula in a surprise assault. Saddam Hussein mobilised more troops for a counter-attack. 'When Iran occupied Fao everybody began to fight back,' said Jafar Ali. 'This was the natural reaction to foreign invasion in all the Shia towns.'[10]

Many Iraqis had divided loyalties. One commando officer from a Shia family had three of his brothers executed by Saddam Hussein, but still fought because he thought it was his duty as a professional soldier and an Iraqi.[11] Others took a wholly opposite point of view. Rasheed Abdul Gafoor, many of whose relatives had been executed by Saddam Hussein, secretly listened to Iranian radio broadcasts in Arabic because only there could he hear religious songs and lectures. He was loyal to Imam Khomeini though it was too dangerous to talk about him with anybody except close family members. It was only after the fall of Saddam Hussein that he felt it safe to decorate the walls of his house with pictures of Khomeini, al-Khoei and al-Hakim.[12]

A simple but compelling reason why Shia soldiers did not desert or fail to fight was that it was lethally dangerous to do so. 'Anybody who failed to fight during a battle was executed instantly,' says one former soldier. 'His coffin was marked with the word "traitor" and his family was charged the price of the bullets used to execute him. Saddam's people were everywhere and when they captured a deserter they cut off his nose and ears and made a special mark on his forehead. On top of this a deserter would be banned from work and his rights as a citizen revoked.'[13] Armies have always used draconian means to stop soldiers running away and in this case mutilations and executions were largely successful in imposing discipline.

There were other reasons why Shia soldiers fought against their Iranian co-religionists. Iranian Shiism was intertwined with Iranian nationalism. Khomeini was able to overthrow the Shah in 1978–9 not only because he was a revered Shia religious leader but because he was a more convincing advocate of Iranian nationalism than the Shah. Ever since the Safavid dynasty forcibly converted Iran to Shiism 500 years earlier Iranian identity has been substantially religious. Khomeini had been expelled from Iran in 1964 when he denounced an agreement to exempt US soldiers in Iran from Iranian law.

The Shia of Iraq were also nationalist though their definition of what this meant in terms of Iraqi national identity was different from that of the Sunni. Their *mujtahids* had been the inspirers of the revolt against the British occupation of 1920. Unlike the Kurds the Shia demand had never been for the destruction or weakening of the Iraqi state but rather a fairer share of power within it and an end to anti-Shia discrimination.[14] This helps explain the surprising popularity of 'Sadrism' when it was re-launched by Muhammad Sadiq al-Sadr between 1992 and 1999 and, under the US occupation, by his son, Muqtada al-Sadr, after 2003. The movement combined Iraqi nationalist and Shia religious identity in a potent blend. Both Saddam and the US were at different moments astonished by the Sadrist success, but Iraq is not the only country where nationalism and religion march together. In Europe, Poland and Ireland are traditionally two of the most nationalist countries, and also two of the most religious, because of the bonding of Roman Catholicism and Polish and Irish national identity.

Saddam Hussein had crushed effective political opposition from the Shia by the summer of 1980. In the first months of the war he felt confident enough to give speeches in solidly Shia areas of Baghdad and Kerbala where he called on the faithful 'to fight with the spirit of Ali'. He paid for gold leaf to decorate the shrine of Abbas. Visiting Najaf he announced that he would 'fight for justice with the swords of the Imams' and made the birthday of Imam Ali a Shia national holiday. For all this there was one voice he wanted to hear supporting the war which remained stubbornly silent. Abu al-Qasim al-Khoei, the paramount religious leader of the Shia, had remained quiescent during the 1970s as persecution intensified against the Dawa party. This angered the supporters of Baqir al-Sadr who accused him of collaboration with the Baath, but al-Khoei's quietism was consistent. He did not approve of clerics becoming politicians or aspiring to become direct rulers of the state. He was vigorously opposed to

Ayatollah Khomeini's doctrine of *wilayat al-faqih* ('leadership of the scholars') under which the senior clergy would be the supreme authority in an Islamic government. In al-Khoei's view the *marji' al-taqlid* must adhere to its traditional role of providing spiritual and moral guidance for the laity.

This apolitical role, and the quietism so frequently criticised by the Sadrists in future, was never quite as otherworldly as it appeared. Al-Khoei genuinely believed – and this was also the belief of his successor Grand Ayatollah Ali al-Sistani – that the main concern of the Shia clergy should be spiritual. Aside from his theological stance there was also a simple but sensible calculation behind his apolitical stance. He could see that in any confrontation between the clerical leadership and the all-powerful Iraqi state the former was bound to lose. Avoiding such a conflict fitted in with the long Shia tradition of *taqiyya* (dissimulation and evasion by the faithful in order to avoid confrontation with more powerful authorities) in order to ensure survival. Allegations that the senior clergy stood idly by while members of the Dawa party were persecuted, arrested, tortured and murdered during the 1970s underplay the fact that there was little the so-called 'quietists' could have done to help their co-religionists. Al-Khoei did not openly support the revolution in Iran but he did not oppose it either. When Faradibbah, the wife of the Shah of Iran, visited Najaf in October 1978 and suddenly turned up at his house accompanied by Iraqi officials, he saw her but during their conversation strongly criticised the Shah's treatment of protestors in Tehran.[15] The following year when Baqir was executed his followers were furious about the religious leadership's mute response. 'It was al-Khoei's duty to eulogise the martyr al-Sadr but he did not,' said one cleric in Najaf. 'Nor did he say anything when seventy-nine scholars were executed on a single day.'[16] In Tehran, Iranian clergy claimed that al-Khoei had secretly supported the Shah in his final days. At a press conference one of them brandished a letter from al-Khoei to the Shah, found after the latter had fled, thanking him for an agate ring sent as a present. Tehran later concluded the letter was a fake.[17] The anger and desperation of the Dawa party supporters was understandable but at this moment the Baath party could have liquidated the surviving institutions of Iraqi Shiism very easily.

With the opening of the war with Iran the regime in Baghdad had a greater need for al-Khoei's support for the Iraqi war effort. It was more difficult to move against him because of the possible impact on the Shia soldiery. Al-Khoei's failure to endorse the war effort spoke volumes. A tone of impatience, if not desperation, began to creep into the government's desire to demonstrate that he supported the war. In October 1980 Iraqi television managed to catch him at a mosque in Najaf where prayers were said for the victory of Iraq's Arab army 'over the Persian aggressors'.[18] In May 1981 the state media proclaimed as a major scoop that al-Khoei had prayed for the health of Saddam Hussein.[19] More brutal but covert pressure was put on al-Khoei and his followers to support the war. When the regime organised the First Popular Islamic Conference in Baghdad in April 1983 the Grand Ayatollah and his family refused to attend. 'The *hawza* was almost destroyed,' says Ghanim Jawad, an important activist in the al-Khoei Foundation in London. 'They arrested activist *ulema* (clergy) or active students and accused them of being supporters of Iran or al-Dawa.' Foreign students were denied visas to stay in Iraq and Iraqi students were conscripted into the army. Iraqi security chipped away at the circle of advisers, friends and relatives around the Grand Ayatollah.[20] The UN Special Rapporteur on human rights in Iraq visited Najaf in January 1992. He said, 'The number of clergy at al-Najaf had been reduced from eight or nine thousand twenty years ago to two thousand ten years later, and 800 before the uprising of 1991.'[21] Al-Khoei himself survived perhaps because his open differences with Khomeini over the clerical control of the state were useful to the government in Baghdad as they denied the Iranian leader primacy over the Shia community worldwide.

For those Shia militants who wanted to oppose Saddam more directly the only alternative to al-Khoei's quietism was to flee the country. Muhammad Baqir al-Hakim was the fifth son of Grand Ayatollah Muhsin al-Hakim, the pre-eminent Shia cleric before al-Khoei. Born in Najaf in 1939 he was a founder member of the Dawa party, and had been jailed and then amnestied after trying to mediate during the bloody Arba'in of 1977. He fled to Syria in 1980 and then to Tehran, the city which, along with Damascus, was to become a base for Islamic militant groups.

The Iranians pressed for a single credible Iraqi Shia Islamic umbrella group to be established under their auspices. This was all the more necessary from the Iranian point of view after Iraqi forces had been driven from Iranian soil in the summer of 1982. If Iran was to advance into Iraq and appeal to the Iraqi Shia to overthrow Saddam Hussein then it needed an organisation uniting its Iraqi Shia friends. On 17 November 1982 al-Hakim announced the formation of the Supreme Council for Islamic Revolution in Iraq (SCIRI) that was to bring together his own following, the Dawa party and the Organization for Islamic Action – the group whose members had carried out attacks in Baghdad in April 1982 – under his leadership. Al-Hakim's family was to pay a fearful price for their opposition to Saddam and alliance with Iran. Sayyid Muhammad al-Musawi, a family friend from Najaf, estimates that sixty-three members of the family were executed by the Baathists.[22] Alarmed by the formation of SCIRI Saddam carried out mass arrests in 1983 of al-Hakim family members still in Iraq. Eighteen were executed and only one – Sayyid Hussein al-Hakim – was released after being forced to witness the killing of his relatives. He was told to go to Tehran to tell Muhammad Baqir al-Hakim about their fate. The cycle of deaths did not end there, Sayyid Mahdi al-Hakim, the brother of Baqir, was attending an Islamic conference in Khartoum in 1988 when a gunman sent by the Iraqi embassy shot him dead in a hotel lobby.

The fortunes of SCIRI were wholly dependent on the success of the Iranian war effort. The Iranians wanted the organisation set up quickly in case the regime in Baghdad collapsed and they needed an Iraqi Islamic leadership to put in its place. It was in a position similar to that of Communist parties that advanced with the tanks of the Red Army into eastern Europe in 1945 and took over local administrations. The difference was that the Iranian army did not advance very far into Iraq. The armed wing of SCIRI, the Badr Organization, drew its recruits from Islamic militants, Iraqi prisoners of war and the one million Iraqi refugees in Iran. Badr was commanded by an Iranian colonel at this time and was wholly under the control of Iran. It swiftly acquired a dubious reputation in Iraq for doing the Iranians' dirty work. 'They tortured Iraqi prisoners during the war,' says one professor at Najaf University. 'They tortured the Sunni and the Shia twice as badly because they used to ask them: Why did you join Saddam's army if you are a Shia?'[23] In the coming years SCIRI never quite shook this reputation in the minds of many Iraqis of being stooges of Iran who tortured their fellow countrymen.

The reign of terror against any sign of domestic discontent in Iraq intensified. Islamic militants arrested anywhere in Iraq knew what fate to expect. Punishment of family members of suspects, including children, became common. After one raid in Najaf in 1980 during which many families were arrested, a former prisoner found a one-month-old baby crying beside the road. The child had presumably been dropped or deliberately left behind by his mother as she was bundled into a security police vehicle. 'Such was the atmosphere of terror in Najaf at the time that the man who found me did not dare ask people whose family I belonged to,' recalls the foundling, now a well-educated twenty-seven-year-old man living in Amara in eastern Iraq. 'The man decided to look after me but this created a further problem because his neighbours would think the baby was a bastard or the child of prisoners which would mean serious trouble with the government. He sent me to Amara to be brought up by an old couple. I have never found out who my real family is.'[24]

It was never likely that Iraq would win a decisive victory in the war though dissidents in Tehran and Damascus optimistically packed their suitcases each time there was an Iranian offensive. The Iraqi defeats of 1981–2, when Saddam Hussein's downfall seemed possible, frightened the US and its allies. Donald Rumsfeld famously visited Baghdad in 1983 to deliver a carefully phrased letter from President Reagan to Saddam saying that Washington backed Iraq. Iraq was the first to start using poison gas on a mass scale since it had been used in the First World War without the rest of the world protesting. The US embassy reopened in Baghdad in 1984 and the CIA provided a flow of satellite photographs of Iranian positions. The US, along with the West Europeans, gave loans and credits and the tide began to turn. Advancing behind a blizzard of chemical weapons, including mustard gas and sarin and tabun nerve gases, the Republican Guard recaptured Fao from Iran in April 1988. Iraqi planes attacked Iranian oil tankers with French Exocet missiles. When the Iranians retaliated against Kuwait, the US agreed that the Kuwaiti oil-tanker fleet should sail under the American flag. The US was effectively joining the Iraqi side in the war. After a US naval vessel shot down an Iranian passenger plane flying to Dubai in July 1988, the Iranians concluded that the odds against them were too great. Ayatollah Khomeini announced that he must 'drain the bitter cup' and agreed to a ceasefire on 8 August 1988.

Saddam Hussein might have been able to unify many Iraqis behind patriotic slogans when an Iranian victory seemed possible. But the long and bloody conflict had served to discredit Iraqi nationalism. When Saddam invaded Kuwait in August 1990 he found the patriotic well had run dry. Iraqis did not want to fight again, particularly in a war they knew Iraq must lose. When officers who had spent their youth in the army were called up in the autumn of 1990 many broke down in tears. The official braggadocio was the same: Saddam pledged to raise a million-strong army. When, on one occasion, Ministry of Information officials took me to see part of this great force being trained, I watched bewildered Sudanese waiters and sullen Egyptian building-workers drilling with elderly Kalashnikovs. In Najaf the most influential Shia religious leader al-Khoei issued a fatwa saying that people should not buy goods looted by the Iraqi army in Kuwait. Another fatwa said that Shia soldiers were forbidden to pray on Kuwaiti territory; if they were already in Kuwait they should pray only in cars or trucks.[25] This, by Shia standards, was a surprisingly direct sign of al-Khoei's disapproval of the invasion. Government-sponsored rallies in Baghdad were ill-attended. The largest gathering I saw in the streets of the capital just before the war started on 17 January 1991 turned out to be a gathering of pigeon-fanciers. Savage punishments no longer maintained discipline in the army. When the US-led forces finally advanced they found that as much as half the Iraqi army had already deserted. Few of the remainder did any fighting. Iraq lost 2,100 tanks in Kuwait, but American damage assessment teams were surprised to discover that only 10 per cent had been destroyed in battle. The rest had been abandoned. Iraqis would no longer fight for Saddam.

CHAPTER FIVE

The Shia Rise Up

Grand Ayatollah al-Khoei was lying on a couch beside a window in a house in Kufa. His straggly white beard covered his chest and he was looking all his ninety-two years. He stared ahead with a detached gaze as if he did not notice the Iraqi security men who had suddenly filled his room. It was a few weeks after the Shia of Iraq had risen up in March 1991, in the wake of the Iraqi army's devastating defeat in Kuwait. At the height of the rebellion mutinying Shia soldiers held every city south of Baghdad and came close to overthrowing Saddam Hussein. Then, as the US-led coalition refused to interfere, Iraqi army units loyal to the regime launched fierce counter-attacks, crushed the uprising and began to exact a terrible vengeance. Along with other reporters I had been expelled from Iraq and forced to go to Jordan when the news of the uprising first reached Baghdad at the beginning of March. Then, to my surprise, I was allowed back in again. The Iraqi government must have wanted to show the media and the world that it was once more in control. Leaving early from the al-Rashid Hotel in Baghdad in a convoy of cars with the Information Ministry minders on 15 April we were told we were going to Kufa and Najaf, but not that we would be seeing al-Khoei. When we reached the nondescript house where he was staying I saw it was surrounded by guards and there were plain-clothes men inside the gates. It was clear he was under house arrest. He seemed to be alone and I could not see any of the myriad of relatives and

retainers whom I would have expected to find around the
Grand Ayatollah who was, after all, the supreme spiritual
leader of 150 million Shia around the world. I have always
felt uneasy interviewing prisoners because it is impossible to
know what pressures or threats have been made against
them. It seemed particularly unfair to badger an old man
surrounded by Iraqi secret policemen. Nevertheless, I asked
al-Khoei what he thought about the uprising. For some
minutes he said nothing and I was beginning to think that he
had not heard my question. Then, speaking very low in a
gasping voice, he said: 'What happened in Najaf and other
cities is not allowed and is against God.' His answer was
carefully ambiguous, not making clear if he was condemning
the actions of the insurgents or the government. He went on
to say: 'Nobody visits me, so I don't know what is happening. I have trouble with my breathing.'[1]

I was right to think that al-Khoei was under intense
pressure from the regime to condemn the uprising. It had
started in Basra on 1 March and by 4 March had spread to
Najaf. Two days later, after the capture of the city by anti-
government forces, al-Khoei had issued the first of two
fatwas urging Muslims 'to look after the holy places' and
guard people's property and government institutions. He
appealed for dead bodies lying in the streets to be buried,
though without success. A second directive, issued as the
insurgents consolidated their victory, set up a Supreme
Committee under which the Shia would provide for security
and public order. To somebody as suspicious as Saddam
Hussein this may have looked as if al-Khoei was authorising
an alternative administration. When Iraqi troops recaptured
Najaf ten days later they arrested al-Khoei. A Najaf resident
who was later interviewed by a human rights organisation
said: 'I watched from a nearby house as some soldiers captured the Imam [al-Khoei], four members of the leadership,
and some of the rebels. They forced the Imam, who is over
ninety years old, to walk without assistance and, since he
cannot, he fell to the ground. Then his son helped him up

and all were taken away.'² Al-Khoei and his son Muhammad
Taqi were taken to the military intelligence headquarters in
Baghdad on the night of 19 March and next morning they
were summoned for a two-hour meeting with a furious
Saddam Hussein. Muhammad Taqi, who sat silent
throughout, later recalled that Saddam said to his father: 'I
didn't think you would do something like this.' The Grand
Ayatollah said he had only been trying to control the
violence. 'No, you wanted to overthrow me,' the Iraqi leader
replied. 'Now you have lost everything. You did everything
the Americans wanted you to do.'³

Saddam compelled al-Khoei to appear with him on television and make a statement denouncing violence. The
Grand Ayatollah had little choice but to comply. The security
police had detained 105 of his associates in Najaf at the same
time as he was arrested including his son-in-law Mahmoud
al-Melawi, the eighty-nine-year-old Ayatollah Murtaza
Kazemi Khalkali and scores of Shia scholars. The al-Hakim
family was once again targeted with two clerics and eight
other family members detained. Despite a long campaign by
human rights organisations to find out what had happened to
the men arrested only one, a Pakistani, was freed. The rest
ended up in mass graves with tens of thousands of other Shia
who were being murdered at this time. Only al-Khoei and his
son Muhammad Taqi were allowed to return to the heavily
guarded house in Najaf where I saw him a few weeks later. √

The rebellion, known in Iraq as the Shaaban Intifada after
the Muslim month of Sha'aban, reshaped the political and
religious landscape of Iraq. It was immediately and
explosively successful in the Shia south and in Kurdistan, but
not in Baghdad and the Sunni heartlands of central Iraq.
Here Saddam Hussein was able to hang on. Sunni terror of
the Shia and Kurds probably consolidated support for him
within the upper ranks of the regime. Sunni generals who
had been planning a coup against him after the debacle in
Kuwait thought again.⁴ I had a friend, a sophisticated

journalist who in private always expressed to me his loathing for the regime and his hope that it would be overthrown. But he was also a Sunni and during the uprising he confessed to me that he was so frightened for the safety of himself and his family if the Shia rebels seized Baghdad that he wanted the uprising crushed. He may have exaggerated the chances of an anti-Sunni pogrom, but he was right in suspecting that as soon as Saddam's iron grip was relaxed a subterranean well of hatred against the regime would instantly burst forth in the Shia community. Sanaa Muhammad, a Shia woman who worked in local government in Kerbala, describes how, soon after the fall of the city to insurgents, she met two women in the street who were asking questions as to the whereabouts of certain men. The women were Shia and explained they had travelled 100 miles across war-torn Iraq because they were 'searching for two of Saddam's security men who killed their brothers and wanted to take their revenge on them'.[5]

The slaughter of Baathist officials during the uprising, and the even more savage retaliation by the government, made the gap between Shia and Sunni in Iraq almost unbridgeable. Each community had a wholly different vision of what had happened during the intifada. For instance, there is no evidence that the Iranian role in it was very significant. This angered many of the insurgents and their sympathisers. Hussein al-Shahristani, an Iraqi nuclear scientist who had been a member of the Dawa party, escaped to Iran from Abu Ghraib prison after twelve years imprisonment during the American bombing in early 1991. He had been arrested and savagely tortured in 1979 for refusing to help Saddam Hussein build a nuclear bomb. He was bitterly critical of the Iranian role. 'They encouraged the uprising and then betrayed it,' he said. 'They only let a few people across the border to help, and they would not let them bring arms. They certainly did not put up posters [of Ayatollah Khomeini] – they were terrified of the American reaction.'[6] But the Sunni community was convinced that the uprising was fomented and sustained by Iran. This made them even more brutal in their treatment of any Shia unlucky enough to be detained during it or afterwards. They saw them as pawns of Iran and traitors to their country. One former Sunni officer, Colonel Othman, stationed in Kerbala at the time of the intifada, is wholly unrepentant about his role in suppressing the uprising, firmly believing to this day that 'Iran was providing aid (to rebels) across the border in the form of food, weapons and secret intelligence agents. Iran was arming the rabble and supporting them psychologically and financially.'[7]

The cause of the uprising was the humiliating defeat of the Iraqi army in Kuwait. This discredited the regime and weakened its instruments of repression. In the six months following Saddam Hussein's invasion of Kuwait, many Iraqis thought that he would do a deal with the US at the last moment. They knew they could not fight the vast coalition President George Bush was assembling. 'We didn't expect a war,' said one general who later fled to England. 'We thought it was all a political manoeuvre.'[8] When round-the-clock bombing of the Iraqi army in Kuwait started on 19 January, the soldiers, mostly Shia and Kurdish conscripts, knew the war could have only one outcome. They deserted in droves. A few months later in Kurdistan I interviewed Captain Azad Shirwan, an intelligence officer of a tank brigade that had been stationed in Kuwait. He told me that by the time the US-led ground offensive started on 24 February most of his men had disappeared: 'In our brigade, positions were mostly defended by officers, because the private soldiers had deserted.'[9] Iraqis of all sorts are astute at sniffing the political winds. They were well informed because they secretly listened to transistor radios. The soldiers in Kuwait knew that the battle was lost before it began. When Saddam Hussein ordered a withdrawal from Kuwait a day into the allied ground offensive the army simply broke up.

'We were anxious to withdraw, to end the mad adventure, when Saddam announced withdrawal within twenty-four hours – though without any formal agreement to ensure the safety of the retreating forces,' one officer recalled bitterly. He and his men suspected that Saddam did not care if regular army units were wiped out so long as he could preserve his praetorian Republican Guard divisions. 'We had to desert our tanks and vehicles to avoid aerial attacks. We walked 100 kilometres towards the Iraqi territories, hungry, thirsty and exhausted.' They arrived at town of Zubair south of Basra. 'In Zubair we decided to put an end to Saddam and his regime. We shot at his posters. Hundreds of retreating soldiers came to the city and joined the revolt; by the afternoon, there were thousands of us. Civilians supported us and demonstrations started. We attacked the party building and the security service headquarters.'[10]

The mutiny soon spread to Basra where the streets were full of angry soldiers separated from their units. It became part of the mythology of the revolt that its opening shot was discharged in Saad Square in Basra on 1 March by a tank-gunner who fired into the smiling face of Saddam Hussein on one of the giant posters that decorated every street in Iraq. This was said to have ignited the uprising and was an iconic moment in the rebellion. Everybody recalls having heard the story, the first cathartic moment of defiance against the dictator, but the tank-gunner himself has proved elusive. There is no doubt, however, about what happened during the rest of the day as anti-Baathist crowds rampaged through the streets. 'The streets were full of people, many of them soldiers,' recalled an exiled Iraqi businessman who had re-turned to Iraq from Iran just before the uprising. 'They were shouting slogans and writing them on the wall, destroying Saddam's pictures and monuments, executing members of the Baath party.'[11] Fighting was particularly intense because some 6,000 loyalists from the Republican Guard held out against 5,000 defectors from the regular army.

So many events were packed into the first euphoric but bloody hours of the uprising that participants had varying accounts of what had happened. A month later, after

Saddam's tanks had recaptured the city, I asked Dr Walid al-Rawi, the cool-headed administrator of Basra Teaching Hospital, about his memories of the revolt. He said it was a little slower to develop than others had related. The first he knew about it was when a policeman told him there were violent incidents in small towns and villages on the edge of the vast marshes between Basra, Amara and Nasiriyah that had always been hiding places for anti-government guerrillas. 'Later that day, a band of fifty rebels came to the hospital and took away three patients who were security men, one of whom they shot in the hospital grounds.' Walking around the city centre I could see burned out Baath party offices, but otherwise the visible damage was limited. From the beginning the insurgents showed their puritanical Islamic beliefs. Muhammad Kassim, the manager of the Basra Tower Hotel, told me that on the first day of the uprising armed men came to his hotel. 'They asked if there were any Baathists staying or any alcohol. I told them no and they went away.' Not every hotel was so lucky. Another band of rebels burst into the Sheraton, notorious for its Filipino hostesses during the Iran–Iraq war. The hotel was closed but I could see from below in the street the dark scorch-marks where the rebels had set fire to its top storey and burned out nineteen rooms.[12]

There were sporadic lynchings in other parts of the city. The military intelligence headquarters were stormed by a crowd on the second day of the uprising and the soldiers inside killed. On the quayside beside the Shatt al-Arab was the dead body of a Baathist official tied by the neck with a spike driven through his chest. Somebody had stolen his shoes and his feet were bare.[13]

Dr al-Rawi was right in thinking that the first incidents in the uprising had started in the villages outside Basra. In a hastily commandeered villa in Baghdad, General Wafiq al-Samarrai, the burly forty-four-year-old head of military intelligence, was monitoring developments for Saddam Hussein in the

disastrous days after the defeat in Kuwait. He had hurriedly
moved into his emergency headquarters before the war in the
correct expectation that the grandiose official offices of
Military Intelligence would be destroyed by missiles and
smart bombs in the first hours of the war. His earliest
intimation that pinprick guerrilla attacks were starting came
in a worrying phone call from Basra. An army general,
Hamid Shakar, had been driving to Baghdad with one body-
guard when insurgents ambushed his car near a paper mill 30
miles north of Basra. This was on the fringe of the marshes
and their vast reed beds, one of the few areas suitable for
guerrillas to hide in the whole of southern Iraq. Al-Samarrai
called Saddam Hussein who rushed to his headquarters. As
he arrived there was a second call, this time from General
Nizar al-Khazraji, who commanded the whole of south-west
Iraq and had his headquarters in Nasiriyah. Shouting his
words over a line so poor that General al-Samarrai could
barely hear him, Khazraji said: 'The rebels are trying to
attack us.' Fearing that he would not be believed he held up
his phone and asked: 'Don't you hear the bullets?' Because of
the bad reception al-Samarrai could hear nothing. Khazraji
asked for a helicopter to extract him. 'I told Saddam, who
was sitting in my headquarters, what was happening in
Nasiriyah and he ordered a helicopter to rescue Khazraji,'
General al-Samarrai recalled. But the Iraqi army was
disintegrating fast. The officer commanding the helicopters
said there was nothing he could do because 'we don't have
any helicopters in the area'. Soon afterwards Saddam and
General al-Samarrai heard that it was too late: the building
Khazraji was in had been stormed by rebels and the general
had been seriously wounded and captured.[14]

Events during the uprising are usually recounted either by
the government or their opponents, but seldom by both.
However, in the case of capture of Khazraji there is a reliable
witness, a Shia notable of Nasiriyah called Kadhum al-
Raysan, who saw what happened. His story is significant
because it confirms what al-Samarrai, who escaped to

London several years later, told me, and shows how scattered bands of Shia guerrillas hiding in the marshes were able to take advantage of the collapse of government authority. Raysan saw fourteen young men with light arms coming from the marshes and heading for the centre of Nasiriyah, a Shia city with a population of one million. The men were chanting *'Allahu Akbar! Allahu Akbar!'* as they advanced. Soon they were joined by hundreds of other young men. As government authority broke down, General Khazraji was caught up in the fighting and besieged in a building with sixty or seventy loyalists. It is at this point that he must have made his anguished but vain plea to Baghdad for help. Raysan says that the fighting went on for hours and everybody in the building was killed aside from Khazraji who was severely wounded. Surprisingly the insurgents did not kill him but took him to the local hospital. From there he was rescued by a helicopter assault team that Baghdad had finally been able to assemble. Raysan, who later fled to Saudi Arabia, did not know why Khazraji was spared when so many minor Baathists were being hunted down and killed.[15]

The intifada spread with extraordinary speed from Basra and Nasiriyah northwards to the Shia cities strung along the Euphrates and Tigris rivers. As the heart of the Shia faith and the home of Grand Ayatollah al-Khoei, Najaf was regarded with suspicion by the regime and was always filled with Baathist security men. Even so there had been signs of dissent earlier in February. On the 14th at the funeral of a well-known cleric called Yusuf al-Hakim, a member of the family famously hostile to the regime, the mourners had chanted anti-Saddam slogans. People knew that the war in Kuwait was going badly. I had stood in the courtyard of the Imam Ali shrine after the start of the bombing campaign watching the simple wooden coffins of dead soldiers draped with the Iraqi flag being carried past. The US air attacks, which killed thirty-five people in Najaf, had also shown that there was nothing the government could do to protect its own people. I visited the pulverised remains of a house, once the home of the al-Habubi family, thirteen of whom had been killed by a misdirected bomb apparently aimed at a nearby electricity substation.

By 2 March angry soldiers who had escaped from Kuwait began to arrive in Najaf. One of them was a professional soldier from the city, named Abdul Hassan al-Khafaji, who bitterly recalls how he and his men were 'chased like rats' out of Kuwait during the lost battle. 'The streets were full of deserters,' he said. 'All structure in the army was lost. Everybody was their own boss. News was spreading that somebody had shot at Saddam's portrait in Basra.' The following day he went to a demonstration in Imam Ali Square close to the shrine. 'At first there were about a hundred people, many of them army officers from Najaf who had deserted. The security forces were well informed and were there as well. The demonstrators were shouting: "Saddam, keep your hands off. The people of Iraq don't want you."' Security men opened fire on the crowd. Only a few of the demonstrators had pistols but they shot back. One important local Baathist was caught and hacked to death with knives. The sound of the shooting attracted more people, mostly young men in their twenties and teenagers. The security men chased them into the bazaar, a warren of small shops and booths in the centre of Najaf, and there was confused fighting for twenty minutes or half an hour, at the end of which the security forces fled to their headquarters. Their retreat was decisive. The crowd took over the shrine of Imam Ali, which had a generator to power its loudspeakers that called the faithful to prayer. Now the jubilant demonstrators used the sound system to rally people against the Baathists shouting slogans such as 'Seek out the criminals'.

A legacy of Saddam Hussein's wars was that every Iraqi male knew how to use a gun. These were available in surprising numbers in Najaf and other Iraqi cities because the Iraqi leader had unwisely stockpiled arms in schools around the country to arm the people in case of an American landing from the air. By the evening of 3 March the increasingly well-armed insurgents had stormed a girl's school used by the Amn al-Khass security police and killed eight or nine people inside. Predominantly Sunni army units that previously guarded Najaf on behalf of the regime had all been sent to Kuwait. The Quds division of the Republican Guard was based just outside Najaf but its barracks were empty apart from administrative staff. These did not resist when the rebels commandeered 82-millimetre mortars and used them against the Baath party headquarters. 'Abdel Amir Jaithoun, my old headmaster, was killed there,' relates Colonel Khafaji. 'So too was Najim Mizhir, who was the only Baath leader in the city who actually came from Najaf and was quite liked, though he shot a demonstrator.' Throughout the city Baathists were hunted down while others hid in the great Shia cemetery that surrounds Najaf.[16] Many, but not all, who were captured abjectly pleaded for their lives. Yunis al-Sammari, the head of the security police in Kufa, rejected an offer to spare his life if he gave information about arms caches. As he was led off to execution he shouted: 'I have lived a Baathist all my life and I will die one.'[17]

In Kerbala, to the north of Najaf, Sanaa Muhammad, a Shia government employee, was astonished at the speed with which the regime was disintegrating around her. From listening to the radio she knew of the retreat from Kuwait but could not believe that Kerbala and the mid-Euphrates region had fallen to insurgents because of 'the terrifying picture of Saddam and his regime we had in our minds'. Then she heard strange noises from the street outside her house. 'Young men were shouting "We have been liberated" and "Saddam is finished". They were cheering for the glory of Imam Hussein and the *hawza*.' Almost immediately revenge killings began. 'Two members of the Baath party were killed in our street,' says Sanaa. 'My family and I were terrified because my brothers worked in government jobs, so they fled from Kerbala. In fact, the killings were of people working for security and the killers knew who they were so they did not need guides. I myself saw a middle-aged man, in the sort of suit that Baath party members used to wear, running down the street until he was out of breath with two or three men chasing him firing their guns. He was dodging right and left trying to avoid the bullets but eventually he was hit and died there. They threw his corpse on to a pile of bodies of people who had been killed earlier in the day.' Retaliatory killings increased when Baath party and security buildings were sacked and confidential documents were discovered revealing who had worked as an informer for the regime.

Liberation was followed by an orgy of looting. Everything was considered fair game. 'I saw how they robbed government institutions and schools,' says Sanaa with deep disapproval. 'They stole machinery from livestock farms that they could not possibly use, just for the sake of destruction. The same thing happened at the Kerbala canning plant: some of the foodstuffs were distributed among the people and the rest just vanished. This happened although there was a declaration by the *marji'iya* forbidding the theft of government property which nobody paid any attention to.'[18] Looting was very much an Iraqi tradition among both Arabs and Kurds, and is probably explained by a history of nomadic raiding in the not so distant past, exacerbated by a hatred of all authority. During the intifada in Najaf even traffic lights were wrecked as symbols of the state.[19] The looters were often in the front ranks of those seizing government buildings (so much so that during the war of 2003 I avoided entering barracks and other state facilities if I could not see looters, on the grounds that if they thought such places were too dangerous to steal from they were probably right). The intifada also revealed that Iraq was full of people desperate for vengeance against the agents of the state. In the city of Kut on the Tigris south of Baghdad, scene of the siege and surrender of a small British army in 1916, the regime only lost control for a single day. But Ali Muhammad, a teacher in Kut, says that even so 'we had the same killing of Baathists, and stealing of government property that happened in other provinces happened here. They stole fabric from the Kut fabric factory. It was only when the authorities regained control and announced by loudspeakers that there was going to be a house-to-house search, that people began leaving stolen goods in the streets.'[20]

The success of the uprising depended on the attitude of the Americans. Clear-sighted Shia rebels saw this from the beginning. 'The biggest reason for the intifada is that they [the rebels] thought the Americans would support them,' Sayyid Majid al-Khoei, the intelligent and perceptive second son of the Grand Ayatollah, told me. 'They knew they couldn't beat Saddam on their own. They thought they could get control of the cities and the Americans would stop Saddam's army from intervening.' In the first euphoric days of the uprising people in the streets believed the same thing. Sayyid Majid kept a diary. On the night of 4 March, just after the insurgents had taken Najaf, he went to the shrine of Imam Ali and wrote down what he heard people saying. Leafing through a battered notebook years later he read their remarks out to me. 'Iraq is finished,' said one man. 'The Western armies are in Basra and Samawa.' People believed rumours that Saddam had fled from Iraq. 'Kerbala and Najaf are in our hands,' said others gathered at the shrine. 'Let us go on to Baghdad.'[21]

For a few days a march on Baghdad seemed possible. The regime was beset by enemies on all sides. On 5 March the Kurds had started their own uprising which was instantly victorious across Kurdistan. In the city of Hilla, only 66 miles south of Baghdad, a tank commander joined the rebels and proposed leading an advance on the capital with his six tanks. 'The way to Baghdad is open,' he said, but his unit disintegrated as his men went hunting for local Baathists to kill. In Najaf there were many army officers who had deserted, including Colonel Khafaji who, with the encouragement of the Grand Ayatollah, set up a military committee to try to organise the thousands of Shia soldiers and armed young men milling about in the streets. The first government counter-attack on Kerbala faltered when a battalion commander shot his chief security officer in the head and changed sides. 'But the committee could not keep his unit together,' confessed Colonel Khafaji. 'We had to tell the men to change into their *dishdashes* [Arab robes] and go home.'[22]

Paradoxically, it was the very sectarian nature of Saddam Hussein's regime, which had provoked the mutiny of Shia units and Kurdish *Jash* (locally recruited pro-government Kurdish militia), that now enabled him to survive. The Shia and Kurds – 80 per cent of the Iraqi population – wanted to overthrow him, but the Sunni, despite recent disasters, did not want him ousted by the other two biggest communities in Iraq. The security services, the Baath party and the elite Republican Guard units of the army were Sunni-dominated and had remained intact. Despite losses in Kuwait the government still commanded a formidable force. According to a March 1991 US Defense Intelligence Agency (DIA) report, seven Republican Guard divisions remained intact (compared to twelve before the war), of which three were armoured, one mechanised and three infantry. This was in addition to twenty-four under-strength regular army divisions of which eighteen were infantry. The DIA estimated the Iraqi army to be less than half the size it had been before its devastating losses in Kuwait, but it was still militarily strong enough to overcome the enthusiastic but unorganised insurgents.[23] These lightly armed rebels had no answer to the regime's tanks and artillery. Had they made a successful dash for Baghdad in the first moments of the rebellion could this have led the badly battered regime to unravel? The Shia were the majority of the population in Baghdad.[24] They might have risen up but it was not very likely. Saddam still had units on which he could rely. In the event, if there was such an opportunity, it was fleeting.

Saddam Hussein was always likely to survive unless the US intervened and stopped him using his tanks and artillery.

After the intifada was savagely crushed President George Bush was accused of encouraging the Iraqis to rise up and then doing nothing. On 15 February he had called on 'the Iraqi military and the Iraqi people to take matters into their own hands and force Saddam Hussein, the dictator, to step aside'. This was not exactly a starting pistol for a rebellion. It had begun, not because of Bush's words, encouraging though these might be, but because the defeat of the Iraqi army in Kuwait led to a military mutiny. This in turn provoked a civil rebellion. Once it began, it was reasonable for the Shia to expect US help in finishing off Saddam. Bush had hoped that the Iraqi military would get rid of Saddam Hussein. He did not expect a mutiny in the ranks but a military coup d'etat at the top by senior army commanders. 'We were concerned that that the uprisings would sidetrack the overthrow of Saddam, by causing the Iraqi military to rally around him to prevent the break-up of the country,' Bush later explained. 'That may have been what actually happened.'[25]

Preventing 'the break-up of the country' was in effect palatable code for supporting the Sunni over the Shia and Kurds. The Shia were not, after all, trying to break up Iraq, but get their fair share of power within it. Using slightly different words Zalmay Khalilzad, then director of policy planning at the State Department, wrote: 'The partitioning of Iraq will not serve our long-term interests. Iraqi disintegration will improve prospects for Iranian domination of the Gulf and remove a restraint on Syria.'[26] The Shia rebels on the ground soon noticed the impact of the American attitude. US forces were close to Basra, Nasiriyah and Samawa, but studiously avoided assisting the rebels. Insurgents saw Iraqi arms dumps containing weapons they desperately needed erupt in flames as American army engineers blew them up. The US was suddenly showing a decorous sensitivity about interfering in Iraq's domestic affairs and offending its Arab allies. In Washington Secretary of Defence Dick Cheney declared piously on 5 March that 'it would be very difficult for us to hold the coalition together for any particular course of action dealing with Iraqi internal politics'.[27] On the same day, US Marine Major General Martin Brandtner, deputy director of operations for the Joint Chiefs of Staff, said, 'There is no move on [the part] of US forces to let any weapons slip through [to the rebels], or to play any role whatsoever in fomenting or assisting any side.'[28]

The evident intention of the US forces to stay neutral while the rebellion was crushed was a frightening development for the people around Grand Ayatollah al-Khoei. Already they could see the Iraqi army using attack helicopters without impediment from the allied forces. They were the leaders of the Shia community in so far as it had any. Sayyid Majid, with the blessings of his father, set off together with Colonel Khafaji and a small party on 9 March to make contact with the allies. 'Find out what are their ideas about us, what are they going to do,' the Grand Ayatollah instructed his son. It was a frustrating journey as they drove south looking for allied leaders to speak to, knowing that Saddam Hussein was beginning to launch a devastating counter-attack they could not hope to withstand. They met American forces outside Nasiriyah and explained their mission to its commander. He disappeared for ten minutes and on his return claimed he was out of touch with his headquarters. This did not seem very likely to Brigadier Ali since American units were loaded down with communications equipment. The officer advised them to talk to the French, 80 miles to the west, who had heard the al-Khoei name and at first were helpful. A meeting with allied commander General Norman Schwarzkopf was promised but never took place. Finally the French explained the problem to Majid: 'The Americans are worried about the Iranians. They asked who brought Khomeini's pictures into Iraq. I explained that I had seen no pictures of Khomeini in any of the cities I had passed through. I said that people were mistaking pictures of my father, Grand Ayatollah al-Khoei, for Khomeini, because both were old men with white beards.'[29]

How far did the Iranians play a role in the uprising, as Baghdad furiously claimed and many in Washington quietly

believed? Hussein al-Shahristani, the nuclear scientist and
prisoner of Saddam Hussein who was to become Iraq's oil
minister in 2006, denounces Iran for encouraging an uprising
and then betraying it. Many in the opposition believed it was
Saddam's men who put up pictures of Khomeini to scare the
US. 'He sent his own *mukhabarat* [intelligence] to the south
with pictures of Khomeini,' the secular Iraqi opposition
leader Saad Jabr told me. 'The Badr brigade never came. We
talked to the Iranians. They swear by the Koran they didn't
send the pictures.[30] But in Basra and Amara, both close to the
Iranian border, there were signs that Muhammad Baqir al-
Hakim, the leader of the SCIRI, the political master of Badr,
was intending to play a role. His picture appeared and a
statement saying 'All parties working from Iranian territories
should also obey al-Hakim's orders, no party is allowed to
recruit volunteers; no ideas except the rightful Islamic ones
should be disseminated.'[31] There is no doubt that Iraqis who
had lived for a long time in Iran did go back to Iraq, but not
always to fight. There were, after all, one million Iraqi
refugees in Iran. Sanaa Muhammad encountered one Iraqi
returnee from Iran who had come to Kerbala to see what had
happened to his property that had been confiscated by the
government. He was angry that his neighbours had not been
more supportive.[32]

Colonel Othman, who played an active role in suppressing
the uprising, was convinced that Badr, Dawa, and Iranian
Revolutionary Guards were flooding into Iraq from Iran
aided by the Shia *ulema* and used Shia *husseiniyahs* (Shia
places of worship roughly equivalent to a small mosque) 'as
their bases and a place to store arms. Iran had a very major
role in these events.' This was the view of most of the Sunni
community inside and outside the Baath Party. 'Sunni
mosques were turned into Shia *husseiniyahs* and religious
chants could be heard from them,' recalls the colonel. 'Badr,
the Qods Organization of the Iranian Revolutionary Guards,
and Islamic Dawa all passed through the border crossing
point between Mehran and Badrah [towns on the Iran–Iraq

border north of Kut and due east of Baghdad].' After assembling at *husseiniyahs* they were guided by *hawza* members to camps and security headquarters of the Baath party 'where they executed the officers and the soldiers'.[33]

The most convincing account of the Islamic militant and Iranian role in the uprising is given by Hussein, a dissident Shia from Basra. He confirms that 'during the war in Kuwait we had continual contacts with the Badr Organization which had a secret headquarters in Kut city which they reached from Mehran [a town just inside Iraq]. They played no part in igniting the uprising, which was a spontaneous reaction to the army's defeat in Kuwait and the reckless and foolhardy actions of Saddam. Muhammad Baqir al-Hakim and his people supported by Badr were supposed to come through Mehran to Kut, but they never came. This was one of the reasons for the hostility later between Sadrists and al-Hakim.' The most likely explanation for the failure of al-Hakim to appear was that the Iranians stopped him. There was a hunger for known leaders among the victorious insurgents. 'In Basra when the province was taken over there was a rumour that Muhammad Baqir al-Hakim had come to the city,' says Hussein. 'There really was a man wearing a turban in the [former] governor's car with half of his body sticking out of the open roof waving to the crowd. They ran after the car but, when they found it was not al-Hakim but a man well known in Basra, they were very angry.'[34] The Iranians seemed to have been as surprised as everybody else by the uprising and were fearful of offending the US. If Badr, a well-equipped and trained military force, had aided the uprising then the Iraqi army would have had to fight harder to regain control of southern Iraq. A week after the insurgents had seized southern Iraq it was becoming grimly apparent that they could expect no help from the Iranians or the Americans.

*

Saddam Hussein was already certain he could crush the insurgency without provoking US intervention. General al-

Samarrai, the military intelligence chief, says the decisive
information on the US position came in the form of an
intercept of two radio conversations between two Shia rebels
somewhere near Nasiriyah. The fact the intercept had been
made, and was passed on by the listening station at
Rashidiya north of Baghdad, shows that the Iraqi military
machine was reconstituting itself. After a glance at the
transcripts, al-Samarrai saw its significance and had a copy
rushed to Saddam. Al-Samarrai recollects that the
conversation opens with one rebel saying: 'We went to the
Americans for their support. They told us, "We are not going
to support you because you are from the al-Sayyid group
[Muhammad Baqir al-Hakim]."

"Ask them again," responds the second speaker. "Go back
and ask once more." '

A second transcript contains the Americans' reply, which
must have been devastating news to the rebels as it was the
death-warrant of the uprising. The first rebel leader reported
back: 'They say, "We are not going to support you because
you are Shia and are collaborating with Iran." ' Al-Samarrai
says this finally convinced Saddam Hussein, as he must have
already suspected, that for now at least the Americans were
not going to allow the Shia to overthrow him. 'After this
message,' says the intelligence chief, 'the position of the
regime immediately became more confident. Now [Saddam]
began to attack the intifada.'

CHAPTER SIX

Saddam Strikes Back

I saw the first signs of the Iraqi army offensive against the Shia rebels at a place called Aoun, east of Kerbala. On each side of the road were the blackened stumps of date-palm trees, which had either been set ablaze by artillery fire or burned by soldiers to deny the insurgents cover for ambushes. The countryside and the outskirts of the city were unnaturally empty with few people about apart from bored soldiers at the many checkpoints. The fighting had been fiercest in Kerbala itself, especially around the shrines of Abbas and Hussein. Just above the gateway into the shrine of Abbas a rocket-propelled grenade had smashed into the blue-and-yellow tiling, exposing the brown bricks underneath. Inside one room in the corner of the rectangular buildings surrounding the inner courtyard our guides showed us a gibbet in the ceiling and dark blood marks on the concrete floor where Baathist officials had had their throats cut. Outside the battered gates were three or four massive British-made Centurion tanks, captured by the Iraqi army during the first few victorious days of the Iran–Iraq war. Their long gun barrels pointed out over a wide empty space that separated the shrine of Abbas from that of Hussein 400 yards away. Two months earlier this had been filled with small shops and twisting alleyways which had been heavily shelled and then bulldozed. I could see mounds of broken bricks and smashed woodwork on either side of the devastated area. I went with other journalists to see General Abdul Khaliq Abdul Aziz, a

vigorous, confident-looking man who had been appointed
governor of Kerbala. He viewed the city very much as
conquered territory and tried to persuade us that the Iranians
had been the driving force behind the insurgents in the city.
He pointed to a few ammunition boxes and TNT charges
that he claimed could only have come from Iran.

We drove south to Najaf where, at first, the golden dome
of the shrine of Imam Ali looked undamaged. When we
entered the courtyard of the shrine itself the flagstones
covering the ground were pitted with little craters where
mortar bombs and rocket-propelled grenades had detonated.
The dome itself had been punctured by heavy machine-gun
fire. Soldiers were nonchalantly guarding the gates. There
was not a single pilgrim in the courtyard where once Shia
from every corner of the world had gathered. A solitary
attendant was sweeping up broken blue tiles from the side
wall of the shrine itself. I went to see the governor of Najaf,
Abdul Rahman al-Dhouri, who told the same tale as his
colleague in Kerbala about how the Iranian revolutionary
guards had swept into Najaf only to be routed by the loyal
forces of the Iraqi government. I left his office and walked
back towards the shrine. Once again I was struck by the
emptiness of streets that had once teemed with people: clergy
in black turbans, intent-looking pilgrims and traders with
their carts selling cheap goods. I was walking slowly on the
pavement, a row of closed shops with heavy metal shutters a
few feet to my left, talking to another journalist. Somebody
must have heard us. Suddenly from behind a shutter I heard
a thin despairing voice say in Iraqi-accented English: 'Help
us! Help us!'

By that time many people in Kerbala and Najaf and the other
cities that had risen against Saddam Hussein at the beginning
of March were beyond help. The government counter-attack
was led by General Hussein Kamel, Saddam's cousin and
son-in-law, who boasted of being the founder of the
Republican Guards. His first probing advance had been

blocked at Aoun but the Republican Guards had swung
south and circled behind Kerbala to cut off the city from
Najaf. By 12 March his forces were entering Kerbala. 'We
started to hear the sound of helicopters overhead and tanks
entering the outskirts,' says Sanaa Muhammad, who found
the intifada anarchic and frightening. 'They distributed
leaflets ordering people to leave Kerbala. We fled to a farm
on the edge of the city. We saw insurgents with ragged beards
and clothes with bloodstains on them who shot at our feet.'
There was food in the farm but all around Sanaa could hear
the sound of shooting and bombing. Her brother brought
news from the centre of Kerbala saying that many people had
sought refuge in and around the shrines thinking these would
be the safest place. Instead they found they were trapped in
the middle of a savage battle that went on for over a week.
As it died away Sanaa's family decided to return to their
house. 'On our way home we saw corpses all over the streets
along with severed heads and burned-out buildings,' she says.

Hussein Kamel issued an order to arrest all young men
over the age of fifteen. A story spread among the Shia that he
had ordered the bombing of the Imam Hussein shrine
declaring, 'My name is Hussein and so is yours: let us see
who is the strongest.' Like the story of the tank-gunner who
fired a round into a portrait of Saddam Hussein in Basra, this
became another iconic story of the uprising but its truth is
impossible to verify (Hussein Kamel is in no position to assist
enquiries because he was shot to death by his relatives in
Baghdad after defecting to Jordan in 1995 and then unwisely
returning in 1996). Sanaa Muhammad heard a nastier story
that reflects the terror felt by people in Kerbala. An old man
was walking with his daughter when they encountered
Hussein Kamel. The general asked them 'Who is better, me
or the Imam al-Hussein?' The old man was afraid and said
'You' but the girl answered unhesitatingly 'The Imam
Hussein'. Hussein Kamel shot her and she died at once while
the old man cried so much because he had abandoned Imam
Hussein that he became blind. The story has the unreal feel

of Christian tales of martyrdom for the faith that were the
staple of medieval Christianity, but the merciless revenge of
the Baath party on the Shia is very well substantiated and no
atrocity can be ruled out.[1]

By 19 March, Kerbala was finally back under government
control. Troops immediately began a reign of terror. A young
lawyer called Abu Muqtad says he saw soldiers throw a
patient off the roof of the al-Husseini hospital.[2] All men of
military age were in danger. Shia were killed simply because
they were Shia. Colonel Othman estimated that 150,000 Shia
were killed in Iraq as a whole during the intifada.[3] Accounts
of what happened next in and around Kerbala, Najaf and
Kufa resemble horror stories about the rounding-up of Jews
in Poland and Ukraine in the wake of the advancing German
army in the Second World War. Whole families were casually
slaughtered. In the aftermath of the 1991 uprising tales of
atrocities were collectively convincing but individually
difficult to prove. But in May 2003 mass graves containing
the bodies of thousands of people killed at the end of the
uprising were found around Hilla and Mahawil, a former
army base 12 miles north of Hilla. In two mass graves alone
2,300 bodies were unearthed. Many of those who had
disappeared during the uprising were identified because their
identity documents were found or some personal item like a
watch was still intact. Often the dead had been arrested at
random and later executed: a fourteen-year-old boy, sent by
his mother to get water from the river, arrested by soldiers on
a bridge; two men who had gone to buy food in a nearby
market; a lawyer and his student son who had gone looking
for a missing relative. Their bodies were all found twelve
years later at Mahawil.

There is only one known survivor of the death pits of
Mahawil and his testimony is convincing. His name is Nasir
Khadir Hazim al-Husseini and he was only twelve years old
at the time. His story is worth telling at some length because
it shows how Saddam's regime deliberately inflicted collective
punishment on the Shia for the rebellion regardless of

whether or not they took part. Nasir came from Hilla, which is about 70 per cent Shia and 30 per cent Sunni. On 16 March his twenty-eight-year-old mother Khulud Abud Naji took Nasir, two other thirteen-year-old relatives, his uncle Muhammad Abud Naji and his cousin Muhammad Yassin Muhammad to see their grandfather in another part of Hilla. On their way they were stopped by a soldier and accused of being looters. They were taken first to a school where they were kept in a classroom that soon filled up with other detainees. 'They blindfolded us and bound our hands, and then they put us in land cruisers with shaded windows and a bus,' says Nasir. 'They took us to Mahawil military base.' There was a perfunctory investigation by senior officers who wrote down their names. They received no food and were taken to a big hall. 'We were sitting in [family] groups, me with my relatives and the others with their relatives. No one dared speak to other groups.' Towards the end of the second day, on 18 March 1991, the detainees were taken outside and lined up in the courtyard of the compound where 'they brought some blankets which they ripped and they tied our hands and blindfolded us with those,' Nasir remembers. 'They covered our eyes and put us inside some TATA buses looted from Kuwait.' Some forty-five to fifty people were crammed together in the bus that drove down a dirt track. Nasir was sitting next to the window of the bus and could just see through a gap in his blindfold. He recalls an abandoned canal and a building, which he later saw was a brick factory.

The bus stopped and executions began immediately. A pit had already been dug and people were dragged off the bus and machine-gunned. 'When they started taking us off the bus, some of us began reciting the *shahada* [Muslim declaration of faith]. My mother told me, "Repeat the *shahada*, because we are about to die." I heard the shouting of the children. We grabbed each other's hands – me, my mother, my cousin, and my uncle. They pulled us, we were all together.' Nasir and his family were flung into a pre-excavated mass grave by one group of men while another group were firing with their guns. 'When I fell down, there were so many bodies underneath me. I lay down on top of them. They started to shoot at us.' After a time the shooting stopped but Nasir felt somebody pull at his clothes and say, 'This one isn't shot yet, shoot him.' He heard shots but still was not hit. An order was given for a bulldozer to bury the bodies but Nasir, still uninjured, was at the edge of the grave. As the bulldozer shovel got close to him he was able to crawl to one side of it. 'I heard the man who was standing on the hill instruct the shovel driver to bury us more – he had seen that I was not yet buried – but the driver left the place and did not do it.' Nasir heard the vehicles drive away and then crawled out of the grave leaving his dead relatives behind. He made his way to the Baghdad–Hilla road and was lucky enough to meet four sympathetic Shia soldiers who helped him return home.[4]

The slaughter was mainly of people from the Hilla area who were selected wholly at random though most of the victims were young men. Among the dead were more than a dozen Egyptian labourers working near Hilla. Few of these were from Kerbala, Najaf or Diwaniyah, suggesting that those who disappeared from these cities, where the resistance to government forces was far greater than Hilla, are buried somewhere else. Iskandar Jawad Witwit, a high-ranking air-force officer based at Mahawil, said that the uprising in Hilla had been crushed by 11 March and was followed by a campaign of mass arrests of men, women and children. 'The executions happened every day,' he says. 'They killed thousands of people.' Witwit was himself arrested on 16 March, accused of sympathising with the uprising, but his testimony is important because as a soldier he mixed with the perpetrators of the massacres. He identified them as being Baath party members, General Security, Special Security, the intelligence services (*mukhabarat)* and leading members of the pro-government Albu Alwan tribe, including its head sheikh. The involvement of the Special Republican Guard –

the elite force recruited from Sunni tribes – is tellingly
revealed by another soldier, Salim Murgan Hitban, returning
from three-day leave in Najaf with a cousin who was also a
soldier. They were picked up by a Special Republican Guard
checkpoint, held in grim conditions in a hall at the base, and
the cousin was then shot. Hitban only survived because a
major on 'the execution committee' had once been his
commanding officer in Mosul.[5]

How many people were killed at Mahawil? Sayyid Jabir
Muhsin al-Husseini, a local farmer who witnessed the
killings, says that the executions started at 9 a.m. and ended
at 5 p.m. with three groups of between 120 and 150 people
being machine-gunned every day between 7 March and 6
April 1991.[6] This means that over 10,000 were killed from
the Hilla area alone which makes Colonel Othman's figure of
150,000 Shia killed in total in southern Iraq seem credible.
Butchery on this scale could only have taken place on the
instructions of Saddam Hussein himself. The aim, if these
mass killings had a rational motive, was to terrorise the Shia
population of Iraq by inflicting on them a collective
punishment so bloody that they would never rise again.

The army counter-attack in Basra quickly retook the city
after three days' fighting. Tanks from the 51st Mechanised
Division, a unit that had not been involved in the mutinies,
captured the road that overlooks the working-class areas of
north Basra. Six weeks later I could see where the heavy
machine-gun bullets had penetrated the thin-walled brick
houses and tank shells had destroyed a fire station which
insurgents had used as a centre for resistance. As in the rest
of southern Iraq there were many atrocities. A man who had
entered the city with relief goods on 7 March saw through
his binoculars a column of twenty tanks heading towards the
city centre through his binoculars. 'I saw that the tank that
was leading had three children tied to its front,' he said.
'They did it because four hours earlier they had tried to
attack in the same way, and a fourteen-year-old girl with

explosives had jumped on the front of the first tank and exploded it (*sic*), forcing the whole column to withdraw.'[7] I did not myself see damage on anything like the scale of Kerbala, which may have been because resistance fighters could escape to Iran. 'I would say there were more than 1,000 dead,' Dr al-Rawi told me at the Basra Teaching Hospital. 'Basra General Hospital issued 600 death certificates. It was a bad time. You could see dogs eating bodies in the streets.'[8] Resistance went on in the suburbs and villages on the east side of the Shatt al-Arab until the end of March because all of the bridges had been destroyed by allied aircraft in January and February and troops could not cross the waterway.[9] As government forces took each area there was the same merciless but haphazard detention of civilians who were then shot or drowned in the river.

In Kurdistan the highly successful Iraqi army counter-attack against the *peshmerga* (Kurdish fighters) had an unexpected result. The Kurds were terrified of Saddam Hussein's revenge, which had killed 180,000 of them in 1988–9. They fled in their millions to Turkey and Iran, leaving their dead and dying by the roadside, and their sufferings were shown on television screens around the world. At first President Bush did not intend to do any more for the Kurds than he had for the Shia, but public pressure to help them became irresistible. A no-fly zone was declared by the US and the Kurds began the first stages of creating a semi-independent enclave in the northern three provinces of Iraq. The sufferings of the Shia were far less visible and therefore provoked much less international reaction. Foreign journalists could interview refugees arriving in Iran or Saudi Arabia with terrible tales, but could not report first-hand while the fighting was still going on.

Surprisingly, film of the repression did emerge and it was taken by the Baath party itself. The party had what amounted almost to a cult of cruelty and seems to have shot the film to encourage its supporters and frighten its enemies by showing their fate. These films sometimes fell into the hands of secret opponents of the regime who smuggled them out of the country.

One such film, shot around the end of March by a Baath party cameraman, records two Baath leaders taking part in the search for insurgents in the marshy lands near the town of Rumaytha about 20 miles from Samawa on the Euphrates north-west of Nasiriyah. The film was later given to me in London and shows what must have been a typical search-and-destroy mission against the insurgents. Clearly visible is the newly appointed Interior Minister Ali Hassan al-Majid, also known as 'Chemical Ali' for his murderous Anfal campaign against the Kurds in 1988 in which poison gas was repeatedly used against civilians. At first I thought the video was only vaguely interesting because it had no soundtrack, but then I found that by turning up the sound to full volume it was possible to hear what was being said. Al-Majid, who had a reputation for savagery second to none in the regime, is heard instructing a helicopter pilot on his way to attack insurgents holding a bridge. 'Don't come back until you have burnt them,' he says. 'And if you haven't burnt them don't come back.' He is joined by Muhammad Hamza al-Zubeidi, soon to be made prime minister because of his reputation for ruthlessness. Al-Zubeidi slaps and kicks prisoners as they lie terrified on the ground. 'Let's execute one so the others will confess,' he suggests. The four or five prisoners in bedraggled civilian clothes look like farm labourers but say nothing except one who pleads softly: 'Please, don't do this.' Al-Majid always has a cigarette in his mouth as he interrogates prisoners and there is the sound of gunfire in the background. Pointing at one prisoner he says: 'Don't execute this one. He will be useful to us.' The soldiers, who appear to be Special Republican Guard, kick the prisoners shouting 'Pimp' and 'Son of a Whore'.

Members of the Baath party dared not be seen as less than enthusiastic in eliminating the enemies of the regime. Any young Shia man was liable to be detained and shot at any

moment. In most cases the executioners showed no reser-
vations. But in one case in Basra, 150 young men, mostly
students, who had been herded into a hall in an office block
belonging to the Oil Tanks Department of the Southern Oil
Company were unexpectedly freed. While they were there
they were visited by a Baath party veteran and friend of
Saddam Hussein accompanied by his son Jassem. Jassem did
not share his father's Baathist sympathies but felt safer with
him while the army was picking people up at random in the
streets of the city. He saw the students crying and begging to
be released because they had done nothing. He also knew
that Ali Hassan al-Majid was due to visit Basra next morning
at 10 a.m. and was likely to order a mass execution of the
young men. In the middle of the night Jassem hit the single
Baathist guarding the entrance to the hall with the butt of his
pistol and opened the door. Holding up a hand in front of his
face so they could not recognise him he told the detainees to
run away as fast and as silently as they could. Jassem then
went back to bed, confident that nobody would imagine that
the son of such a stalwart Baathist as his father could have
knocked out the guard and freed the prisoners. The story
does not have a happy ending. 'When the other Baathists saw
the guard unconscious and the prisoners gone they panicked
because Ali Hassan al-Majid was coming expecting to order
the executions,' says a friend of Jassem. 'The Baathists rushed
out into the street and seized everybody they saw until the
hall was full again with 150 people who were executed as
had been planned.'[10]

CHAPTER SEVEN

Sadr II: The White Lion

Saddam Hussein reasserted his grip on power with surprising speed in the wake of his defeat in Kuwait and the uprisings by the Shia and the Kurds. Few other rulers could have survived the self-inflicted catastrophes of 1991 but Saddam had a sure knowledge of the Iraqi political landscape, its lethal pitfalls and how to escape them. This was in sharp contrast to his ignorance of other countries that led to his disastrous decision to invade Iran in 1980 and Kuwait ten years later. In the twelve years after 1991 no plot or second uprising came near to unseating Saddam despite several attempts. 'We have got the worst of all possible worlds,' an Iraqi friend said gloomily to me in 1992. 'We have been completely defeated and we still have Saddam Hussein in power.'

In successfully stabilising his regime the Iraqi ruler made one serious mistake. It was a strange and atypical error by a man who regarded even his closest aides and relatives with suspicion and slept in different houses every night to confuse potential assassins. For once in his career Saddam trusted somebody too far. He had drawn the lesson from the Shia intifada that the Shia masses detested the regime and the Shia religious leaders like Grand Ayatollah al-Khoei could not be trusted. Savage though repression of the Shia had been, he did not rely on it alone. After the death by natural causes of the ninety-three-year-old al-Khoei in August 1992, Saddam conceived a plan to install his own candidate as head of the

Shia religious hierarchy. He would choose somebody who was of Arab rather than Iranian origin like al-Khoei as paramount *marji' al-taqlid*. He would be an Iraqi nationalist as well as a religious leader and must back the regime in its confrontation with the US. Persecution of the Shia community and their clergy was intense in 1991–2. Saddam Hussein himself was believed to have penned a series of anti-Shia articles in the Baath party newspaper *al-Thawra* in which they were accused of believing in 'deviant' doctrines and not being fully Iraqi.[1] Many of the *hawza* were dead, imprisoned or scattered; their schools and colleges were closed. It was Saddam's idea of a political masterstroke to relax this persecution and reconcile with the Shia community by co-opting a member of the al-Sadr family who would be a cat's paw of the regime in Baghdad. Saddam's nominee would have all the more legitimacy because of his blood relationship with the revered Shia martyr Muhammad Baqir al-Sadr whom the regime had executed so brutally twelve years earlier.

The man Saddam chose as his candidate to be religious leader of the Shia community was Muhammad Muhammad Sadiq al-Sadr, a cousin, student and senior aide of Muhammad Baqir al-Sadr. To easily distinguish the two Sadrs, Baqir became known as Sadr I and Sadiq as Sadr II. At the time he struck his deal with the regime in 1992 his family was well known, but he was not. He was highly intelligent, had an original mind and was cunning enough to deceive the Iraqi *mukhabarat,* an organisation devoted to smelling out treachery, into believing it could manipulate him in its own interests. He used the breathing space this gave him and his supporters to revive the morale and religious commitment of the Shia after the slaughter of the 1991 uprising and the oppression thereafter. His mixture of Islamic revivalism, nationalism and populism had a deep appeal to angry, alienated but terrorised young Shia men. 'He made us feel self-confident while before we were controlled by fear,' recalls Ali Hussein Khidr, a pious seventeen-year-old from Nasiriyah who travelled with his teenage friends to see

Muhammad Sadiq in Najaf in 1997. 'We felt that a strong man was standing with us so we were afraid of nothing.'[2] As a religious leader al-Sadr was interested primarily in reviving the faith among the Shia masses, addressing the immediate problems of their daily lives and subtly undermining the propaganda of the regime. At first he expressed his real feelings indirectly but they would have been clear to any Iraqi. He would begin Friday prayers, which he had introduced, in a radical break with Shia tradition, by leading thousands of worshippers in the mosque in Kufa in chanting: 'Yes, yes to Islam; yes, yes to the faith; no, no to injustice; no, no to Israel; no, no to America; no, no to the devil.' There was nothing here that the regime could object to, but his congregation would have noticed that there was no call to support the Iraqi leader. Sheikh Yassin al-Assadi, who heard him speak, says: 'What he said was an intelligent and deliberate contradiction of the regime's slogans such as "Yes, yes to the leader Saddam Hussein" and "With our soul and blood we will sacrifice ourselves for you, Saddam" and many others.'[3]

There was a fundamental difference between Sadiq al-Sadr's approach and that of his mentor and relative Baqir al-Sadr. The new leader did not intend to make a direct attack on the state, trying to gain power by supporting a political party or through a coup. He seldom mentioned, at least at first, political issues in his fatwas (judgements). Muhammad Hassan Ibrahim, a seventeen-year-old from the impoverished Shia city of Kut south of Baghdad, saw clearly the different approaches of the two al-Sadrs. 'The first al-Sadr set up a political party linked to the elite of the *hawza*, while the second was immersed in the world of tribes and issues of daily life,' he said. 'The first wanted a political revolution while the second aimed for a Shia cultural revival in which it was important what you saw at the cinema and the music you listened to. He wanted to establish an Islamic popular base strong enough to stand up to a murderous and tyrannical regime.'[4]

Muhammad Sadiq was extraordinarily successful in his mission, given his own slender resources and the power of the Iraqi state. Today it is his face that has replaced that of Saddam on posters pasted on walls in Shia areas of Iraq. Pictured standing alongside his cousin Baqir al-Sadr and his son Muqtada, he looks older than his years, his features dominated by his long, silver-coloured, straggly beard, which led to him to being nicknamed 'the White Lion', *al-layth al-abyadh*. In 1998 he began to wear a white shroud over his shoulders, a sign that he expected to be martyred. Observers did not have to be told who he thought would kill him. At about the same time he recorded a CD, widely distributed before and after his death, in which he gave details of his career. It is as if he wanted to set the record straight and rebut calumny from rival Shia religious leaders who repeatedly denounced him as a police agent.

Muhammad Muhammad Sadiq al-Sadr was born in Najaf on 23 March 1943, the only son of his father Sayyid Muhammad Sadiq al-Sadr. Confusingly he was normally referred to by his father's name. He lived with his mother's father, Ayatollah Muhammad Reza al-Yassin, married young and had four sons – Mustafa, Muammal, Murtadha and Muqtada – and two daughters. Intellectually precocious, he began his study in the *hawza* in 1954 at the age of eleven. There he was to meet and study under the men who were to reshape the Shia world in Iraq such as his cousin Ayatollah Muhammad Baqir al-Sadr and the Ayatollah al-Khoei. He entered the *faqih* (law) college in 1960 and studied science and languages, gaining a working knowledge of English. He completed his studies under the future leader of Iran, Ayatollah Khomeini, and Sayyid Muhsin al-Hakim, then the most prominent member of another great Shia clerical family that were to become his fierce opponents. By 1977 Muhammad Sadiq became a *mujtahid* at the early age of thirty-four, which qualified him not only to interpret Shia law but to give judgements on political and social questions.

A decade earlier these undoubted academic achievements,

together with his membership of the Shia clerical aristocracy, might have opened the door for Muhammad Sadiq to enjoy a sedate and well-respected career in Najaf. There would have been spats and rivalries with other religious families such as the al-Hakim or religious notables such as Ali al-Sistani. Clerical rivalries, whether Islamic or Christian, have a long tradition of extreme rancour at odds with the supposed other-worldly concerns of opponents. Even in as decorous a religious establishment as the Church of England in the nineteenth century, Anthony Trollope describes with accurate relish the fierce feuds of clergymen in their struggles for jobs, promotion and power. In twentieth-century Najaf, as in nineteenth-century Barchester, the fictional English cathedral town where Trollope's novels are set, the fact that contestants had grown up together or rubbed shoulders for decades made their disputes all the more venomous. But after the Baath party staged its coup d'etat in 1968, all parallels between the Shia clergy of Iraq and ecclesiastical hierarchies in other countries and in Iraq in the past ceased to be valid. Hitherto the Shia clergy had led a cloistered existence in which it seldom faced persecution. The worst punishment faced by the *mujtahid* who had promoted the rebellion of 1920 against the British occupation was a short spell in prison and enforced or voluntary exile. All this was now to change as Shia religious leaders entered an era during which they endured unrelenting persecution. From the beginning it was clear that the Baathists did not intend to share authority with anybody. They identified the Shia clergy, and above all those sympathetic to the Dawa party, as dangerous antagonists and moved to crush them with the brutality that was their party's hallmark.

Muhammad Sadiq was arrested twice, the first time in 1972 when he was detained along with his cousin Muhammad Baqir al-Sadr and Muhammad Baqir al-Hakim. His second arrest was in 1974 when he was tortured in the *mukhabarat* office in Najaf. When he protested against the brutal treatment of other prisoners he was taken to another security office in Diwaniyah to the south of Najaf where he was tortured even more severely. His mistreatment had an understandably serious impact on his personality and his religious views. When he was released from prison in 1975 he devoted himself so intently to prayers that he began to damage his health, and his teacher Muhammad Baqir was forced to ask him to moderate his religious observances. The young cleric remembered this as a time of isolation because, although he was out of jail, he was under house arrest and few dared enter his home. When he was allowed a little more freedom he was still closely watched by Iraqi security and people were too frightened to say 'hello' to him when he visited the Imam Ali shrine.[5] During this period there were the first signs that his ideas were moving in a dramatically different direction from that of other *mujtahid*. He developed an interest in mystical Islam, explaining later that he was taught this by an ordinary worker in Najaf called Hajj Abd el-Zahra al-Gara'wi. This in itself was a surprising and telling admission for a member of a clerical class where knowledge and advancement came through tuition by scholars of proven learning, acquired by years of study.[6]

In the 1980s Muhammad Sadiq did little to draw attention to himself but he developed original ideas about how Shia Islam and its leaders should respond to persecution by the state. Endurance and passive resistance, the traditional Shia recipe for surviving tyrannical governments, were not enough. He opposed the principle of *taqiyya* (dissimulation and concealment) when dealing with Saddam Hussein arguing that, on the contrary, this was the moment for Shia religious leaders to stand up openly for their faith. He would later speak scornfully of the silent or pacific *marji'iya* compared with the active or militant *marji'iya*. Many of his ideas about the creation of an Islamic state he owed to Muhammad Baqir al-Sadr but he gave priority to starting an Islamic cultural revolution which would precede seizing state power. The latter option was in any case impractical in the 1990s given the disparity between the feeble resources of the

Shia community and strength of the Baathist regime. Sadiq al-Sadr believed that by withdrawing from the world the Shia hierarchy had abandoned their own people whose sufferings, already great, had become a great deal worse after 1991. His plan was to persuade the regime that he was under its control so he could build a mass movement, making Shiism once more relevant to the spiritual, psychological and economic needs of the faithful. His status as the successor to Muhammad Baqir, Sadr I, was reinforced by marriages between Sadr I's three daughters and Sadr II's three sons. Jafar al-Sadr, the son of Sadr I and principal assistant of Sadr II, says: 'Muqtada married my youngest sister in 1994, Sayyid Mustafa the eldest in 1987 and Sayyid Muammal the second oldest in 1992.'[7]

The Iraqi economy and society were collapsing under the weight of UN sanctions imposed at the time of the invasion of Kuwait in 1990 and never lifted until 2003. Millions of Iraqis saw their lives being ruined. This explains why they were so receptive to Sadiq al-Sadr's religious message. The severity of sanctions and their devastating impact on ordinary Iraqis were never understood by the outside world. They were not like past sanctions, such as those imposed on South Africa or Rhodesia as a sign of international dis-approval, but were more akin to a medieval siege, a siege furthermore that lasted thirteen years. They were supposedly aimed at denying the Iraqi government access to its oil revenues, but in reality it was the mass of the population and not the political elite who were hit hardest. The latter could increase their personal wealth through black-market operations and state-sanctioned smuggling. Sanctions were a disaster for ordinary Iraqis because so many of them were directly or indirectly employed by the government which now had no money to pay them. Officials, teachers, army officers and pensioners were all suddenly penniless. A friend of mine called Jawad, a highly qualified professor of engineering at Baghdad University, was unlucky enough to return to Iraq in the summer of 1990 in order to see a much valued student through his PhD. When Saddam invaded Kuwait Jawad found he was trapped because no country where he had previously held teaching jobs would give him a visa. He found his income had fallen to the equivalent of $5 a month. By 1995 he was shyly asking me if I could find him a job as a driver with the UN office in Baghdad. The Iraqi currency collapsed after the invasion of Kuwait and savings were wiped out. When I first went to Iraq a dollar was worth about a third of a dinar but by 1992 a single dollar would buy you 2,000 dinars. When I changed a hundred-dollar bill with the money changers in Saadoun Street in central Baghdad they would hand me a weighty black plastic bag full of greasy bundles of dinar notes held together by rubber bands.

Iraqis were bewildered and frightened by the ongoing catastrophe that so cruelly dislocated their lives and showed no sign of ending. Many had hoped up to the last minute that the war over Kuwait would be averted. Even the most pessimistic had not foreseen that in the space of a few days bombs and missiles would wreck the infrastructure of power stations, oil refineries, telecommunications centres and water-treatment plants that had turned Iraq into a modern country over the previous half-century. Some of the better-off had stocked up their deep freezes with meat to see them through the conflict. But when the electrical system ceased to work during the first days of the bombing in 1991, the freezers stopped working and the carefully stored meat began to rot. Soon there was a penetrating stench in middle-class neighbourhoods because people were forced to throw out the maggot-ridden meat only to find it was not collected by garbage collectors and was left on the ground. The garbage men had no gasoline for their trucks because Saddam had not even taken the simple precaution of storing fuel in the weeks before the refineries were put out of action. When garbage removal eventually resumed after the war, the collectors made a discovery with sinister implications. Previously one third of what they collected had consisted of food scraps but this was no longer the case. In a country where ever more people were not getting enough to eat, nothing edible, not even the toughest melon rinds, was being thrown away.

The closest approximation to the disaster that befell Iraq and Iraqis in 1991 is the Great Crash of 1929 in the US. In both cases the collapse was sudden and totally unexpected by its victims. In the three years between 1929 and 1932 unemployment in America rose from 1.5 million to 13 million. In Iraq there was full employment in 1990 and there were an additional one million Egyptians working in the country. Two years later, the Iraqi Ministry of Labour recorded that unemployment had risen to over 50 per cent of the work force. When US troops invaded Iraq in 2003 and saw the miserable shanty towns on the road to Baghdad they thought this was the normal state in which Iraqis lived; in fact for many Iraqis this grinding poverty was a new experience. In the 1970s the Iraqi health system had been similar in quality to that of Greece. But when I visited a hospital on the outskirts of Baghdad in 1996 its car park was full of trucks on blocks because their wheels and engines had been cannibalised to keep a couple of vehicles going. While I was there, a child was dying because there were no more oxygen bottles available.

In fact, what happened to Iraqis in the 1990s was far worse than the experience of Americans in the 1930s. In the US, the folk-memory long persisted of desperate men and women forced to pick through maggoty trash in a search for food. But it was a recollection of a disaster that was safely in the past and unlikely to be repeated. For Iraqis there was no comforting sense that, if they endured a few years' deprivation, life would begin to improve. Sanctions would stay as long as Saddam Hussein governed Iraq and there was no sign of his rule ending. Indeed sanctions seemed designed more to keep Iraq weak than remove him. For all the brutality and unpopularity of his regime more Iraqis were dying because of UN sanctions in the 1990s than were being shot, tortured and imprisoned by the regime.

At this time the Ministry of Information in Baghdad insisted that any foreign journalist travelling outside the capital should be accompanied by a 'minder' from the ministry. I used to ask minders to take me to their home village which they were always eager to do. Many were well-educated men who secretly blamed Saddam Hussein for forcing them into a job they considered below their talents. One day we went to a fruit-growing village in Diyala, a well-watered province north-east of Baghdad. Ten years later this area was devastated by tit-for-tat massacres between Sunni and Shia, but at this time the villagers here were doing better than most in Iraq. They grew their own food and sold fruit in the markets of Baquba, the provincial capital, and Baghdad. But their prosperity was only relative. 'It looks as if we are well off,' Buhha'a Hussein al-Sayef, a local farmer, told me as we sat on the shady balcony of his house overlooking his groves of pomegranate trees and date palms. Then he went on to explain that their water purification plant had long ceased to work so they were drinking polluted water from the canals that made many of them sick. Driving away from the village I saw people chasing after our car. It turned out they thought I was a foreign doctor. When we stopped I explained I was a journalist but they still seemed to imagine I must have some medical expertise. Several people went back to their houses to get dusty old X-rays of their children, many of whom were ill. The X-rays had been taken years before, either in Amman, Jordan, or in a local clinic that was now closed. One man called Ali Ahmed Suwaidan was determined that I should look at an X-ray of the head of his daughter Fatima who was playing on the ground nearby. 'There is something wrong with her balance,' he said sadly. 'She cannot stand up.' He held the little girl upright for a few seconds and then removed his hands. She immediately crumpled at our feet.

The devastating impact of sanctions explains why Muhammad Sadiq's open hostility to the US and covert opposition to Saddam Hussein spoke straight to the heart of millions of Iraqi Shia. They hated the regime in Baghdad but also detested an American government that they blamed for the sanctions that were destroying their lives and those of their children. I could see the terrible results of sanctions in the village and city streets. If further evidence was needed there was a grim procession of medical reports and statistics. A survey of 2,120 children under the age of five in Baghdad was carried out by a foreign team in the summer of 1995. It showed that 29 per cent of them were underweight compared to 7 per cent in 1991. The number of children who were 'stunted' had risen from 12 per cent to 28 per cent. The authors of the report said that only in Mali had they seen conditions comparable to Iraq.[8] One foreign medical delegation had reported watching with horror as Iraqi doctors tried to carry out an operation in which they could not even cut the patient's skin because the scissors they were using were too blunt.

The mass impoverishment of Iraqis, and the failure or inability of the government to do anything about it, was the essential precondition to the swift rise of Muhammad Sadiq al-Sadr in the early 1990s and his son Muqtada after 2003. The Shia community was worse affected than the Sunni because it had always been poorer and such well-paid jobs as did exist were likely to go to Sunni loyal to the regime. Saddam Hussein might have money to build palaces and mosques, but he no longer controlled revenues sufficient to buy off dissent. It was a tactic which, in common with the rulers of other oil states, he had used effectively in the past. In the first couple of years of his unpopular war with Iran Saddam had rebuilt much of central Baghdad, using large loans from Saudi Arabia and Kuwait, partly in a bid to show Iraqis that the conflict was not stopping economic development. He gave jobs, contracts, cash, scholarships, cars and houses to those whose cooperation he needed. After 1990 this was no longer possible. In 1989 Iraq's oil revenue was $13 billion. Three years later it was down to $400 million a year derived from Turkish truck drivers, whose smuggling of oil across the northern border was tolerated by the US because Turkey and the Iraqi Kurds both benefited. One consequence of the state's lack of money and inability to supply services was a greater demand for the work of religious charities established by Sadiq al-Sadr and later by Muqtada. The oil-for-food programme introduced in 1996 fended off starvation, if not malnutrition, but it did little more.

The US, Britain and other supporters of sanctions claimed for years, contrary to all evidence from international aid organisations, that the burden of sanctions on the Iraqi people was exaggerated. They argued that if they were being impoverished it was all the fault of Saddam for diverting money into his own pockets and wasting resources by constructing giant palaces. But in the three Iraqi provinces of Kurdistan where Saddam had lost control after 1991 the impact of sanctions was as bad as or worse than further south. In 1996 I went to a village called Penjwin in Sulaimaniyah province in Iraqi Kurdistan. It was on the Iraqi side of the border with Iran and, because of its front-line position during the Iran–Iraq war, it was liberally sown with mines. In the village street I noticed that an astonishing number of people were missing hands or legs. Villagers explained dolefully that in order to feed their families they had to undertake one of the most dangerous jobs in the world. They would locate an Italian-made mine called the Valmara that jumped into the air, propelled by a small explosive, if you touched it. At waist height the main explosive would detonate, spraying hundreds of lethal ball bearings in all directions. People from Penjwin would defuse this lethal contraption in order to make a few dollars by selling the aluminium wrapped around the explosive. Some did not survive the operation and many others, like those I had seen, were mutilated for life.

There were those who understood exactly what sanctions were doing to Iraqi society but their warnings were ignored or derided in Washington and London. Denis Halliday, a fifty-seven-year-old Irish Quaker appointed UN humanitarian coordinator in August 1997, said simply that 'the infrastructure is collapsing and it will take ten to twenty years to restore'. After resigning in protest over sanctions a year later he spelled out their calamitous long-term effects not just on health but on the fabric of Iraqi society: the great increase in crime, fewer marriages because people could not afford to marry, the bitterness and rage of young men without a future. He compared them to the orphans of the Afghan war who had formed the core of the Taliban movement. He saw a generation growing up in Iraq that was filled with hate. 'What should be of concern is the possibility of more fundamentalist Islamic thinking developing,' said Halliday prophetically. 'It is not well understood as a possible spin-off of the sanctions regime. We are pushing people to take extreme positions.'[9]

Muhammad Sadiq's brief but explosive career as a Shia religious leader illustrated the growing strength of fundamentalist Islam. It is a dramatic story that falls roughly into three unequal parts. He had been imprisoned after the Shia uprising like many of the Shia clergy. After his release, between 1992 and 1996, he appeared to cooperate with the regime, dwelling on social and religious topics and avoiding politics. Speaking in an interview of his relations with the government he said: 'They avoid harming us so long as we avoid harming them.'[10] It was not a relationship that was likely to last long. Saddam and the Baath party were never able to tolerate allies who showed any degree of independence. 'The regime was afraid of internal opposition so they were looking for a cleric they could control,' says Jawad al-Khalasi, a cleric with extensive contact with the Sadrists. 'They thought Sadiq al-Sadr was perfect, that he was weak and was easily controlled. But he tricked them.'[11] His initial priority was to establish a network of preachers and organisers to revive Shiism among the Shia masses in Baghdad and southern Iraq. 'He used very intelligent tactics by establishing a sort of truce [with the regime] in order to give himself space to operate,' says Sheikh Yassin al-Assadi who knew him during this period.[12] At moments his ambivalent relations with the authorities seem to have amused him. In the mid-1990s, at a time when they still trusted him, a senior Iraqi security officer offered him some bodyguards. Sadiq turned him down categorically, saying that to accept protection would destroy his credibility as a religious leader, and adding that many people 'already consider me a government agent. If I accept this protection that means nobody will pray with me. Thank the president for his concern about my safety but Allah is the one who will protect me and I accept God's will.'[13] The moment of trust did not last long. As the ever-watchful Iraqi security forces saw with dismay that their protégé was creating a mass movement, they tried to rein him in. From about 1997 Muhammad Sadiq started to become more confrontational and the government restricted his activities more and more, limiting the number of worshippers at Kufa mosque where he preached and banning religious processions. This period of growing friction was followed by a few months at the end of 1998 and early 1999 when he became convinced that Saddam Hussein intended to kill him.

The attempt by the regime to co-opt Sadiq al-Sadr was part of its broader effort to use religion as cement to keep itself in power. The Baath party had been highly secular in the 1970s, but just before the opening of the war in Kuwait '*Allahu Akbar*' (God is Great) was inscribed on the Iraqi flag. In the wake of defeat there was a surge in popular piety among both Shia and Sunni. Arab nationalism had been discredited by Saddam's costly military adventures and the failure of corrupt elites in other parts of the Arab world. The Iraqi leader now wanted to ride the wave of Islamic revivalism. He started his so-called 'Faith' campaign in 1994. Restaurants along Abu Nawas Street, where I used to drink *arak,* an aniseed-flavoured liquor, and eat *mazgouf* fish from the Tigris, went dry. In 1996 I visited a favourite Lebanese restaurant called al Mudhif on Abu Nawas that had formerly served wine and spirits. Knowing of the new 'dry' policy I brought red wine concealed in an anonymous flask with me. 'Put it away,' whispered a waiter who caught sight of it, and turning pale he pressed his wrists together to indicate that he feared being handcuffed. 'Do you want me to go to jail?' In the streets of Baghdad there were noticeably more women wearing the veil. Saddam, who carried everything to excess, announced that he would build a hundred new mosques, including one at the old Muthanna municipal airport which would be the biggest in the world. It was to have a dome the size of a football pitch and would rise from the centre of an artificial lake in the shape of the Arab world. My friend who had been a professor of engineering at Baghdad University – he only succeeded in evading a ban on resignations from official jobs by faking a heart attack – was a consultant on the design of the giant mosque. He lamented the absurdity of the project that could never be completed because Iraq lacked the basic construction materials and equipment. 'We do not have high-tensile steel, pile drivers, reinforcement bars, or additives for the cement,' he said. The only part of the mosque to be completed was an elegant pavilion from which the self-appointed chief engineer of the project, Saddam himself, could view its progress.

Muhammad Sadiq later played down his cooperation with the authorities but at first it was extensive. 'They gave him money and the key to the school taken from Muhammad Baqir al-Sadr in 1980,' says a former Dawa militant, who is generally unsympathetic to him. 'They also gave him the right to authorise residence visas for non-Iraqi Shia students and scholars in Najaf which was a very important right because so many of them came from other countries.' Muhammad Sadiq was allowed to speak and travel and to send his emissaries all over Iraq. His main platform for reaching ordinary Shia was Friday prayers, a central feature of Sunni Islam, but hitherto regarded as heretical by the Shia *ulema*. To a non-Iraqi this introduction of Friday prayers did not appear a radical move, but when they were instituted in the mid-1990s it was viewed by Sunni and Shia in Iraq as an extraordinarily significant development. The theological justification for not having Friday prayers was that to do so would be to recognise the legitimacy of earthly rulers. It appeared that al-Sadr was now prepared to do so. 'We saw it as a sign that the Shia were reconciling with Saddam,' recalls the Iraqi journalist Ghaith Ahad Awab who was living in Baghdad at the time. 'I remember the dinar rose against the dollar as the news spread.'[14]

Muhammad Sadiq began to send out emissaries to all Shia areas of Iraq, paying particular attention to the very poor and to the clans and tribes. 'Muhammad Sadiq's movement started in 1992 and was from the beginning a mass popular movement which attracted the poor and deprived,' says Jafar al-Sadr, the son of Baqir al-Sadr, who was one of Sadiq's chief lieutenants. He says this distinguished it from his father's movement which was more 'intellectual, cultural and elitist'.[15] His representatives tried to penetrate even to the most remote parts of the country such as the marshes of the south, notorious for bandits and disease. Iraqis identify strongly with their home districts and the representatives were encouraged to go back to the areas they came from where they were known and trusted. Their arrival created great excitement, particularly among the young, and dismay among local Shia religious dignitaries. Muhammad Hassan Ibrahim was seventeen years old in 1996, when missionaries from Sadiq al-Sadr arrived unexpectedly in Kut in 1996 and announced they would hold Friday prayers. 'The announcement that prayers were to take place was by posters on the walls and by word of mouth,' he remembers. 'We went to the prayers in an unknown mosque because all the mosques and *husseiniyahs* were strongly connected to each other and all supported [Grand Ayatollah Ali] al-Sistani. There were a great many people there and it was a beautiful scene. The prayers were important for us and most of the sermon was about social problems.'[16] Sometimes none of the Shia mosques could be used. Ali Hussein Khidr, also seventeen years old at the time and living in the large Shia city of Nasiriyah on the Euphrates, says: 'I was in Nasiriyah in 1997 when Friday prayers were announced for the first time by loudspeaker. They were led by Sayyid Muammal [Muhammad Sadiq's second son] and, because all the mosques and *husseiniyahs* were controlled by followers of Sayyid al-Sistani we gathered in the Hbubi street, the main street in Nasiriyah. People came to see this strange event. They had not seen Friday prayers. Most of those who came to pray were young people who stood in lines and held hands with each other.'[17]

What sort of topics did Sadiq al-Sadr's representative talk about? It was not merely to avoid confrontation with the authorities that they concentrated on social and economic rather than dangerously political issues. It was the Sadrist belief that the traditional *marji'iya* had lost touch with life as it was really lived by ordinary Iraqis, and al-Khoei and al-Sistani dwelt in aristocratic isolation from the world of their followers. Given that most Iraqis were desperately trying to cope with a permanent economic crisis in the 1990s, there was a vigorous appetite for advice and counselling on how to survive. One former disciple of Muhammad Sadiq tells an anecdote illustrating his master's pragmatism. 'One day, I was sitting with Muhammad Sadiq in his office, when a man came in to ask the price of tomatoes,' he says. 'The question infuriated me: I thought he had come to mock us. But al-Sadr, wiser and smarter than I am, gave him a detailed answer, giving him the price of different kinds of tomatoes. He had understood what the question was about. I caught up with the man as he left the office and asked him why he had asked the question. He replied: "In selecting a *marji'* [a religious figure to emulate and whose rulings he would accept], I choose the one who knows my suffering, who is close to the poor and the disinherited." '[18]

The Sadrists, as they were later known, sought to involve themselves in all aspects of life. The aim was less to establish an Islamic state than to restore Islamic beliefs and *mores*.

Muhammad Sadiq set up a court that did not have penal powers, but dealt with divorce and payment of donations to clergy. He issued rulings on tribal law covering questions which the *ulema* had previously avoided like the payment of blood money after a killing or arranged marriages to prevent or end a blood feud. It was during this period that Sadrists became strong in areas that were to be their political and religious bastions under both Muhammad Sadiq and Muqtada. The most important of these was Sadr City renamed in 2003 after Sadiq al-Sadr. With a population of two million people it was almost entirely Shia, impoverished and tribally linked to Maysan province in southern Iraq. Yassin Sajad, a young man from Sadr City, explains why its people followed Muhammad Sadiq. 'Sayyid al-Sadr had a very good relationship with the tribes of Sadr City, which includes a large number from the south. When he held prayers we found him the only *marji'* who spoke directly and in public about the disintegration of Iraqi society as a result of the economic blockade. He also talked about services, electricity, water and other things we were short of. Since he had a good relationship with the tribes most of them followed him and did not follow [Grand Ayatollah Ali] al-Sistani because Sadiq al-Sadr talked to the poor and needy. This is what the *marji'iya* did not do before.'[19]

There was a social revolutionary element in Sadrism as it developed in the 1990s, all the more potent because so many Iraqi Shia had always been poor and many more were becoming so. 'Sadiq al-Sadr's power base was well-defined, and Muqtada's present-day followers belong to the same social class,' concludes a highly informed study by the Brussels-based International Crisis Group. 'The relatively well-to-do, urbanized, educated or commercial classes eyed him [Sadiq al-Sadr] warily, viewing his plebeian, militant Shiism as a source of instability and a threat to their interests.'[20] The former possessing classes of the Shia community were being destroyed by sanctions or were emigrating abroad. The highly educated could be seen standing for hours outside Arab embassies, clutching CVs showing they spoke three or four languages, hoping for some ill-paid teacher's job in Libya or Syria.

The Sadrists emphasised activism and missionary zeal. They persistently, and sometimes unfairly, contrasted their public campaigns for the Islamic faith and opposition to the authorities with the 'quietism' of the followers of al-Khoei and al-Sistani. This militancy was not always well received. Sadiq al-Sadr sent a representative to the marshes around Basra to preach to the impoverished rice-growers and buffalo breeders. He was travelling in a small boat when its owner asked him a question about a religious issue and, on receiving an unsatisfactory reply, promptly threw the representative into the water forcing him to swim to safety. The man returned to Najaf bitterly complaining to Muhammad Sadiq about his treatment but was persuaded to return to the marshlands to try again.

Religious revivalism is often accompanied by self-righteous puritanism and this was true of the Sadrist delegates. In Basra, the largest Shia city with a population of two million, prayers took place in the street because the mosques were not big enough to accommodate the number of worshippers. Ali Kassem, a local Sadrist militant, says the prayers were led by Sheikh Saleh al-Jizani who gave a sermon in which 'he called the gypsies to repentance and he explained why the voice of Islam did not reach them and how they wallowed in their lusts and we must reform them by talking to them. In fact this is what happened: There is a street in Basra called Bashar, the Hayaniya district and the Five Miles area all of which have bad reputations but soon there were less noisy dances and the brothels closed.'

The Sadrists' greatest appeal was to the embittered Shia youth that was coming of age in the 1990s, as the UN representative Denis Halliday had forecast, without a future and without hope. Speaking about Kut, Muhammad Hassan Ibrahim says that eight or nine weeks after the first Friday prayers were held there was 'a sorting out between those who follow al-Sistani and those who follow al-Sadr. Truthfully, those who supported al-Sistani were more numerous but the majority of the young were with Sayyid al-Sadr.' The Sadrists consciously targeted the young. A high point of cooperation with the regime came in 1997 when it allowed them to publish a magazine called *al-Huda* which was edited by Muqtada, Sadiq's youngest son. 'The vast majority of al-Sadr followers were young, the oldest among them born in 1964,' says Ali Hussein Khidr, the young religious enthusiast from Nasiriyah. 'We were highly motivated by the revolutionary sentiments of al-Sadr and we had had enough of the submission and silence of *taqiyya* (concealment and dissimulation).' There had always been a strong Messianic theme in Shiism in which the world would be put to rights by the return of the Twelfth Imam, the hidden Mahdi who has never died. But, as with the return of the Christian Messiah, the postponement of revolutionary change on earth until the Mahdi's reappearance at an uncertain future date conveniently allowed the present generation to get on with their lives without having to trouble themselves too much about it. Muhammad Sadiq rejected this. Ali Hussein says approvingly: 'Sayyid al-Sadr was telling us in his speeches that the Mahdi is not happy with this kind of *taqiyya* and we must create the right kind of conditions for him to reappear.'

The content of the Sadrists' preaching was about restoring traditional Islamic customs or restrictions such as the prohibition on the sale or consumption of alcohol. His followers started telling taxi drivers not to pick up women if they were not wearing the veil. There was a fatwa forbidding people from watching Shabab television channel, owned by Uday, Saddam's playboy son, which, though popular because it showed Western films, was considered a source of corruption (when the Americans took Baghdad in 2003 they thought that Iraqis would be eager to see the latest Hollywood movies only to find that they had already seen pirated versions on Shabab).

Confrontation was inevitable. Under Saddam's rule, the

date of the founding of the Baath party and a highly fictionalised account of its history were drilled into students in Iraqi schools, while there was nothing about the Shia Imams and little about Islamic Iraq. Muhammad Sadiq was pushing Islamic and Shia culture as a direct antidote to Baathism. Soon there were menacing signs that Saddam was beginning to realise that his plan to install his own candidate as religious leader of the Shia had spectacularly backfired. One man had no doubts about the final outcome of the escalating struggle between the government and its erstwhile protégé. 'It will all end with one bullet,' predicted Muhammad Sadiq to his disciples.[21]

CHAPTER EIGHT

Sadr II: The Assassination

Students entering their classroom in the *hawza* seminary in Najaf at the beginning of the school year in 1998 were greeted by a strange request from their professor. He asked them all to remove their turbans and disassemble them so they became just a long piece of cloth. When the students had complied with this curious demand their professor immediately asked them to remake their turbans and put them on again. Some, who came from religious families, speedily did so but others, mostly those who had entered the seminary recently, struggled to rewrap the cloth so as to recreate the turban. The purpose of the exercise, recalls Sheikh Akram al-Assadi, who witnessed it as a student in the *hawza* at the time, was to identify those students whose ignorance in the matter of turbans revealed that they might be police spies. 'The government sent 100–150 young security and intelligence officers to be students and teachers inside the *hawza*,' says Sheikh al-Assadi. 'Some of those who had important jobs in [Muhammad Sadiq] al-Sadr's office became students only after the uprising of 1991 and after al-Sadr himself became important. So many new and strange people were entering the *hawza* that we knew they were from the intelligence agencies.'[1]

The unwrapping of the turbans might be taken as a symptom of the paranoid anxiety inevitable among people living in any police state. Sheikh al-Assadi's very high figure for the number of Baathist spies infiltrating the *hawza* is

suspect since they could scarcely all have been so incom-
petent as to be readily identifiable. It is also true that in an
authoritarian state security services spread rumours that their
all-seeing eye is everywhere in order to demoralise dissenters.
But in Iraq the state had a multitude of informants, easily
recruited through cash payments, fear of arrest and favours
granted or withheld. Saddam would not have started so risky
a tactic as devolving power over the *hawza* to Sadiq al-Sadr
and allowing him to appoint prayer readers in hundreds of
cities and towns without monitoring his actions closely.

Right up to the moment that security agents ambushed
and killed al-Sadr and his two elder sons Mustafa and
Muammal at a roundabout in Najaf on 19 February 1999,
many of his Shia opponents openly denounced him as a
collaborator with the regime. After his death when they saw
Sadiq al-Sadr's vast popularity among the Shia masses these
critics were deeply embarrassed by their previous allegations.
There was an unseemly scramble to suppress denunciatory
pamphlets and articles by the exiled groups, notably the
Tehran-based SCIRI of Muhammad Baqir al-Hakim and the
remnants of the Dawa party, by now divided into several
different factions. Today these documents are difficult to
obtain, closely guarded by their authors who are reticent
about the re-publication of their ill-timed criticism of a man
whom many Shia regard as having saintly attributes. Among
the Sadrists there lingers a bitter sense of betrayal by other
Shia religious leaders, a belief that, while they were fighting
Saddam and dying doing so, others, like Grand Ayatollah al-
Sistani, stood by in silence or lived comfortably in exile like
al-Hakim in Tehran or Sayyid Majid al-Khoei in London.

The feuds of the Shia religious parties are important
because the divisions and hatreds stemming from events in
the 1990s are vital to an understanding of the men who, a
decade later, had come to dominate the Iraqi government. By
2007 the leader of the Dawa party was Nouri al-Maliki, no
longer a hunted exile in Damascus but the prime minister of
Iraq who spoke by video phone to President George W. Bush

every fortnight. The most powerful party within his coalition of Shia religious parties was SCIRI. Their sometime ally and frequent opponent within the Shia community was Muqtada al-Sadr, by now leader of a movement whose Mehdi Army militia was identified by President Bush as one of the greatest threats to the US in Iraq. Grand Ayatollah Ali al-Sistani, whom Muhammad Sadiq denounced as a pawn of Sayyid Majid al-Khoei, retains immense influence over the Shia community.

The allegations against Sadiq al-Sadr are worth looking at in greater detail because they illustrate the subtle as well as the crude methods used by Saddam Hussein to shore up his authority during his last decade in power. Sheikh Akram al-Assadi explains the case against al-Sadr though he says he does not necessarily believe all the charges. The essence of this is that he was the creature of the Baathist regime when they released him from prison in 1991 three months after the uprising. He was naïve, often changed his mind, was easily influenced by those around him and had made a full confession to his interrogators in 1972 and 1974. In 1991 he first supported the uprising and later criticised it when it failed. The regime wanted to use him to control the *hawza,* so it gave him control of all religious schools and all new students had to have his authorisation. Only he was able to obtain residence visas for the many students from elsewhere in the Shia world. The Iraqi authorities funded him and allowed him control over what religious books were published in Najaf. It was further claimed that Rokan Ghafour al-Majid al-Tikriti, the nephew and aide-de-camp of Saddam, acted as liaison between the regime and Sadiq al-Sadr through his eldest son Mustafa. By 1998 SCIRI in Tehran was saying in pamphlets that militants should be very careful in dealing with al-Sadr and 'not reveal their real names because he was surrounded by members of the security and intelligence services'.[2]

Muhammad Salem, a student of Muhammad Sadiq, rebuts these and other charges saying that 'Sayyid al-Sadr wanted to exploit the weakness of the regime after the uprising though he was absolutely against the government. He was waiting for his moment to fight the regime, but first he needed a truce with it.' Salem agrees there were security agents infiltrated among Muhammad Sadiq's students though he contends this was also true of other clergy. As for Rokan Ghafour al-Majid al-Tikriti, one of whose jobs was liaising with the southern Shia tribes, Muhammad Salem says he only came to see Sadiq al-Sadr once at the end of 1998 and this was to tell him to stop his Friday prayers. 'Sayyid al-Sadr's response was to put the head of his brown walking stick on Rokan's chest and say defiantly: 'Tell your master I will not stop prayers as long as I am alive.'[3]

Whatever Saddam Hussein and his security forces expected from Sadiq al-Sadr, he betrayed them. This was why they assassinated him and his two elder sons. There were obviously police agents in his entourage, as there were everywhere else in Iraq. But Muhammad Salem argues convincingly that not many of al-Sadr's representatives can have been double agents since 'more than 120 imams and preachers who followed al-Sadr were arrested or executed before or after his assassination'. At the same time Muhammad Sadiq, for several years at least, must have convinced the Baathist authorities, some of the most suspicious men in the world, that he was genuinely cooperating with them. The rumour about Rokan's contacts with Mustafa is interesting because Rokan played a central role in another Saddam tactic aimed at securing his power during the 1990s. The plan was to cultivate the Shia tribes of southern Iraq, both urban and rural, pay off their leaders, and use them as one more instrument of government control. Saddam knew the Iraqi state machine was getting weaker because of lack of money and that the Shia tribes, whose power the Baath party had previously sought to eliminate, were getting stronger. Instead of opposing this process he sought to bring it under his control so his authority would be strengthened. At an early meeting with the Shia tribal sheikhs Saddam even apologised for land reforms that had destroyed their feudal power. Where there were no sheikhs to cultivate, or where they were hostile to the regime, new ones were appointed. These were known contemptuously among Iraqis as 'Taiwan Sheikhs' because they were deemed fake or second-hand copies like cheap products made in Taiwan.[4]

I used to see these sheikhs from distance provinces staying at government expense in the al-Rashid Hotel. They were known to hotel staff as 'the flying sheikhs' because they were fascinated by the hotel lifts which they had never seen before. Accompanied by their heavily armed bodyguards they would take the lifts up and down for hours with evident enjoyment. But though despised as hillbillies by the staff of the al-Rashid hotel the Shia tribal leaders had real authority. The differing levels of financial compensation for victims of violence is revealed in an agreement signed by four clans in Baghdad at this time: 'For physical assault with the bare hands ID [Iraqi Dinars] 75,000; for an assault with a wooden club causing no bleeding ID 100,000–150,000; for an assault with a sharp instrument which involves no loss of leg or limb ID 200,000-300,000. If death is caused the blood money runs into millions depending on the victim's gender, age or work.'[5]

Much of Muhammad Sadiq's missionary zeal was directed towards the tribes, particularly those in the slums of what was then known as Saddam City (now Sadr City) in Baghdad. The laws and customs of the tribes were often at odds with those followed by the traditional Shia clergy. This made them particularly open to the Messianic revivalism of Sadrist prayer leaders. 'The integration of Iraqi tribalism and Shiite puritanism has yielded a potent and cultural force,' suggests Mahan Abedin, an analyst of Iraqi and Iranian politics. 'It is partly for this reason that the government sponsored Muhammad Sadiq al-Sadr. In his controversial book *Fiqh al-Asha'ir* [Tribal Jurisprudence], Muhammad Sadiq al-Sadr has sought to reconcile tribal customs with sharia and conferred upon tribal leaders the right to administer religious law.'[6] Saddam saw the role of

Muhammad Sadiq as being one way of securing his authority over the poorest and most tribal of the Shia who had revolted in 1991.

For people like Muhammad Sadiq, living on their nerves because violent death is always around the corner, petty disputes become magnified out of all proportion. Friction with other Shia religious leaders is evident in episodes witnessed by his students and is sometimes captured in tape-recorded remarks. At one moment Muhammad Sadiq issued a fatwa permitting smoking during fasting and was asked why other members of the hierarchy made an opposite ruling. He replied impatiently: 'Habibi, go and ask the others why they permit the chewing of gum [during fasting]. Are they only forbidding smoking because al-Sadr is in favour of it?'[7] A tape-recording made by Muhammad Sadiq in 1998 refers to a quarrel with the al-Hakim family over rights to control a school in Najaf and their questioning of his scholarly credentials. He says he wanted to make up the quarrel but his overtures were rejected. When al-Sadr visited al-Sistani in his home he was wounded by the failure of the Grand Ayatollah to address more than a few cursory remarks to him or accompany him to the door to say goodbye. Elsewhere Muhammad Sadiq wonders what right had Sayyid Majid al-Khoei, by then running the al-Khoei Foundation in London, to spend funds donated because of the great prestige of his father.[8]

Looking at these squabbles it is easy to forget that opposing Saddam Hussein in Iraq while he was still in power was an act of great courage. Death and detention were never far away. Nor was this courage confined to the Sadrists. Many of those in exile had lost members of their families. Of Muhammad Baqir al-Hakim's eight brothers, six had been killed by Saddam. The so-called 'quietist' clergy following al-Khoei were not immune. Over one hundred of them, including al-Khoei's son-in-law, had disappeared during the mass arrests in 1991. His son Muhammad Taqi was killed in what the al-Khoei family believe was a government-arranged car accident between Najaf and Kerbala on 21 July 1994. These deaths were in keeping with the Shia tradition, stretching back to Imam Hussein, of martyrdom in opposing tyranny.

Furthermore, many of the issues furiously debated by Shia spiritual leaders are not unique to Iraq. They have been at the core of religious and philosophical dispute in other countries down the course of history. The al-Sadr family advocated direct political involvement by the Islamic clergy in defence of the people and against Saddam Hussein. Grand Ayatollahs al-Khoei and al-Sistani opposed it, arguing that they must remain above the political fray or the purity of religion would be sullied and discredited. Their attitude was not so very different from that of Jesus two thousand years earlier when, asked by opponents of the Roman occupation of Palestine about paying tribute to the authorities, he famously retorted: 'Render unto Caesar that which is Caesar's.'

Relations between Muhammad Sadiq al-Sadr and the regime in Baghdad reached their high point in 1996 and began to sour thereafter. The immense numbers attending Friday prayers alarmed the Iraqi security services. They were also beginning to suspect that al-Sadr's cooperation with them was temporary and tactical and he was, in practice, one of Saddam Hussein's most dangerous enemies. This revelation was slow in coming and Muhammad Sadiq tried to put off a final confrontation, which he correctly assumed would lead to his own death, as long as possible. 'He realised that with Friday prayers he could fight the oppressor indirectly by confronting him ideologically and building a mass base,' says Sheikh Yassin al-Assadi, a contemporary eyewitness in Najaf. 'He was wary at first of saying a word that the authorities could use as evidence to arrest him, and his criticism of the authorities was only by means of hints.'

Friday prayers led by Muhammad Sadiq only started in Kufa in 1998 but in other southern governorates they were initiated earlier. In Kut they began in 1996[9] and al-Sadr issued a fatwa inaugurating them in Thawra in Baghdad in 1997.[10] He was also eager to resume the ritualised pilgrimages to Kerbala and Najaf that were so central to the popular Shia religious tradition. These had been banned or curtailed over many years. Muhammad Hassan Ibrahim from Kut heeded a call by al-Sadr to take part in the walk to Kerbala in 1997 to celebrate the birthday of Imam Mehdi. What followed shows that neither the authorities, al-Sadr himself nor rival Shia religious leaders were quite ready for a confrontation. Muhammad Hassan recalls that the Baathist officials rejected al-Sadr's request for the march to be authorised because 'they feared the march would turn into an Islamic political demonstration against the regime. Al-Sadr ordered the marchers, who had already started the pilgrimage, to stop and go home in order to prevent bloodshed. I was among the marchers. It was wintertime and the weather was cool. Sometimes we would walk in the main road and at others we would go through the farms where people would hide us from the police or disguise us as one of themselves. Sometimes we saw police in plain clothes walking with us but they did not do anything to us but just collected information.' Despite hearing al-Sadr's order to stop the march, Muhammad Hassan continued walking to Kerbala with two friends. He stayed on in Kerbala to go to a sermon delivered by Muhammad Sadiq who 'hinted clearly that the regime in Baghdad had done a service to colonialism and the colonialists and Zionists when it stopped visits to the Imam Hussein shrine'. He went on to attack the passivity of the leaders of the *hawza* on the question of the march. Al-Sadr said: 'One notices that on the question of the march and the ban on the march the traditional silent *hawza* or their representatives said nothing, as if they don't know what is happening in Iraqi society.'

By the following year Muhammad Sadiq was addressing hundreds of thousands of people gathered in and around the mosque in Kufa. It is worth giving at some length the story of Ali Hussein Khidr, the seventeen-year-old from Nasiriyah,

whose account conveys the enthusiasm of young Shia
teenagers for the Sadrist movement. He and his friends went
repeatedly to Kufa to attend Friday Prayers. 'We travelled on
Thursday afternoon by car to Kufa,' he says. 'In winter we
slept at friends' homes or sometimes somebody working with
al-Sadr found a place for us to sleep despite the very large
number of people in the same situation. In summer we either
slept in the mosque or in the street. We were prepared to
endure the hot weather in order to see al-Sadr. The regime
began harassing young people in Nasiriyah travelling to
Kufa. The Baathist authorities gave the driver of a bus a piece
of paper that was meant to make it easier to enter Kufa, but
when he handed it over to the guards at the entrance to the
city (there were always checkpoints on roads leading into
Iraqi cities and towns) they arrested him.' This cut down the
numbers going to Kufa but only marginally, and Ali Hussein
and his friends would simply hitch lifts in private cars or go
in vehicles owned by committed Sadrists. He says the number
of arrests was not large 'because the regime did not want a
clash with so many people, especially with the youth, after
the uprising'.

Ali Hussein describes typical Friday prayers as delivered by
Muhammad Sadiq in the great mosque in Kufa. 'There were
very large throngs of people singing songs and shouting
slogans to welcome him. He got out of an old Mitsubishi car,
model 1982, accompanied by his sons Muammal, Muqtada
and Mustafa. They had difficulty getting into the mosque
because of the immense crowds. Once inside he would retire
to a small room, close the door and nobody saw him again
until he mounted the podium and began his speech. He would
first pray to the Prophet and then start a topic without
preamble. Once, when he delivered the second of his sermons,
I saw people trying to touch his cloak and kiss his hand. He
was wearing a white shroud and leaning on a brown stick.
During his walk he saw a small child with a beautiful face and
walked with him to where he would speak. He then thanked
all those who were attending the prayers and asked the

security and intelligence officers observing them to also join in the prayers. He repeated his well-known slogans starting with "No, no to America!", "No, no to Israel!" Then he delivered a sermon aimed at ending differences between Sunni and Shia and invited Sunni to pray in Shia mosques and asked Shia not to refuse to pray before a Sunni prayer leader.'[11]

All the while his tone was getting sharper and his opposition to the regime less discreet. For instance in October 1997 there was a referendum, the result carefully fixed in advance, on the position of Saddam Hussein as a leader. The regime's slogan was 'Yes to Saddam Hussein'. But in a sermon delivered on 15 October 1997 Muhammad Sadiq said: 'NO! Yes is just for God.'

The personality of Muhammad Sadiq is elusive because those who came to talk to him in Najaf or Kufa mostly saw him as a living saint. Many of these were young men who found him approachable, modest and willing to discuss matters they found it embarrassing to talk about such as 'temporary marriages'. His approach was deliberately democratic and his sermons were delivered using common Iraqi speech whereas his lectures to his students were in more complex Arabic. This may explain why his opponents accused him of naivety and simplicity. He succeeded in giving his followers, often very young, confidence in themselves. 'When we entered Najaf city we felt as if al-Sadr was telling us that you are the owner of the land,' recalls Ali Hussein Khidr. 'It was as if he was saying you are Shia, you are one of Imam Ali's followers, you are strong.'[12]

For most of his short public career Muhammad Sadiq focused on immediate practical issues facing the Shia community. Avoiding political questions was also part of his effort to postpone confrontation with the state. At the same time he believed that the active and militant *marji'iya* must prepare the way for the Twelfth Imam, the return of the hidden *mahdi* who would end oppression on earth. In the longer term his support for an Islamic state ruled by the learned jurists (*wilayat al-faqih*) was in the tradition of

Muhammad Baqir al-Sadr and Ayatollah Khomeini. He did not see this spiritual primacy as being exerted over all Muslims as did the Iranian leaders. The question was in any case theoretical in Iraq under the iron rule of Saddam. It was also going to remain theoretical in future since Iraq may be 60 per cent Shia but it is also 40 per cent Sunni if Sunni Arabs and the Kurds, who are overwhelmingly Sunni, are taken together. The complete primacy of a Shia religious leader was never feasible. But when al-Sadr proclaimed his leadership over the Iraqi Shia, the move was deeply resented in Iran. His offices in Iran were immediately closed and his representatives expelled. 'All ties were broken as soon as he [Muhammad Sadiq] proclaimed his *wilayat al-faqih* because . . . it contradicted Ali Khamenei's [the Iranian supreme leader] *wilayat al-faqih*,' said one of Muqtada's representatives. 'I think that is the reason why Iran shut down al-Sadr's offices in Iran at the time.'[13]

The escalating confrontation between the Sadrists and Saddam in 1998 took place against a background of ever-increasing pressure on Baghdad by the US. The crisis over the access of UN inspectors looking for Iraq's supposed weapons of mass destruction (WMD) finally boiled over on 16 December 1998 when the US launched 'Operation Desert Fox'. Once again bombs and missiles fell on Baghdad and other Iraqi cities. Iraqi officials guessed that the brief bombardment was a diversionary tactic by President Clinton as impeachment proceedings began in Washington over his affair with Monica Lewinsky. But the international crisis over WMD made the regime nervous. Its tolerance of al-Sadr was already wearing thin. A more repressive policy towards the Shia was presaged by the mysterious assassinations of two leading Ayatollahs, Ayatollah al-Gharawi and Ayatollah Burujurdi, earlier in 1998. These killings were universally blamed on the regime by the Shia community. The UN reported that 2,500 people had been executed in Abu Ghraib prison since the end of 1997, including some who had taken part in the 1991 uprising.[14]

The regime was impatient at Sadiq's equivocations concerning overt support for Saddam Hussein. It wanted him to praise openly the Iraqi leader at Friday prayers. It ordered him to cancel the march to Kerbala at the end of 1998 and to limit the vast congregations attending his prayer meetings. According to Sheikh Yassin al-Assadi, Muhammad Sadiq realised that an open breach with the regime was now inevitable and would end with his death. He therefore 'refused to invoke Saddam's name at Friday prayers despite the insistence of Saddam and his aides who said it was a political necessity because of US–British aggression'.[15] In a sermon on 12 February 1999 he called for the release of the 101 clergy and students arrested at the same time as Grand Ayatollah al-Khoei in 1991. As he shouted this demand the vast audience of tens of thousands in Kufa mosque echoed back his words, chanting: 'Immediately! Immediately! Immediately! We want! We want! We want!' Al-Sadr's aides reportedly said that he had been telephoned by Saddam himself asking him to withdraw the demand and when he refused the Iraqi leader slammed down the phone.[16] Even if Saddam did not make the call himself, he sent a series of intimidating messengers such as Muhammad Hamza al-Zubeidi, the notoriously brutal governor and Baath party leader for the mid-Euphrates region who had been video-taped mistreating Shia rebels in 1991. He told Muhammad Sadiq: 'There is a presidential order forbidding Friday prayers this week.' Al-Sadr responded: 'I will pray, I will pray, I will pray.'

The government was also worried by signs that for the first time since 1991, Shia militants were switching to armed resistance. The most serious outbreak was in Nasiriyah. Ali Hussein Khidr, a committed follower of Muhammad Sadiq, gives an account of an abortive Shia uprising which took place at this date. 'I was with Sheikh Abdel Karim Ismail with groups of Sayyid [Muhammad Sadiq] al-Sadr's followers who planned to overthrow the government. Its agents knew of our plan, ambushed us and arrested Sheikh

Abdel Karim with a group of young people. There were violent clashes in Nasiriyah and the governor's headquarters had been attacked with rockets. The government lost control of the city for several days. I fled with family to the villages so as not to be arrested or executed like other young people. We were in a village whose people were from the clan of Jouber and the village had the same name. Muhammad Hamza al-Zubeidi deployed the Republican Guard. But the village and the clan were well armed with anti-aircraft and anti-tank weapons supplied by the Badr corps in Iran. When al-Zubeidi came to the village he completely destroyed it: he cut off the water supply, bombed and executed many villagers including women and children. My family and I escaped miraculously because we were some distance from the village. We heard the sound of the bombs, the shooting and the screams until they died away. The situation was very difficult in the city and all the cities of the south.'[17]

People in Najaf saw ominous signs that the regime was preparing to act against Muhammad Sadiq. Dr Hassan Mustafa, about thirty years old at the time and now a professor at Najaf University, came from a religious family that had good relations with the *hawza*. He was an attentive witness to the last days of al-Sadr. He says the atmosphere in the city was very tense. When Sadiq al-Sadr entered Kufa mosque, an official approached him and told him not to hold prayers. He rejected the advice. Security forces were very visible in the mosque says Dr Mustafa: 'We knew the faces of most of them but this time there more of them and they looked hostile. None of them were from Najaf and from their appearance they appeared to be from the west not the south of Iraq.' (In other words they were light-skinned men from the overwhelmingly Sunni Anbar province that covers western Iraq and not darker men from the Shia south.) In Najaf, checkpoints began to spring up every 150–200 yards manned by soldiers from the Hammurabi Republican Guard division. This started a week or ten days before the assassination and then the faces at the checkpoints changed again: 'There was a special force called the Fedayeen Saddam, brutal people trained to murder and sabotage, known for their ferocity and frightening appearance.' The regime was also sending fresh troops to Shia areas like Thawra (now Sadr City), Hurriya and Bai'aa in Baghdad as well as to Kufa and Najaf. It had offered Muhammad Sadiq guards but he refused them. There is evidence from another source that Muhammad Sadiq knew what was about to happen. Around 15 February Mustafa al-Khadimi, an ex-Dawa militant then living in London, got a message from Jafar al-Sadr, the son of Muhammad Baqir and a senior lieutenant of Muhammad Sadiq. It was to be passed on to Ahmed Chalabi, one of the leaders of the Iraqi opposition. The message read simply: 'I need help. Saddam is going to kill me.'[18]

On 19 February July Muhammad Sadiq was returning to his house with his two elder sons Mustafa and Muammal and their driver. By Dr Mustafa's account, as they were entering the 1920 Revolution roundabout a second car, later identified as an Oldsmobile, was waiting. It was filled with gunmen armed with machine guns. They riddled al-Sadr's car killing his sons and the driver immediately. Al-Sadr alone remained alive but was badly wounded in the head and legs. He was taken to the Saddam Hospital about two miles away. 'I was with one of my friends and they stopped us from going through the main gate of the hospital so we tried and failed to get in through a side entrance,' says Dr Mustafa. There were security men everywhere, from other parts of Iraq but not from Najaf. Outside the gates a crowd was shouting and trying to get in. Staff in the hospital later told Dr Mustafa that these men prevented doctors entering the room where Muhammad Sadiq and his two sons had been taken. 'One of the doctors said that Sayyid al-Sadr was alive when they brought him into the hospital but they let him bleed to death.'

*

In Thawra and in other Shia cities of southern Iraq there was an explosive reaction as news of the assassination spread. Nobody had any doubt who was behind it. The regime was prepared for an angry popular reaction to murder but even so it must have been aghast at the extent of the outbreaks of popular violence. The willingness of so many people to die or face arrest while making hopeless protests, shows the extent to which al-Sadr was seen as a Messiah. 'I was one who loved Sayyid al-Sadr,' says Sajad Ali from Sadr City, 'because he was the only man who tried to assist poor and needy people, especially the young, at a time when there was widespread unemployment, the economic blockade and injustice by the authorities.' Protestors gathered around the Muhsin mosque in Thawra and chanted: 'Down with the regime!' They called for revenge. The clashes between the demonstrators and the security forces there lasted for hours. Fifteen of the latter, including a major, were killed and several of their cars burned. They opened fire indiscriminately, killing and wounding numerous demonstrators. Sajad Ali said 400 people died in the hail of bullets. Foreign diplomats estimated that the number was forty to eighty dead and an Iraqi government official privately told a foreign aid worker that the true figure was fifty-four.[19] 'When I heard the news of his [Muhammad Sadiq's] death I was shocked (I was twenty-eight at the time) and I went with my friends to the mosque to ask for weapons to resist,' says Sajad Ali, 'but at the mosque we agreed with its Imam Sheikh Ali al-Ka'abi to hold prayers as a protest the following Friday, when he chanted and shouted against the regime. Afterwards there were clashes and Sheikh Ali al-Ka'abi was arrested. They said they would release him if he agreed not to criticise the government but he refused. At the time of his arrest he hit one of the investigators so he was held for a long time and severely tortured.' Surprisingly he was released but continued his attacks on the government and was then arrested again and finally executed.

The courage and determination of Sadiq al-Sadr's

supporters is astonishing. On the second Friday after the killing his followers returned to the Muhsin mosque. They were determined to die. Sajad Ali says: 'This time we tied our feet and ankles together with strong rope so we could not escape when the security forces attacked us and we would continue to pray until martyrdom. Instead they beat us with sticks that gave us electric shocks that did not kill us but stopped us praying.' However, some of the worshippers in the mosque were shot and killed. 'The authorities would only return the bodies to their families if they paid for the bullets that killed them and promised not to perform mourning ceremonies.'[20] Repression was finally effective. Resistance ebbed away because of the mass arrests and executions of the very young. Sajad Ali makes a surprising admission for a man so committed to Sadiq. He says that even in Thawra opposition to Saddam was not total because 'in many houses, though not in all, there was a brother and sister who was a Baathist'.

A month after these first outbreaks of spontaneous violence there was an ill-coordinated uprising which became known as the 'al-Sadr intifada'. It was not on the scale of the 1991 rebellion and the regime crushed it so swiftly and ruthlessly that little news of these bloody events surfaced outside Iraq. A general uprising in all the cities of southern Iraq was originally planned for 28 February but instead the outbreaks took place one after another. The most serious revolt was in Basra on 17 March 1999 when, at night, groups of armed men attacked government buildings, intelligence headquarters and Baath party offices. There was heavy fighting in which at least forty Baath party members were killed.[21] Jassem, then a thirty-six-year-old Sadrist sympathiser and one of the few survivors of this little-known episode, says that the uprising was the work of a mixture of groups. 'There were about 168 students from the Faculty of Engineering in the University of Basra,' he says, 'as well as a group from Hezbollah [an Iraqi movement not connected to the Lebanese movement of the same name] and the Badr corps. There was meant to be a simultaneous uprising in all the southern provinces.' The rebels waited for the arrival of the 10,000-strong Badr Brigade stationed in Iran, its participation essential if there was to be any chance of success because they were well-trained and well-armed professional soldiers. Jassem says the leaders were to be Karim Mahoud, a famed guerrilla leader from Amara who was also known as 'The Lord of the Marshes' and led the Hezbollah group, Sheikh Saleh al-Jizani from Basra and Sheikh Abdel Karim Ismail from Basra itself. But at the last moment Muhammad Baqir al-Hakim, the leader of SCIRI who controlled the Badr group, postponed the uprising. 'We don't know the reason for the delay to this day but we felt let down,' says Jassem. The rebels went ahead with the plans anyway and 'many martyrs fell during their attack on the party and security headquarters where we killed large numbers of the security forces including senior Baathists and intelligence officers'. Jassem says that they gained control of the centre of Basra for two nights before troops from the 3rd [Iraqi army] Corps and the Baathists retook it.[22]

Government vengeance was savage. A four-page document listing 120 men who were executed was found by looters in the office of the General Security Directorate, after British troops took Basra in 2003. The youngest victim was sixteen and the eldest was thirty-six. Some were executed by the families of Baathists who had been killed in the uprising, according to notes on the list. The bodies were buried in mass graves by Basra airport. The executions were carried out under the authority of Ali Hassan al-Majid who was in charge of southern Iraq. He summoned Shia clan and tribal leaders to a meeting where he furiously berated them, saying those who went to Friday prayers were criminals, claiming a fatwa had been issued by Shia clerics allowing brothers to marry their sisters and demanding that they cease helping the Sadrists and cooperate in hunting them down.

Muhammad Baqir al-Hakim probably called off Badr support for the uprising because he could see it was doomed.

The Iranians, who had veto power over his actions, are also likely to have forbidden Badr troops to cross into Iraq from Iran. But the failed intifada and the assassination of Sadiq al-Sadr himself, the very man whom al-Hakim had been denouncing as a police agent, deepened the hostility that amounted at times to hatred between the Sadrists and the exiled groups. This had significant repercussions after 2003 when the Shia leaders began to assert themselves as the new leaders of Iraq.

There is a final, dramatic episode in the story of Muhammad Sadiq, which illustrates the cult-like devotion he attracted among ordinary Iraqis. It took place in Qom, the Iranian holy city where there were thousands of Iraqi refugees, guerrilla fighters from Badr and religious students from Iraq. They heard the news of al-Sadr's murder the day after it had happened. Horrified, many of them immediately rushed to the house of his representative in Iran, Sayyid Jafar al-Sadr, the son of Muhammad Baqir al-Sadr. It was Jafar who had relayed the message from Muhammad Sadiq to London a few days earlier saying that he expected Saddam to kill him. 'The masses gathered in front of his house and in the street to express their pain and sorrow at what had happened,' recalls an eyewitness. 'They chanted against Sayyid Muhammad Baqir al-Hakim and Saddam and some scuffled with those who had criticised al-Sadr but the situation did not get out of control.'[23]

The murder of Muhammad Sadiq by the Iraqi leader put both al-Hakim and the Iranians in an embarrassing position. The former had publicly denounced him as a collaborator and the Iranian government had closed Jafar's office when Muhammad Sadiq had declared himself the supreme leader of the Iraqi Shia, thus contesting the claim of Ali Khamenei. In a conciliatory if hypocritical gesture, the office of Khamenei arranged for a mourning ceremony at the A'azum mosque, one of the largest in Qom. It was filled to overflowing with Iraqi exiles, Iranian officials and Shia clergy so latecomers had to stand outside the mosque. Al-Hakim unwisely decided to attend. As he took his seat the crowd in the mosque began to shout: 'Long live al-Sadr! The al-Hakim family are traitors!' The preacher pleaded with them to drop this slogan but without result. Jafar al-Sadr, who had been receiving delegations, then tried to calm down the congregation but was also ignored. 'Some people began to throw their shoes, cigarette packets and anything that came to hand at Sayyid al-Hakim to express their anger and even their hatred,' said an Iraqi observing the scene. 'He decided to leave the mosque as soon as his car and security guards arrived. While he was moving towards the car more shoes were hurled at him.'

The explosive growth of the al-Sadr movement, the assassination of its leader, and the 'al-Sadr intifada' which followed were, taken together, the most serious domestic crisis faced by Saddam's regime between 1991 and 2003. It was an extraordinary achievement for Muhammad Sadiq to have created such a powerful mass movement under the eyes of the Iraqi authorities. His blend of Islamic revivalism, populism and Iraqi nationalism had a powerful appeal to the mass of Shia. Depleted by death, flight and mass arrests, his movement went deep underground but did not disappear. It was to re-emerge after the fall of Saddam with Sadiq al-Sadr's youngest son Muqtada at its head. The most convincing explanation for his rapid rise, according to a member of the Dawa party, is that 'Muqtada's movement was built by his father. All he did was help it to evolve and continue the process initiated by Muhammad Sadiq al-Sadr.'[24]

CHAPTER NINE

Muqtada Survives

Muqtada was lucky to survive. He probably owed his life to the hypocrisy of the regime that pretended it had nothing to do with the assassination of his father and his two brothers, Mustafa and Muammal. Government officials brazenly attended the mourning ceremonies in Najaf to commiserate with him. Muqtada, now responsible for his mother and his brothers' wives and children, was careful to play along with the pretence and sent a letter formally thanking the government for its sympathy. Even so an office he set up to receive condolences from more credible mourners was swiftly closed by the *mukhabarat*.[1] The regime produced its own unlikely explanation of what had happened. The official government newspaper *al-Jumhuriyah* described the killings as 'among the many conspiracies against Iraq' and an effort to 'disturb internal security' but reassuringly added that several suspects had been arrested. The Iraq News Agency on 6 April 1999 announced that two clerics, Sheikh Abd al-Hassan Abbas al-Kufi and Sheikh Ali Qazim Hajman, and two religious students, Ahmed Mustafa Ardebili and Haider Ali Hussein, had been executed for the crime. The statement said the four men were 'foreigners', implying they were Iranians. In other media the regime blamed paid intelligence agents who were part of an American–Zionist plot. The claims impressed few people inside or outside Iraq. One of the men, Sheikh al-Kufi, had been arrested in Najaf on 24 December 1998 and could not have taken part in the assassination.[2] 'Baghdad television showed the confession of the detainees,' says Dr Hassan Mustafa, 'who were dressed as Shia clerics, in which they spoke of the assassination of al-Sadr and his two sons, Mustafa and Muammal. But the confessions were obviously made in a torture chamber and did not fool anybody or obscure the fact that Saddam's regime was responsible.'[3]

This clumsy cover story had the advantage from Muqtada's point of view that, after claiming to have caught the assassins of his family, the regime could not easily move to kill him as well though, going by Saddam's history, it would have done so if its security men had suspected he posed the slightest threat. In later years Western news agencies were to use the cliché 'firebrand cleric' to describe Muqtada, but the phrase, implying spontaneous and ill-considered militancy, is highly misleading. On the contrary, his success in Iraqi politics has often been due to his ability to make swift retreats, politically and militarily, when faced with an adversary superior in strength. His politics might be radical but he would scarcely have survived after 1999 unless his behaviour had been carefully calculated not to arouse any suspicion on the part of the *mukhabarat* that he was a danger to the regime. He neither accused the Iraqi security services of murdering his father and brothers nor did he play any role in the sporadic uprisings that followed. Saddam may have feared that the murder of another al-Sadr could transform these outbreaks into general Shia rebellion. 'The government baulked at killing Muqtada al-Sadr because it feared this would provoke a popular uprising,' says Sheikh Ali, the *nom de guerre* of one of Muqtada's aides and later a leader of the Mehdi Army. 'Members of the *marji'iya,* senior religious figures, advised Muqtada to stick to attending religious classes and to reduce the number of people he met to the minimum so as to preserve his own life. They pointed out that there was nobody left in his immediate family, just himself and his surviving brother Murtadha who did not have an important position.' (Murtadha is variously described as being sick or a recluse and to have died in about 2005.)

Muqtada's low profile over the next four years was not just a matter of choice. His every action was closely monitored. 'The security forces tracked his movements even inside his own home,' recalls Sheikh Ali. 'Everybody and everything had to be inspected before it was allowed into his house which was surrounded by security men.'[4] The regime's excuse for this close surveillance was that it was intent on protecting Muqtada from the same dire fate as his relatives. One commentator suggests that the permanent stress under which Muqtada lived during these years 'may have psychologically scarred the young cleric'.[5] Certainly these years of living on his nerves, never knowing if he would end the day in prison or be killed by the regime like all his close relatives, would help explain Muqtada's continual wariness and suspicion of those around him.

Muqtada is the fourth and youngest son of Muhammad Sadiq al-Sadr. He was born on 12 August 1973 which would make him twenty-five years old when his father and brothers were assassinated. He married a daughter of Muhammad Baqir al-Sadr in 1994, but they have no children. Even so he is sometimes called by his nickname Abu Hashim (father of Hashim). His many enemies were later to claim that his father paid little attention to him and did not rate his talents highly,[6] though this is strenuously denied by his followers. Muhammad Sadiq al-Sadr operated very much through his three politically active sons who were his closest aides. Ayatollahs normally rely on their sons as their political lieutenants, but Sadiq was doubly dependent on them because of his need for tight security as he double-crossed the regime while claiming to be its ally. His eldest son Mustafa was much better known among Shia than Muqtada himself and Sadiq was sometimes called Abu Mustafa (father of Mustafa). But Muqtada still played a number of crucial roles. In late 1997, at the moment when the Baath regime had its greatest confidence that the Sadrist movement was working in its interests, it had taken the unprecedented decision to allow the Sadrists to produce their own Islamic magazine. This was called *al-Huda* and Muqtada was its editor-in-chief. It published his father's speeches and fatwas, decisions on what was *al-haram* and *al-halal* (forbidden and permitted) as well as articles by Shia scholars. 'It sold out quickly,' says a witness, 'because it was the only non-government magazine issued in that era of political persecution and intellectual monopoly. It was bimonthly and we were working to make it a weekly when Sayyid al-Sadr was assassinated.'[7] The role of Muqtada was to oversee contributions, printing and distribution.

He had various other jobs. Sheikh Ali says he was responsible for his father's security, particularly when Muhammad Sadiq was addressing vast crowds at the mosque in Kufa when 'two guards were placed in front of him and three behind'. Muqtada was also dean of a religious university set up by his father in Najaf. Most important of all, he was responsible for Thawra in Baghdad, which was to become the main bastion of his strength. Several men who later became his lieutenants, such as Mustafa al-Yaqubi, were appointed by him. Exact details of Muqtada's biography are contentious because of the adoration and hatred he was to inspire after the fall of Saddam Hussein, but there is no doubt that he was politically highly experienced and well connected by the time his father and brothers were assassinated.

Supporters of Muqtada admit that his isolation under house arrest prevented him leading any Sadrist underground in the four years following his father's death. He did cautiously seek to contact religious sheikhs, but the *mukhabarat* surveillance was too great to hold meetings. Persecution of the Sadrist remnants was intense and it was difficult and dangerous even to visit his father's tomb in Najaf without courting arrest. Many of those who had been leaders of the movement, like Ali al-Ka'abi in Thawra, were dead, in prison or had fled abroad. There were attempts to hold commemorative prayers for Muhammad Sadiq in Diwaniyah and the Baghdad districts of Shuala and Kadhimiyah in 2000, a year after his death, but those who turned up were immediately detained.

Muqtada continued his theological studies which were essential to his rise in the clerical hierarchy. He had started these under his father, studying alongside Mahmoud Hassan al-Sarki, Sayyid Hassan Husseini and Qassem Al-Ta'i. He had entered the *hawza* in 1988 but never got beyond pre-graduation research which was interrupted when his father was killed. Asked what Muqtada did in the 1990s Jafar al-Sadr, Sadr II's chief lieutenant, simply says: 'He was working hard in his father's office.'[8] It is a rule of the *hawza* that studies have to be continued under the same teacher in order to progress to the next clerical rank. Muqtada transferred to Muhammad Ishaq al-Fayadh, an Afghan ayatollah living in Najaf whom his father had recommended as a man to be consulted, though al-Fayadh was closer in belief to the quietism of Grand Ayatollah Ali al-Sistani than to the militant activism of the Sadrists. They considered him 'a generous and good hearted man but far from political life'.[9] As his official successor – or rather as a man whose words he had advised his followers to heed – Sadiq had appointed Ayatollah Kadhim al-Haeri, who was an Iraqi by origin but had lived in Qom in Iran for two decades. In practice neither man had the energy or the experience to play a leading role in Iraq's complex and violent politics.

Muqtada was keen to burnish his religious credentials and, despite his much enhanced status after the overthrow of Saddam, came back for further study under Ayatollah Fayadh. His opponents later criticised him for his lowly place in the Shia religious hierarchy, implying that he lacked intelligence or academic ability. The next four years showed that Muqtada was a highly astute politician, but his enemies, both Iraqis and Americans, persistently underestimated him. His lack of the right religious qualifications mattered little in the turmoil of post-Saddam Iraq. In any case, the Sadrist movement under Muqtada's father had always had an anti-clerical strain, accusing the *marji'iya* of failing to do anything to alleviate the misery and oppression of ordinary Iraqis. Muqtada's very youth was an advantage because it meant that he had grown up in the 1990s, in the wake of the Iraqi army's defeat in Kuwait, the merciless crushing of the Shia uprising and the destruction of the Iraqi economy and society by UN sanctions. His very lack of official status as a member of the *marji'iya* made him all the more attractive to many impoverished young Shia who were distrustful of all religious and political authorities. They found it easier to identify with Muqtada who had stayed in Iraq than to trust people like Sayyid Majid al-Khoei who had lived for twelve years in London or Muhammad Baqir al-Hakim, the leader of SCIRI, who had spent twenty-three years in Iran. Muqtada himself was very conscious of the status that his continued presence in Iraq gave him. In an interview in June 2003 he acknowledged that he had not reached the rank of *mujtahid,* but claimed the right to leadership because of the sacrifices of those 'who never left the country and remained with their people in Iraq to share their burdens'.[10]

Muqtada's greatest strength was that he was the son of Muhammad Sadiq al-Sadr and the son-in-law and cousin of Muhammad Baqir al-Sadr, the two great martyrs in the modern history of the Shia. He spent a large part of his time when he was under house arrest between 1999 and 2003 archiving their work and speeches. When he was asked in later years to define what was meant by the 'Sadrist Movement' he denied it was a political party. He said it was simply made up of people who followed the teachings of Muhammad Sadiq al-Sadr (Sadr II). He added that in a broader sense the movement included anybody who honoured the 'Speaking Hawza' and followed the teachings of Ayatollah Baqir al-Sadr (Sadr I). Both wanted an Islamic society which would prepare the way for the return of the Imam Mehdi, the redeemer who would end the rule of tyrants and establish justice in the world.[11]

At times Muqtada seemed to merge his identity with his revered and martyred relatives. He not only articulated their theology but imitated their personal behaviour. His manner of giving speeches was clearly modelled on that of his father, each word emphasised by the same abrupt gestures until, as one observer put it, 'he makes you feel dizzy'. Where he differed from Muhammad Sadiq was that he was unwaveringly serious, in contrast with his father who often lightened his conversation with jokes. In public Muqtada cultivated an image of melancholy gravity, as if to rebut charges that he was a youthful lightweight, while in private discussions he is described as businesslike, moody and, at times, short tempered. 'He can't endure any question or fact to be repeated twice,' comments one of his supporters. 'And if the topic has deviated from the topic under discussion he will return to the main point quickly. His own comments are short.'

Groping to describe Muqtada, Western commentators often note that he is 'charismatic' (or occasionally that he is 'uncharismatic') and for once the cliché has a kernel of truth. The word has been devalued by overuse so that it now means little more than that a person has glamour, charm and allure. But the original meaning of the word 'charismatic' was to suggest that the person so described had a special kind of holiness or semi-divine grace. This was certainly true of Muqtada who acquired a cult-like status and whose followers believed he had a special relationship with God. This belief was never shared by a majority of Shia, but there was a core of people around Muqtada who saw him as the true redeemer for whose return the Shia had prayed for over a thousand years.

The Sadrists were surprised by the scale of the surge in support for them as Saddam's regime fell apart in early April 2003. Like every other Iraqi political group they under-estimated the extent to which ordinary Iraqis were suspicious of returning Iraqi exiles. Class differences were very deep in the Shia community and only they represented the millions of labourers and unemployed. The Sadrists were also a religious movement in a country in which secular politicians had to struggle to get a hearing. At the same time they may have been too conscious of their own weakness because, although they had many sympathisers and a limited number of militants on the run, they had no real political structure. Right up to its final collapse on 9 April, Saddam's regime was fearful of a repeat of the Shia uprising of 1991. Its security forces were everywhere on the alert. The only action carried out by the Sadrists, by their own account, was the organisation of protests in October 2002 after Saddam had declared a general amnesty for all prisoners except those imprisoned for political reasons. 'Women, children and the elderly took part in peaceful demonstrations demanding the release of prisoners linked to the Sadrist movement,' recalls one Sadrist militant. 'The authorities did not stop such demonstrations because they were peaceful and there were no slogans against the regime.'[12] Foreign journalists in Baghdad at the time were astonished to find these demonstrators standing outside the Ministry of Information in central Baghdad calling for the release of their relatives. Wider protests took place in what was to become Sadr City. 'These demonstrations were the first sign of the unexpectedly strong movement that was developing behind Muqtada,' the Sadrist militant adds.

There was never any likelihood of a second Shia rebellion. Unlike 1991 the regime was forewarned. Its security men had large-scale maps of every district in Iraq in which the houses of potential opponents were marked in black ink. A Shia shopkeeper from Baghdad who fled to Kurdistan told me in early March 2003: 'If there is any sign of weakness on the part of the government there will be an uprising.' But the Shia remembered the terrible price they had paid for the failed rebellion in 1991 and were cautious about risking a second failure. The US ground offensive had started on 19 March: there seemed no point in an Iraqi risking his or her life if the Americans were going to overthrow Saddam Hussein regardless of what Iraqis did or did not do.

I spent the weeks of the initial invasion of March/April

2003 in Kurdistan. I knew the government in Baghdad was not going to give me a visa because it was offended by a book I had co-authored with my brother, Andrew, titled *Out of the Ashes: The Resurrection of Saddam Hussein*, which was an account of how Saddam survived defeat in the first Gulf War. I had heard that the regime was particularly angry about the chapters dealing with the Shia and Kurdish uprisings, as well as the murderous activities of Saddam's family. For a time I feared I would be unable to reach Iraq before the war started, but in February Hoshyar Zebari, later Iraq's Foreign Minister and then spokesman for the Kurdistan Democratic Party, called me in Washington to say jubilantly that he had persuaded the Syrian government to let me cross the Tigris from north-east Syria into Iraqi territory controlled by the Kurds.

Four days after the start of the war I spoke to two Shia soldiers called Haider Abdul Hussein and Abdul Hassan Ali who had deserted from the Iraqi army in the north. 'I heard the war had started on a little radio the size of a cigarette packet we had smuggled into my unit, although radios were forbidden,' said Haider. 'I did not want to die for Saddam.' He did not expect a Shia uprising, pointing out that the one in 1991 had only happened because the army had already broken up.[13] The Americans were in any case against action by Iraqi armed resistance. The one Iraqi city to be taken by Iraqi insurgents opposed to Saddam was Amara, 200 miles south of Baghdad, which fell on 7 April. It was captured by guerrillas led by Karim Mahmoud al-Muhammadawi, nicknamed Abu Hatem and also 'Lord of the Marshes', who had taken part in the failed uprisings in 1999 after the assassination of Muhammad Sadiq al-Sadr. But no sooner had he captured Amara than he was ordered out by the CIA with the implied threat that he would be bombed if he did not withdraw.[14]

Muqtada moved more quickly than anybody else in Iraq to organise his supporters as the regime began to crumble. On 8 April he was deputised by Ayatollah al-Haeri, whom his father had appointed as his official heir and who lived in the Iranian holy city of Qom, to act as his representative in Iraq and issue fatwas to his followers. None of his rivals was as energetic. He had a web of supporters who could be activated at speed. Many of them were very young. In Thawra, the vast Shia slum, a twenty-three-year-old cleric and local leader, called Sayyid Ali al-Rawawi, said the Sadrist movement was able to take control of the area with just ninety trainee clerics. He had a letter from Muqtada appointing him his *wakil* or representative. Mosques and *husseiniyahs* were used as meeting places and centres for organising neighbourhoods. Within a couple of months the Sadrists controlled 90 per cent of the mosques in Sadr City and had taken over schools, hospitals and welfare centres. Much of this happened in the first few days after the fall of Saddam Hussein. A week after he fled the Sadrists claimed to have 50,000 volunteers organised in predominantly Shia East Baghdad, collecting refuse, directing traffic and distributing hospital meals.[15]

The euphoria and anarchy in Sadr City during those first hours of freedom is captured in the account of a highly committed young Sadrist militant called Abbas. 'We believed Sadr II [Muhammad Sadiq al-Sadr] was like the Prophet Muhammad because he did so many things for our community,' he says. 'We, his followers, had a sense of failure and guilt that we had not been able to stop him being killed so we felt it our duty to support his son and complete his work.' He says nobody organised his activities or those of his friends: 'We knew that the regime had fallen on the morning of 9 April when we found that people had started to rampage and loot. We heard people running through the streets screaming hysterically, "Saddam has fallen! Saddam has fallen!" After a few hours the crowds began to disappear and we thought that they had gone to celebrate but unfortunately they were looting. In the afternoon they came back carrying stolen objects, large and small. This situation went on for a few days and then we, the young men, organised ourselves and volunteered, without anybody leading us, to guard public property. Communications were cut so we did not know what was happening in other provinces. We guarded the power stations, transformers and electricity cables, so if there was any electricity at all in Baghdad after the fall of Saddam it was because of al-Sadr's followers.'[16]

Muqtada never doubted his right to lead the Sadrists despite challenges from important lieutenants of his father such as Muhammad al-Yaqubi, more senior than him in the Shia hierarchy, who was to set up his own party *Hizb al-Fadhila* which later won control of Basra. After the murder of Muhammad Sadiq there were half-smothered disputes between Muqtada and al-Yaqubi over the control of donations and the official stamps from Sadiq's office. Generally, the followers of Muqtada gained control in villages, towns and city districts where his father had also had many followers. One difference was, however, that Muqtada was more reliant than his father on the impoverished urban masses, people whom his opponents denounced and feared as a dangerous, criminalised mob.

Muqtada succeeded in asserting his authority over swathes of Shia Iraq in a few days because of his own abilities and the legacy of his father, in terms of both prestige and organisation. But he was also riding a wave of Shia self-assertion that was as overpowering as it was unexpected. Suddenly there were pictures of Sadr I and Sadr II and other Shia religious notables pasted on every wall. The new post-Saddam Iraq had no secular heroes. More surprisingly, there were traditional signs of Shia identity everywhere. Shia waved green date-palm leaves and green banners, symbolising Imam Ali. People held up clay tablets known as *turba* made from soil taken from Najaf. These were placed in front of the worshipper so, as he prayed, his forehead would touch the sacred earth of the city where Imam Ali was buried. As Saddam's statues were torn down, Shia demonstrators would beat their chests in a ritualised sign indicating their Shia identity. 'By God we swear never to forget Imam Hussein,' chanted the vast crowds and 'No God but Allah'. It was already evident that the future belonged to the Shia religious leaders and a struggle was already beginning as to which of them would come out on top.

CHAPTER TEN

Murder in the Shrine

The enemies of Saddam Hussein always attributed the extreme violence in Iraq to him and his regime. They optimistically imagined that once he was overthrown Iraqis would be able to resolve their differences peacefully. But within twenty-four hours of Saddam's fall on 9 April 2003 one of his ablest and most important opponents, Sayyid Majid al-Khoei, the son of Grand Ayatollah al-Khoei, was hacked to death by fellow Shia after being dragged, his hands bound, from the Imam Ali shrine in Najaf. It was further alleged that he had not been more or less accidentally killed by an out-of-control mob, but was deliberately murdered on the instructions of Muqtada al-Sadr as part of a long-running family feud. The death of al-Khoei, a charming and intelligent man, was an early sign that the new Iraq was going to be just as dangerous as the old, possibly even more so. The Shia leaders wanted to use the overthrow of Saddam by the US to displace the Sunni as rulers of Iraq, but the savagery of the attack in Najaf revealed the bitter divisions within their own community.

I last saw Sayyid Majid four months before he died at a rancorous conference of the Iraqi opposition in London in mid-December 2002. As Londoners held pre-Christmas office parties in the Metropole Hotel on a rain-swept Edgware Road, they could not have guessed that they were rubbing shoulders with Iraqis engaged in the first battles to decide who would succeed Saddam. I saw Sayyid Majid, an alert good looking forty-three-year-old man in a black turban, short dark beard and flowing robes, sweep through the hotel lobby, attracting curious glances from partygoers sipping their margaritas. He had a slightly amused smile on his face, his normal expression, which suggested that he was not going to be surprised by anything that happened at the conference. I had first met him a decade or so earlier. On fleeing Iraq in 1991 after trying and failing to get American support for the Shia uprising, he had come to London. When his brother Muhammad Taqi was murdered in 1994 he became head of the al-Khoei Foundation, an influential and well-funded Shia charity with its headquarters in north London. He gathered a group of very able Iraqis around him and cultivated good relations with the British Foreign Office and the US State Department. I saw him often. He would say that the Shia had made a mistake in 1920 by rising against the British occupation enabling the Sunni to take power in their stead. This became something of a cliché later, but I first heard it from Sayyid Majid and it represented an important political truth. The Shia community, a majority of Iraqis, was not going to oppose a US attack on Iraq to overthrow Saddam. Sayyid Majid was also openly scathing about clerical supremacy in Tehran though distressed when his criticisms of the Iranian regime appeared in print.

That December conference in London was all too accurate a guide to the chronic disunity of Saddam's opponents in the years to come. It had almost failed to convene at all. I had seen Hoshyar Zebari, then a leading member of the Kurdistan Democratic Party and later Iraqi Foreign Minister, a few days earlier in the hotel where he was staying in Knightsbridge. I had known him when he was a student at Essex University twenty years earlier and always been impressed by his energy, ability and unquenchable optimism in the worst of circumstances. But on this occasion even he, slumped in a hotel armchair, was sounding depressed. 'If we can't discuss things democratically between ourselves now, what will it be like when we are part of a (post-Saddam) government?' he asked gloomily – and, as it turned out, prophetically.

It was a good question. Many of the differences that were to cripple future Iraqi governments were already surfacing. The delegates at the conference were overwhelmingly Kurds or Shia Arab. There were very few Sunni. The Tehran-based SCIRI of Muhammad Baqir al-Hakim wanted to be accepted as the main representative of the Shia community. Its members were secretive, well organised and effective. The Sadrists were not present and nobody at the conference supposed they still existed as a significant force. The US envoy to the conference was Zalmay Khalilzad, a suave and experienced diplomat who was later to be US ambassador to Baghdad. He sought to unite the opposition in public but steered away from allowing it to form a provisional government or promising it real power. It is easy in retrospect to deride the delegates as naïve, but at the time their main fear was that the US would baulk at the last moment at overthrowing Saddam. There was also an unspoken anxiety among the Shia and Kurds that Washington would doublecross them by removing Saddam and his clique but sustaining Sunni Arab dominance under American tutelage. This would be a repeat of the old British formula for controlling Iraq. Khalilzad had to deny that the US wanted 'Saddamism without Saddam'. I wrote, somewhat cynically, that the most ominous sign at the conference was the absence of smokefilled rooms. Most Iraqis in Iraq were and are chain-smokers, seldom without a cigarette in their mouths – understandably, given the strain under which they live. Few of the delegates at the conference were heavy smokers. They had been in exile for years living in cities like New York, Chicago and Los Angeles where smoking is frowned on. In other words they had very little experience or knowledge of present-day Iraq.

Few realised how deeply Iraqis inside the country had changed since 1991 as a result of the crushing defeat in Kuwait, the Shia and Kurdish uprisings, the savage repression that followed and the deadly weight of UN sanctions which had destroyed their economy. Sayyid Majid was eager to remove the American suspicion of the Iraqi Shia as pawns of Iran. He was heavily influenced by his experiences in 1991 when he had seen the Americans so decisively shy away from aiding the Shia rebellion to overthrow the Baathists. He said that at that time the US was full of people who were 'scared to shake hands with a man in a black turban'. After talks with politically active Americans a few months previously he told me he found them more open to the idea of Shia predominance in Iraq and even a separate Shia state in the south. He was commonly described in the press as 'a pro-American' cleric but his pro-Americanism had the very practical intention of making the Iraqi Shia acceptable to Washington. He underestimated the extent to which many Iraqi Shia hated the US and its friends just as much as they did Saddam Hussein.

The US was eager to see Sayyid Majid back in Iraq. The US State Department and the CIA liked him. On 28 March 2003 he flew with a party of supporters and friends from Gatwick airport to the US military base in Bahrain. With him was Abdul Hassan al-Khafaji, also known as Abu Tariq, the former Iraqi army colonel who joined the uprising in 1991 and had accompanied Sayyid Majid on his agonising journey across southern Iraq in a vain search for American aid. As an ex-military man he was in charge of security for the group. Other members of the party included Ma'ad Fayadh, a journalist from *al-Sharq al-Awsat* newspaper, Maher al-Yasseri, a Shia cleric from Detroit and Hazem al-Shalaan, later a highly controversial Iraqi defence minister. On 3 April they boarded a US military plane which flew them to Nasiriyah. The road north to Najaf was deemed unsafe and the group was taken in a US helicopter to Najaf but thereafter they refused American protection. 'People in Najaf were amazed to see him,' says Ma'ad Fayadh, the Iraqi journalist who was also a friend of Sayyid Majid. 'Some abandoned their cars in the middle of the street so they could greet him.' But there were also signs of popular suspicion of returning exiles as people who had lived in luxury abroad on the payroll of foreign intelligence services, while Iraq sank into ever deeper misery. Fayadh heard people ask: 'Who is this coming from London?'[1]

Early on some members of the group had raised the question with Sayyid Majid of visiting Muqtada al-Sadr who was in Najaf. Fayadh, who does not conceal his loathing for Muqtada and blames him for the bloody events that were about to happen, says nevertheless: 'It was clear that he was a power in Najaf. He was supported by all the people who were Fedayeen Saddam [a militia force established by Saddam. Opponents of Muqtada routinely accused him of recruiting them but never produced evidence that he did so]. They were all the poor and the unemployed and they had Kalashnikovs in their hands. They shouted at us: "Muqtada is our Imam." '[2] The long feud between the al-Khoei family and the al-Sadrs played a role in Sayyid Majid's fatal decision not to see Muqtada and try to resolve their quarrels. In a tape-recording in 1998 Muhammad Sadiq al-Sadr, Muqtada's father, had denounced Sayyid Majid publicly as not being worthy of a place in the *marji'iya*, the Shia hierarchy, and had questioned his right to control the al-Khoei Foundation funds. Presumably Sayyid Majid believed that as the scion of a revered clerical dynasty he was untouchable. 'We said "Muqtada has power. Talk to him," ' says Fayadh, recalling that the conversation took place on 7 April. Sayyid Majid retorted grandly, 'Why should I? Who is this Muqtada?' Members of his group noticed black-clad supporters of Muqtada, possibly precursors of the Mehdi Army, shadowing them through the streets of Najaf, but they were not too worried. None of them thought they were in danger. 'They looked at us like enemies, but we never supposed they would attack us,' says Fayadh.[3] Colonel al-Khafaji, who was in charge of security, recalled that at first people in Najaf were nervous on seeing them. 'They were frightened that Saddam might come back and said, "Maybe the same thing will happen as in 1991." But day by day the number of people coming to the shrine with us increased.'⁴ Sayyid Majid distributed $350,000 to the poor from al-Khoei Foundation funds; his staff later denied rumours circulated by his political rivals that he had ever received $13 million from the CIA.

On the morning of 10 April, al-Khoei took a dangerous step, much riskier than he supposed. As part of his campaign to reconcile different factions in Najaf he went to the house of one of the most unpopular men in the city, Haidar al-Rufaie al-Killidar, and asked him to come to the shrine. Haidar came from a family in Najaf that for centuries had been hereditary custodians and keyholders of the shrine of Imam Ali. It was not an easy job. Radwan Hussein al-Rufaie, a cousin of Haidar, said, 'I turned it down because I was against the regime and my brother took it over, but he disappeared in 1991, accused of plotting against Saddam. Haidar, on the other hand, was seen as completely affiliated with the government. He appeared on television talking with Saddam Hussein and was a member of the Iraqi parliament.'⁵ Haidar, a portly man with a plump face, had sensibly not been to his office in the shrine since the war began. Though visibly nervous he now allowed himself to be persuaded by Sayyid Majid that he should return.

Leaving Haidar's house, Sayyid Majid and his party went at about 8.45 a.m. to the shrine and entered the spacious wood-panelled office of the custodian. Surviving photographs show Sayyid Majid in a long dark robe sitting on a sofa and smiling gently but confidently at his companions, unaware of any impending danger. Above his head on the wall is a painting of Imam Ali and Imam Hussein. An hour passed before there were the first signs of hostility. A crowd began to gather in the courtyard outside the office and there were shouts of 'Long life to al-Sadr' and 'Give us Haidar or we will kill you'. A few moments later a window was smashed. At first Sayyid Majid tried to calm the crowd, which by now numbered some 400, but the microphone he picked up did not work. By one account the cable had been cut. As he stood in the door of the custodian's office somebody lunged at him with a knife and he jumped back for safety. Al-Khafaji told me that the first shot was fired into the air by Maher al-Yasseri, the cleric from Detroit, where there is a large Iraqi community. 'He became frightened and fired a shot. Many of the crowd ran away, but only to get their own guns.' A gunfight started. There were two Kalashnikovs and two pistols in Haidar's office. The trapped party inside started to shoot back though they had little ammunition. Al-Yasseri was mortally wounded by a bullet and fell down. Al-Khoei took off his turban and pressed it to the wound in the chest of the dying man, shouting as he did so, 'Don't shoot! This young man is dying! He is a Shia! He is a Muslim!'

The shooting went on for ninety minutes. Ma'ad Fayadh, who fired a pistol at somebody trying to get through the door, describes the last desperate moments of the fight. 'Somebody threw a grenade,' he says. 'I heard Sayyid Majid call out, "I am hurt."' One of his fingers had been blown off and another was hanging by a piece of skin. Fayadh tried to staunch the bleeding with a towel. There was no sign of help coming. Colonel Khafaji had managed to get away and those remaining in the custodian's office believed he would call the Americans on his satellite Thuraya phone. 'I do not understand to this day what happened,' says Fayadh. 'He left early, returned to the house [where they had been staying] and did not call the Americans.' Even had he done so it is unlikely that US forces would have entered the shrine, one of the holiest of the Shia faith. The alleged inaction of Colonel Khafaji was a source of bitterness and recriminations afterwards. The siege ended when al-Khoei's group ran out of ammunition and one man went outside with a white shirt and a Koran to surrender. Some of the crowd burst into the office and tied the hands of those inside behind their backs.

What happened over the next hour was to spawn almost as many different versions as the Kennedy assassination. Sheikh Salah Bilal, one of those who were tied up, says his captor told him: 'We are taking you to Muqtada al-Sadr to pass sentence.'⁶ Ma'ad Fayadh, whose own hands were bound, says that Riyadh al-Nuri, the head of the Sadrist movement in Najaf, said: 'I am from Muqtada and you are the hostages of Muqtada.' They were then led out of the room though the gate of the shrine in the midst of an angry, jostling crowd, many of whom were armed with guns, swords and knives. Ma'ad Fayadh recalls: 'The first thing I saw was swords and knives flashing in the sun. I thought, "Oh my God, that's it."' Within moments he saw Haidar al-Rufaie, the hereditary keyholder, hacked to death in front of him and al-Khoei repeatedly stabbed with knives. While the attention of the crowd was on its two main victims he was able to slip away.

Muqtada's house was a few hundred yards away down a narrow lane crowded with small shops. Sayyid Majid was badly wounded though his dark robe hid the bloodstains. He slumped down by the door when they came to Muqtada's house. 'Most of his body was bleeding and he lay down on one side,' says Sheikh Salah Bilal. 'I put his head on my leg.' After some minutes, he says, a message came from Muqtada saying, 'Don't let them sit by my door.' Sayyid Majid, Sheikh Bilal and a man called Hamid al-Timimi took refuge in a sewing-machine shop in the same street. The owner of the shop tried to save them by telling the crowd that Sayyid Majid was dead but they did not believe him. After a few minutes they smashed down the door, dragged Sayyid Majid out and shot him at the end of the street. His lifeless body lay where it fell for some hours until it was claimed by his in-laws, who washed and buried him. Muqtada, denying any responsibility, attended the mourning ceremonies claiming that he had sent men to help Sayyid Majid.

Over the following months stories multiplied among Muqtada's many enemies about how his senior lieutenants had mocked Sayyid Majid as they dragged him from the shrine and Muqtada had directly and publicly ordered his execution. These accounts are dubious. It is unlikely that so cautious a man as Muqtada – and anybody who survived Saddam had well-honed survival instincts – would have openly incriminated himself by issuing instructions before witnesses for the murder of a rival. At the same time there is overwhelming evidence that the mob that besieged and then stormed the office in the shrine was led by Sadrists. Riyadh al-Nuri, Muqtada's office manager, was identified as taking Sayyid Majid away. The siege went on for an hour and a half and if Muqtada did not know that al-Khoei was being done to death it may well have been because he did not choose to know.

The Sadrists' version of what happened in the days after Sayyid Majid arrived in Najaf and during his last bloody few hours at the shrine makes sense on most points, but is not quite convincing concerning their complete lack of responsibility for his death. According to Sheikh Ali, the *nom de guerre* of a man who later became a leader of the Mehdi Army, Sayyid Majid had returned to Najaf at a bad moment when nobody controlled the city. His account largely confirms the story of the survivors of Sayyid Majid's group. He says: 'Majid al-Khoei came to Najaf on the back of an American tank. He was with Haidar al-Killidar who was a Baathist and a member of parliament. Followers of al-Sadr were in the shrine at the time performing their religious duties when they saw turbulent people surrounding Majid and Haidar so they interfered to protect Majid and tried to get him out of the shrine. What happened was that one of Majid's bodyguards fired a shot from his gun killing one of the crowd. When people saw this they killed them with their knives.' The shot he refers to was probably that fired by Maher al-Yasseri, the young Shia cleric from Detroit. Sheikh Ali also argues that Muqtada himself had only just been released from prolonged house arrest by Saddam's security services a week before the murder of Sayyid Majid. 'Sayyid Muqtada did not know him and did not meet him. Abdul Majid al-Khoei came [to the shrine] the day after the fall of the regime so how could Muqtada have had men ready to kill him since he had been under house arrest for so long? The main point is that the people were furious and wanted to retaliate against any Baathist they could get their hands on. Al-Khoei's visit was badly timed because law had broken down and nobody controlled Najaf.' This may have been true of the original riot at the shrine, but does not explain why a desperately wounded Sayyid Majid was turned away from Muqtada's house, dragged out of his last refuge in the sewing-machine shop and killed in the street.[7] As I discovered at a Mehdi Army checkpoint in Kufa a year later the Sadrist movement contained many violent young men loyal to Muqtada, but only loosely under his control. It was a convenient excuse for the Sadrists in the coming years that they were not responsible for much of the violence carried out in their name.

CHAPTER ELEVEN

Muqtada Seizes his Moment

Muqtada's dramatic rise to prominence immediately after the fall of Saddam mystified the outside world as well as many Iraqis. His most important advantage was that he was the son and son-in-law of the most revered Shia martyrs. He was also ideally placed to take advantage of the political vacuum in Iraq as the old regime collapsed on 9 April. The exiled parties were still out of Iraq, unfamiliar with their country after years abroad and suspected by Iraqis of being pawns of the US or Iran. The tragic fate of Sayyid Majid al-Khoei underlined the dangers exiles faced if they did not carefully prepare the ground for their return. The Grand Ayatollah Ali al-Sistani had immense prestige, but a central theme of his theology was that the clergy should avoid direct political involvement. Saddam's *mukhabarat* had long ago destroyed the secular opposition parties and his own ruinous wars had discredited secular Arab nationalism. The triumphant US military forces, having made no coherent plans about what to do after overthrowing Saddam Hussein, were still on the sidelines. The way was open for the Sadrists to step into the gap and seize as much power as they could.

Muqtada was highly active. His resources were limited but he deployed them with energy and skill. Abbas, the young Sadrist militant from Sadr City, says Muqtada was in touch with about twelve to fifteen religious sheikhs on legitimate matters during the last days of Saddam (a sheikh is a cleric not descended from the prophet who wears a white turban; a

sayyid wears a black turban).[1] This gave him a nucleus of
local leaders on whom to rely. He swiftly appointed others
such as Sheikh Muhammad al-Fartousi who became his
representative in the Rusafa or eastern side of Baghdad.
Fartousi immediately set up a Sadrist office in a building until
recently occupied by the Baath party in Sadr City. Committees
were established to try to restore normal life. Sadrists picked
up where they had left off at the last high point in Shia
political activism before state repression intensified following
the assassination of Sadr II four years earlier in February,
1999. In Sadr City people reopened the Muhsin Mosque that
had been closed since the day when Shia worshippers were
arrested there. 'Immediately after the fall of Saddam,' says an
eyewitness, 'people broke all the locks and opened the doors
of the Muhsin Mosque, cleaned it and brought out the
headdresses and shoes which belonged to those who had been
praying for the last time before they were arrested.'[2]

Muqtada himself did not come to Baghdad until July, but
on 11 April he gave his first Friday sermon in the Grand
Mosque in Kufa (this small city, unlike Najaf, was dominated
by Sadrist supporters) where his father had so often spoken.
'There were many people in Kufa who came from all of the
southern provinces to hear him speak,' says Abbas. 'He
talked about the fall of Saddam and the collapse of his
regime and urged people to obey al-Haeri's orders. He also
urged them to make the Arba'in pilgrimage to Kerbala
because it had been banned by the old regime. Sadr II had
called for it just before he died but then cancelled it, fearing
the cruelty of Saddam. This ritual was revived in memory of
him and his son. It was at this time that we changed the name
of Thawra to Sadr City [after Muhammad Sadiq al-Sadr] and
there were pictures of Muqtada everywhere.'[3] As we saw, up
to one million Shia – some authorities claim three million –
obeyed Muqtada's instructions and ignored the dangers of
travel in wartime to make the pilgrimage to Kerbala.

The weekend of 11–12 July saw the mass looting of
Baghdad and all other Iraqi cities and towns. Any building

remotely connected to the government or the Baath party was fair game. Looting was an Iraqi tradition born of tribal raiding and poverty and it should not have come as a surprise. After the invasion of Kuwait the Iraqi army had systematically looted everything of value from bulldozers to hotel cutlery. In the Shia uprising of 1991 looters had promptly ransacked the factories as well as state institutions. During the Kurdish civil war in 1996 some 5,000 cars had been stolen in a single day in Arbil. There was a social revolutionary ferocity in the robbery and destruction that now swept across Iraq. Houses of the Baathist leadership were targeted in acts of political revenge and on the wholly correct supposition that it was there that the richest pickings were to be found. It was not only the impoverished masses of Sadr City who saw their opportunity. Government officials seized ministerial cars, computers and photocopiers. The destruction often seemed driven by hatred of the powers-that-be and all their works. In the Natural History Museum in the Wazzariyah district of north-east Baghdad looters systematically smashed the display cases showing Iraqi wildlife with the butts of their Kalashnikovs. Only a stuffed white horse, given, when alive, to Saddam by the King Morocco remained intact, for no obvious reason. Outside in the museum forecourt were enormous model dinosaurs which the looters had sprayed with machine-gun fire. One of them had even shinned up the long sinuous neck of a dinosaur to lop off its concrete head. A Sadrist militant from Sadr City explains that this apparently senseless vandalism was born of a new sense of empowerment and freedom from fear. 'When people started to steal and destroy state property,' he says, 'they wanted to demonstrate to themselves that fear was gone and there was no longer any authority to watch, trap and kill them. When a young man smashed up a police car he was really saying: "This is the Saddam state and I am destroying it." '[4]

The looting posed a dilemma for the Sadrists. On the one hand it was deeply offensive to pious and puritanical young

Sadrists like Abbas. On the other the mass of the looters were the very same poor and angry young men who were the main support of Muqtada. Sadrism was a social as well as religious movement, though it was also true that Sadr City had long been famous for its thieves' markets. Abbas was proud of what he and other self-appointed guardians of order achieved though his claims are a little too good to be true. 'We guarded the hospitals from thieves after many things had been stolen,' he says, 'and we got the telephone numbers of doctors from the remaining staff and contacted them to get them to come back to work. We guarded them when they were treating people and we turned some of the mosques and *husseiniyahs* near looted clinics into medical facilities. We directed traffic in the streets because there were many cars and no traffic policemen. We did all we could to regulate and direct social life.' An appeal was made from the mosques for the return of loot and many stolen objects were returned. 'I personally was responsible for the electricity sector,' he adds proudly. 'Thousands of electricity transformers were returned and until now the Electricity Ministry is grateful for what we did for them. We were astonished when we saw people returning wads of dollar bills.' This was hardly typical behaviour but Sadrist clerics did try to recover some of the stolen property. One woman went with a friend, also female, to a house in an alleyway in Sadr City where two men in turbans were in charge of receiving loot, such as fittings from street-lights, that was being returned. 'The two clerics wrote down what was given back but they did not thank the young men who were returning stolen goods,' she says. 'They were upset by our presence and insisted that we wear the *abaya*, long black cloaks, which were borrowed from a neighbouring house.' Enough electrical equipment was returned for the electricity in Sadr City to be switched on again on 16 April, a week after the fall of Saddam, an event immediately marked by young men rushing into the street and firing their machine guns into the air in celebration.

Muqtada was more ambivalent on the question of loot

than Abbas supposed. The looters became universally known in Iraq as *al-hawasim* meaning 'the finalists'. The term was a derisive reference to Saddam Hussein's claim that an American invasion of Iraq would provoke 'a final battle'. In May Muqtada issued what became known as the *al-hawasim* fatwa saying that looters could hold on to what they had expropriated so long as they paid a donation (*khums*) of one fifth of its value to their local Sadrist office. Many, including Sadrist supporters, found this deeply shocking. Sheikh Ali, later a Mehdi Army commander, claims that the original fatwa was issued by Ayatollah al-Haeri, the nominal head of the Sadrists, in far off Qom, and Muqtada loyally issued the same instruction. This is difficult to take seriously. Given that al-Haeri complained that his orders were routinely disregarded by Muqtada it is unlikely that he would have singled out this instruction to obey. The impact of the instruction was to frighten and alienate the Shia establishment and property-owning classes from the Sadrists; many of the better off Shia began to see Muqtada as a dangerous Islamic Bolshevik and demagogue leading a mob of robbers and thieves. Four years later Dr Ahmed, a supporter of al-Sistani living in Najaf, gave his opinion that 'most of the followers of the Sadrist trend are thieves and I was convinced of that after the fatwa by their *marji'iya* permitted the stealing of public property that turned them from poor people into rich people overnight'.[5]

There were other reasons for the *hawza* establishment to be frightened. They were shocked by the murder of Sayyid Majid al-Khoei, the first time that the rivalry between the leading Shia clerical families had ended in killing. In the aftermath of the murder in the alleyway near Muqtada's house pro-Sadrist mobs besieged the house of al-Sistani, who was of Iranian origin, and Ayatollah Muhammad al-Fayadh, who was Afghan, demanding they leave Iraq and return to their own countries. Al-Sistani called on local tribes to provide 1,500 armed men to protect him and the other ayatollahs. The incident showed that the so-called 'quietist'

Shia leaders could mobilise support if they had to. The news of the siege of al-Sistani's house was spread by radio and the response by the Shia showed that the Grand Ayatollah still had great popularity and moral authority. 'I was sleeping in a village near Basra that night,' recalls Hussein al-Shahristani, the nuclear scientist who had been imprisoned and tortured by Saddam before escaping in 1991. 'Suddenly I saw the villagers grabbing their guns and preparing to rush to Najaf hundreds of miles away. "al-Sistani is under attack," they told me. That was all they needed to know. The same thing happened all over Iraq.'[6] The rift between Muqtada and al-Sistani was evident, but it was not complete, and in the anarchic conditions of post-Saddam Iraq the Sadrists could disclaim with some credibility the excesses of their supporters. In Samawa, on the Euphrates south of Najaf, at a demonstration on 16 April, demonstrators carried pictures of both Grand Ayatollah al-Sistani and Muhammad Sadiq al-Sadr. They chanted, 'No to colonial occupation, no to America, blessed be Iraq.'[7] They denied there was any division between al-Sistani and Muqtada and said both should be honoured. The demonstration is interesting because it showed that Muqtada, despite his youth and lack of religious qualifications, was regarded with reverence almost equal to that al-Sistani. Within a week of the fall of Saddam Hussein he had successfully identified himself with Sadr I and Sadr II.

The high tide was soon reached for the Sadrists. They had moved faster and more effectively than other opposition movements but their organised support was spread thin. The *hawza* was at first caught by surprise when its authority was challenged but began to reassert itself. For all their religious rhetoric, the Sadrists relied on religious students and followers of Muqtada's father who had not achieved high religious rank. Courts established by the Sadrists in Baghdad were imposing their own interpretation of Islamic law by arbitrary arrests, closing video shops, attacking liquor stores and insisting that women wear the veil. 'We had some imams saying women will be beaten in the streets if some of their hair is showing and liquor stores burned down,' al-Fartousi told a reporter. 'This is not what we are about. Gentle advice to such women or a tap on the shoulder should suffice.'[8] This was hardly reassuring. The Sadrists might claim they were trying to control anarchy but for many Iraqis, including almost all the middle class, they were the anarchists. Other opponents of Saddam began to arrive in Iraq. Muhammad Baqir al-Hakim, the leader of the Supreme Council for Islamic Revolution in Iraq (SCIRI), returned to Iraq on 10 May 2003 with 400 guards in a convoy from Iran. His re-appearance had been pre-advertised for several days by loud-speakers in the mosques. He was greeted by vast welcoming crowds as he passed through Basra, Samawa and Diwaniyah. But the crowds noticeably diminished in size as he moved north and in Najaf, where local leaders including Muqtada went to see him, there were only 300–400 supporters to greet him.[9] Soon, however, al-Hakim was leading Friday prayers in the Imam Ali mosque in Najaf in competition with Muqtada who was doing the same thing a few miles away in the Grand Mosque in Kufa.

The bitter rivalries of the past did not diminish. The Sadrists remembered al-Hakim's past denunciations of Sadr II as a Baathist with anger. But al-Hakim had a powerful asset in the shape of the Badr corps which at this time had about 4,000 to 8,000 well-trained and armed men. These returned to Iraq without fanfare, leaving their heavy weapons and artillery behind in Iran so as not to alienate the US. The Sadrists pointed out that Badr, the one professional military Shia force, had failed to cross into Iraq to fight in support of the Shia uprisings in 1991 or 1999. Muqtada did not mince his words. Before al-Hakim returned he was quoted as saying he 'betrayed the people of Basra and the south when he urged [them] to fight [in 1991] and didn't help them, causing the intifada to fail'.[10] Baqir al-Hakim's men had fought on the Iranian side during the Iran–Iraq war and were believed by many Iraqis to have savagely tortured Iraqi prisoners. 'Hakim does not represent Iraq,' said Muhammad Fartousi, Muqtada's representative in Sadr City soon after Hakim's return. 'He represents outside forces and works with Iran, the US and Israel. We need someone from inside who suffered with Iraqis and represents the people's voice. We don't want an Iranian state'.[11]

It was bizarre that President Bush was to claim repeatedly over the next four years that Muqtada and the Mehdi Army were Iranian pawns when SCIRI and Badr, by now allied to the US, were demonstrably Iranian creations. The lack of US criticism of SCIRI was because it had shown itself ready to work with the US after the occupation. SCIRI had started cooperating with the US in the mid-1990s and took part in the opposition conferences, notably the one in London in December 2002 described in the previous chapter. Muhammad Baqir al-Hakim was opposed to permanent US occupation but he was prepared to aid it in the short term. SCIRI joined the US-appointed Iraqi Government when it was set up in July 2003 and took part in all local elections. Unlike Muqtada's movement, SCIRI was well organised and well disciplined; it had a clear strategy of becoming the representative of the Iraqi religious, political and tribal establishment. It intended to conciliate the Americans and this aim was all the easier to achieve since Washington quickly came to detest SCIRI's rivals, the Sadrists. SCIRI always had limited popular appeal, but it was expert at infiltrating the institutions of the new Iraqi state, notably the Interior Ministry, the police force in the south and, after the provincial elections of January 2005, the local government.

SCIRI usually moved in the shadows. The extent to which it still took orders or advice from Iran was a question often asked by Iraqis and Americans alike over the coming years, but never convincingly answered. Was SCIRI the ungrateful child of Iran that had transferred its affections to America? This interpretation was open to the challenge that it had starting cooperating with the US in the 1990s, when it was still based in Tehran and was very much under Iranian control. It was possible that Iran had decided to bet on all possible contenders for power in Iraq so it would win whoever came out on top. Covertly supporting its enemies as well as its friends was a devious but traditional Iranian approach. An experienced Iraqi Shia commentator who was hostile to Iran told me dolefully a year later that, after travelling widely in southern Iraq, he had concluded that 'it is impossible to oppose Iran because they are paying all the pro-Iranian parties – and they are paying all the anti-Iranian parties as well'.

Muqtada could have gone on playing the anti-Iranian card but it was a measure of his growing skill as a politician that he did not. For all his astonishing success in the first month after the fall of Saddam Hussein he had also acquired an impressive list of enemies: The US, the *hawza*, SCIRI and Dawa. The secular middle class found his black-clad militants frighteningly like the Taliban in Kabul. In June 2003 Muqtada first went on the *hajj* to Mecca and on his return travelled to Iran, the overt reason being to consult with Kadhim al-Haeri, the nominal leader of the Sadrist movement. According to another Sadrist leader, Muqtada also talked about the idea of starting his own militia, to be called the Mehdi Army.[12] But his most important meetings in Iran were not with al-Ha'eri but with the Iranian supreme leader, Ayatollah Ali Khamenei, and, reportedly, also with Qasim Suleimani, the commander of the Qods Brigade (a special foreign department of the Intelligence arm of the Iranian Revolutionary Guards).[13] Iranian journalists in Tehran at the time were perplexed as to why their government was devoting so much time to supporting a young man whose staying power in Iraqi politics seemed so uncertain. Four years later President Bush was to denounce the Mehdi Army as an arm of the Qods Brigade in Iraq. His accusation sounded like an Americanised version of the Iraqi habit of seeing the sinister hand of Iranian intelligence behind everything that happened in Iraq. Much of this was paranoia and allegations of significant Iranian involvement in Iraq were seldom backed up by evidence, but Iran did provide a useful safe haven and potential source of supplies and money for the nascent Mehdi Army.

The attraction of Muqtada for the Iranians was that he was vigorously opposed to the US occupation from the beginning. It was only grudgingly at a time when his movement was weak at the end of 2003 that he had described them as 'guests'. This made him and his movement different from all the other important Shia political and religious leaders who either supported the occupation or were prepared to cooperate with it. From the first day of the occupation after the overthrow of Saddam Hussein, Muqtada said, 'The smaller devil has gone but the bigger devil has come.' Other Shiite clerics made the point during the first days of the occupation. 'We thank the Americans if they have come here to liberate us,' said Ali al-Shawki in Sadr City. 'But if they are here to colonize us, we will regard them as enemies and fight them with all means.'[14] This was in keeping with the vigorous Iraqi nationalism of Muqtada's father and was central to the Sadrists' appeal. In the summer of 2003 there were still many Shia who were uncertain about what benefits the US occupation might bring but within months they were becoming soured by the failures of US rule.

These developments were not quite so obvious at the time as they appear in retrospect. The US set up the twenty-five-member Iraqi Governing Council (IGC) on 13 July, but it had little real power and its members were widely regarded as corrupt American stooges. Muqtada was to benefit from being excluded from this body while SCIRI, Dawa and secular Iraqi leaders were discredited by joining it. From the beginning he denounced its legitimacy, saying: 'The government is the result of an illegitimate order by the IGC, which in itself is illegitimate because it was appointed by an illegitimate occupation.' He concluded: 'We do not recognise it, directly or indirectly, since it exists contrary to the wishes of the Iraqis.' The IGC was 'a US toy'. These words resonated with Iraqis because by the end of 2003 and beginning of

2004 the Americans and the IGC were increasingly unpopular. They were also widely heard because Muqtada's speeches were being carried on al-Jazeera, the Arab satellite channel.[15] One of the big changes in Iraq at this time was that rooftops were blossoming with satellite dishes which had been forbidden under pain of six months in jail under Saddam Hussein's regime.

A few days after the IGC was formed Muqtada told thousands of worshippers in the Kufa mosque on 18 July that it was made up of 'non-believers'. He said he was setting up a religious army, to be called the Mehdi Army, and called for 'a general mobilization to fight the American and British occupiers'. He was careful to stress that his army was going to use 'peaceful means' and he condemned armed attacks on coalition soldiers, but it was evident that these could not be ruled out in the future.[16]

At first the Mehdi Army was very amateur. Most Iraqi men have guns, and know how to use them, and many had been drafted into the Iraqi army and received some military training there. 'At the beginning the Mehdi Army was weak and had no real units such as companies and divisions but was just groups of armed men,' says Sheikh Ali, later one of its leaders. 'The only condition for somebody who wanted to be a soldier in the Mehdi Army was to be a believer and per-form prayers. You registered at the mosque, *husseiniyah* or a Sadr office in any part of Iraq. The applicants had to be recommended by well-known people and all followers of the *marji'iya* could join, though no one came apart from followers of al-Sadr.'[17] The Mehdi Army's first battalion graduated in Basra on 6 October 2003.

These new initiatives by Muqtada all worked to his advantage over the next year, but this did not happen immediately. On the contrary at the height of the scorching Iraqi summer of 2003 there were fewer and fewer portraits of Muqtada pasted on to walls in southern Iraq. Observers dismissed the Mehdi Army as a paper force. The great majority of the Shia leaders were intent on their original strategy of forcing the US to hold elections, which the Shia were bound to win as the majority of the population. They feared that Muqtada's confrontational approach would alienate the Americans whom they were so carefully cultivating. Among the Shia population as a whole there was less unanimity about cooperating with the US. American political and military leaders seemed to be doing everything possible to discredit themselves but they had not quite succeeded yet. On 13 August, for instance, a US helicopter stripped a Shia banner from a tower in Sadr City provoking widespread protests. The US military at first denied that the incident had occurred, only to find that it had been recorded on video.

The US was absorbed in combating the developing threat of guerrilla war by the Sunni community but on 29 August a suicide bomb killed Muhammad Baqir al-Hakim, the founder of SCIRI, and 125 people who were with him. There were allegations that the Sadrists might be behind the attack, but it turned out that the bomber was Yassin Jarad, the father of the second wife of Abu Musab al-Zarqawi, the *salafi* (bigoted anti-Shia ultra-orthodox Sunni) leader of the suicide bombing campaign.[18] This was one of the first attacks planned by Zarqawi and showed that the Sunni insurrection was going to be directed against the Shia community as a whole and not just against the Iraqi government and US forces. This inability of the US or Iraqi government forces to provide effective security against Zarqawi was to be a great recruiting sergeant for the Mehdi Army. It also undermined Grand Ayatollah al-Sistani's strategy of patient endurance in the face of the *salafi* attack while the Shia took power through the ballot box.

In the second half of 2003 Muqtada overplayed his hand several times and his support began to look uncertain even in Sadr City. On 10 October he announced he was setting up a shadow government with its own ministries of the interior, finance, justice, information and foreign affairs. A few days later on 15 October his supporters tried and failed to take over the shrines in Kerbala and there was shooting in which

dozens were killed. The control of the shrines was important
not just because they were a potent religious symbol but
because they received large donations from the faithful.
There were angry denunciations of the Mehdi Army in Najaf.
One furious circular read: 'The [Mehdi] army is composed of
suspicious elements, [including] individuals from the extinct
regime and its security officers and members of the [Baath]
party who have wrapped their heads with white and black
rags to mislead people into believing that they are men of
religion when in truth they are only devils . . . We do not
need your army which you have slanderously and falsely
called the Mehdi Army . . . The Imam (al-Mehdi) is in no
need of any army made up of thieves, robbers and perverts
under the leadership of a one-eyed charlatan.'[19]

   In Sadr City, the US installed a hand-picked council to
replace the Sadrist council. The Sadrists had promised a
massive street demonstration to protest against the US
action. I went along to see if the support for the Sadrists was
on the wane compared to earlier in the year. Security for the
protest was well organised with lines of men politely
searching all attending to detect suicide bombers. But the
number of worshippers attending Friday prayers at the al-
Ahrar mosque in Sadr City was only 10,000. Prayers were to
be followed by a march on Sadr City town hall, which was
guarded by American soldiers and tanks. The sermon by
Abdel Hadi al-Daraji, one of Muqtada's senior aides, was a
mixture of religious and nationalist appeals but the crowd
chanted 'Yes, yes to Muqtada!' without much conviction.
After prayers were over, only about 3,000 people were
prepared to march. A few days later in early November
Muqtada announced that the coalition forces were 'guests' in
Iraq and the main enemy were survivors of Saddam's regime.
His retreat was a little humiliating after his previous
denunciations of the occupation, but he was already showing
a sure instinct for the swift tactical retreat when confronting
an opponent of superior strength. It was a talent that was to
prove essential for his survival over the coming year.

CHAPTER TWELVE

The Siege of Najaf

In early March 2004 I went to visit the office of *al-Hawza*, Muqtada's newspaper in Baghdad. There were only a few members of the staff there but they were relaxed and friendly. I talked to a young man called Hussein who was a student in the French department at Mustansariyah University on Palestine Street near Sadr City which was increasingly under Sadrist control. He was explaining the Sadrist positions on various questions when he was interrupted by the roar of an explosion nearer to the centre of the city. I said I would have to cut short our talk to go to the nearest hospital to talk to the injured. It was almost impossible to get to the site of a bomb blast in central Baghdad unless one was very close by when it happened because the explosion immediately caused immense traffic jams. I had discovered that the best way to find out what had happened was to go directly to the hospitals receiving the casualties and talk to survivors and their friends. Hussein wanted to see them too, but said he had no car and asked if we could give him a lift. We drove to al-Kindi hospital, but the uniformed policeman at the gate said he was under strict orders not to let anyone in. Hussein, who was sitting in the back seat, leant out the window and said quietly, 'We are from the office of Sayyid al-Shahid [the Office of the Martyr, named after Sadr II but in practice Muqtada's office].' The policeman froze for a second and then ran to open the gates for us, saying in an awed voice to the other police as we drove through, 'They are from the

Sayyid's office.' Clearly, the popularity and influence of the Sadrists in Baghdad had increased markedly since I had gone to the ill-attended protest march in Sadr City four months earlier.

I thought of this small incident when the US viceroy and head of the Coalition Provisional Authority (CPA), Paul Bremer, closed *al-Hawza* for sixty days a few weeks later on 28 March. I suspected that the US officials in the Green Zone were going to get a bigger reaction than they expected. The reason for the closure of the newspaper was that it had carried a sermon from Muqtada praising the 9/11 attack on the World Trade Center in New York as 'a miracle and bless-ing from God', though the letter handed to the editor said only that it had broken the law on fomenting violence.[1] 'Close the rag down,' Bremer had said to aides when he read a translation of the offending issue. In his account of his disastrous year ruling Iraq, Bremer shows extreme animus towards Muqtada, describing him as 'a rabble-rousing Shiite cleric' and even comparing him to Hitler. As early as June 2003 he quotes himself as thinking: 'Muqtada al-Sadr has the potential of ripping this country apart. We can't let this happen.'[2] In the second half of 2003 Bremer repeatedly portrays himself as decrying the timidity of the US military, the CIA and the British, all of whom hesitated before con-fronting Muqtada. Their fears were understandable and, as events soon demonstrated, wholly justified. Given the escalating armed resistance by the Sunni community it did not make sense to provoke a Shia uprising at the same time.

For months Bremer hovered on the edge of ordering the arrest of Muqtada and his closest lieutenants for the murder of Sayyid Majid al-Khoei. An Iraqi judge Raad Juhi had even issued an arrest warrant for Muqtada in November, saying that he had two eyewitnesses who said they had heard Muqtada give the order for al-Khoei to be killed (the pretence that there was an independent Iraqi judiciary operating at the time was never going to cut much ice with Iraqis). Bremer held two beliefs that were dangerously contradictory. For him, Muqtada was at one and the same time a powerful and menacing figure capable of tearing Iraq apart, and simultaneously so weak that he would tamely submit to arrest, while his following would be too small to make effective protests. Iraqi ministers were struck by the degree to which Bremer hated and belittled Muqtada. They were told not to refer to the 'Mehdi Army' but to call it 'Muqtada's militia'. Ali Allawi, the highly intelligent independent Islamist who was a member of the Iraqi Governing Council, once tried to explain to Bremer how the Sadrists were the political representatives of the millions of Shia poor. Bremer furiously retorted that he 'didn't care a damn about the underclass and what they [the Sadrists] represented'.[3]

Though Muqtada and the Sadrists were not strong enough to stand on their own against the US, their support, which had dipped in the second half of 2004, was growing once more. This was principally because they were the only Shia movement against the occupation, the unpopularity of which was increasing by the day. Not only was there friction with US soldiers on the street, but the US-led Coalition Provisional Authority (CPA) was manifestly failing to restore services and provide jobs. Teachers and civil servants were paid more, but the vast 'underclass' which Bremer so despised was seeing few benefits from the overthrow of Saddam Hussein. Some 70 per cent of the population was unemployed according to the Ministry of Labour. SCIRI and Dawa were members of the Iraqi Governing Council, which brought them little real power and did them political damage because they were seen as pawns of the occupation. The murders of Muhammad Baqir al-Hakim and Sayyid Majid al-Khoei also removed the two most active scions of the Shia clerical aristocracy who might have competed with Muqtada.

Yet the Sadrists were still a minority movement. The Shia might not much like the US occupation, but most were still far from wanting to fight it. The most prestigious and influential Shia leader was Grand Ayatollah Ali al-Sistani. The Sadrist distinction between the politically active and inactive *marji'iya* was always an over-simplification. Al-Sistani might not want the clergy to actively take part in politics as in Iran or seek to create their own clerical government. But this did not mean that he believed in a legal division between church and state as in the US and France, or wanted a secular Iraq. He was not so much apolitical as acutely conscious of the corrupting effect of political power on the Shia clergy, as evidenced by Iran. He kept his distance from the CPA and would meet none of its officials. This lack of personal contact combined with distortions of al-Sistani's views when passed on by self-interested go-betweens led Bremer and the CPA to underestimate the determination of the *marji'iya* to force elections, which the Shia community was bound to win, and to insist on a new constitution in which Islam was the primary source of legislation. On 26 June 2003 al-Sistani issued a crucial fatwa which said bluntly: 'First of all there must be a general election so that every Iraqi citizen who is eligible to vote can choose someone to represent him in a foundational Constitution preparation assembly. Then the drafted Constitution can be put to a referendum.' This was a recipe for revolutionary change. If it happened then Iraq, which had been part of the Sunni order in the Middle East for hundreds of years, would become a Shia state. Al-Sistani's position was immensely powerful because of his own great influence on the Shia. For a few months after the overthrow of Saddam Hussein, Washington and its emissaries in Baghdad had an arrogant and self-deceiving sense of being in control of Iraq. As the Sunni insurrection began to take off Washington and its emissaries in Baghdad became more and more desperate for local Iraqi allies. They could not afford to fight the Sunni and offend the Shia at the same time. If al-Sistani's limited cooperation was rebuffed then the alternative to him would be Muqtada, who was against the occupation root and branch.

Muqtada had come close to an all-out fight with the CPA in August and October when Bremer was eager to order his arrest but was always frustrated at the last moment. Bremer optimistically hoped that the arrest itself would be carried out by the Iraqi police – something which was unlikely to happen. The coalition military force outside Najaf at this moment was Spanish and had no intention of entering the holy city to snatch Muqtada.[4] Muqtada himself went on denouncing the occupation, but was chary of a direct military confrontation with the US army. This was a pattern we were to see twice in 2004 during the Mehdi Army's battles with the US military. Muqtada adopted similar tactics in 2007 when he stood down the Mehdi Army in February at the start of the US 'surge' and in September when he declared a six-month ceasefire after fighting with the police and Badr Organization during the 15 Shabaan pilgrimage to Kerbala. For all his white martyr's shroud and messianic rhetoric he was a cautious man.

Bremer's errors are glaring in retrospect and in later years his superiors were swift to hold him responsible for much that went wrong for the US during the first catastrophic year of occupation. This was unfair or misleading since it was evident in Baghdad at the time that US actions were determined by the Washington political agenda and above all the upcoming Presidential election in 2004. Bremer also got disastrously poor advice from the returning Iraqi exiles, senior members of SCIRI and Dawa, and from Shia clergy hostile to Muqtada, all of whom had their reasons for wanting to see the US dispose of a dangerous rival. The animosities between the different Shia leaders and groups were very evident to American officials in the Green Zone, but, confusingly, the divisions could suddenly be replaced by solidarity in the face of a common threat. Failure to see this was a principal reason why they were outmanoeuvred by Muqtada and failed to eliminate him. In their hearts the Shia Islamists, whether SCIRI, Dawa, Sadrist or just supporters of al-Sistani, knew that the US disliked not only Muqtada but all the Shia religious parties that were led by, or were under the influence of, black-turbaned clerics. At critical moments the Shia leaders saw that, however much they detested each other, they would be wise to hang together, if they did not want to hang separately. There were signs of this on the street. In October the Mehdi Army had fought guards loyal to al-Sistani for control of the shrine in Najaf, but by January 2004 supporters of both had united to take part in marches in Baghdad called by al-Sistani to demand direct elections for the next Iraqi parliament. Enormous chanting crowds, waving their banners, carried portraits of Sadr II and Muqtada along with those of al-Sistani.

Bremer was probably right in thinking that Muqtada was at his most vulnerable in the last half of 2003 though he was not nearly as vulnerable as Bremer supposed. He still controlled the great Sadrist fortress of Sadr City and this alone made him an important political player in Iraq. An area of twenty square kilometres of close-packed housing in east Baghdad with a population of 2–2.5 million, it was routinely described in the media as 'a suburb of Baghdad' but it was a lot more than that. If it had been a separate city it would have been the second biggest city in Iraq, larger than Basra or Mosul. It was always obscure how big it really was because Saddam Hussein's regime, the CPA and succeeding Iraqi regimes found the existence of such an area, covertly or openly hostile to the powers that be, intimidating. Its population was almost entirely Shia, many of them from Amara, the province in the south from which they had fled to escape the tyranny of the feudal landowners by coming to Baghdad in the 1950s. But, as Ali Allawi points out in a description of the area based on unpublished Iraqi government studies dated 2004. 'All the main tribes of the south, that is, up to 164 different tribes and clans, were represented [in Sadr City]. The power of the local tribal leaders, numbering over 300, was generally acknowledged, but with the rise of the Grand Ayatollah Muhammad al-Sadr [Sadr II], who had specifically reached out to the inhabitants of Sadr City, most of the tribal elders had deferred to his overarching authority.' Following the fall of Saddam, the religious, tribal and professional leaders in the area gave their backing to

Muqtada.[5] By the summer of 2003 some 90 per cent of the mosques in Sadr City were under Sadrist control. Islamic mores were enforced in institutions like orphanages run by the Sadrists. Boys and girls were separated and girls were forced to wear the veil. Even so the latter said they preferred the orphanage to the danger of the streets.[6] 'The growing power of the clerics means that the chief of a clan has less influence in Sadr City,' says Fadhil Muhammad, a professor of sociology and an expert on the area. 'The big change since 2003 had been the growth of religious parties and groups such as the Mehdi Army, SCIRI and Dawa, but the strongest of these is the Sadrist movement. Thousands of young men belong to these organisations so the clans have lost their authority over them. When there is a dispute the clans themselves ask for a sayyid or a sheikh to be the judge.'[7]

Enforced Islamic puritanism became the norm. Gypsy villages, to give one example, were seen by the Sadrists as centres for prostitution and came under attack. Munawar Mashelah, who now works as a guard in a building in central Baghdad and disguises his gypsy origins, recalls how a dozen or so young men in five saloon cars approached his village (known as a *kawliya*). They shouted warnings to leave by the following morning. 'As soon as they left, families fled quickly,' Munawar recalls, but they didn't know where to go, though some hid in Rashid military camp. Others who stayed were attacked and one woman in each family killed. As so often when it comes to violence attributed to the Sadrists, it is impossible to make a precise distinction between their actions and those of freelance and criminal gangs. It is a measure of the failure of the CPA and Iraqi government to provide personal security that the surviving gypsy families thought their only chance of survival was 'to pay large bribes to join and take the names of well-known tribes and clans who would then protect them in central and western Iraq.'[8]

There was a further reason why the political tide favoured Muqtada in the first months of 2004, ensuring that he was going to be a more dangerous opponent that Bremer

imagined. The sectarian bombing campaign orchestrated by
Abu Musab al-Zarqawi showed that the US was incapable of
providing security to ordinary Shia. On 2 March millions of
Shia marched and prayed to celebrate Ashura, the most
important event in their religious calendar commemorating
the battle of Kerbala when Imam Hussein and his seventy-
two companions were massacred in 680 AD. It was a
peculiarly triumphant moment and the first Ashura to be
celebrated since the fall of Saddam at which ancient rituals
could be performed openly without fear of arrest. Men
slashed their scalps with swords so blood ran down their
faces in memory of the death and suffering of Hussein and
those with him. People cried 'Hussein! Hussein!' and beat
their chests in ritualised grief. The walls of the shrine in
Kerbala were decorated with scenes from the battle 1,400
hundred years earlier: Hussein's half-brother Abbas fighting
his way to the bank of the Euphrates to bring water to the
thirsty but refusing to drink himself; Hussein's infant son
pierced in the neck by an arrow when clasped in the arms of
his father; the severed head of Hussein stuck on a pike by the
victorious Umayyad army. These modern-day Shia mourners
felt a sense that, so many centuries after their historic defeat,
they were finally on the winning side. Outside Kerbala a
group of Sadrists chanted warnings against those who might
try to deny the Shia their victory. 'The oppressors tore apart
your land, my people,' they cried. 'The envious ones sowed
discord among you, but do not attack us to the sound of
your drums or we will crush you – Iraq! Iraq!'[9]

At about 10 a.m., a series of bombs exploded near the
shrines in Kerbala and Kadhimiyah in Baghdad. Some 270
people were killed and 570 wounded. Limbs torn off by the
blast and mangled and bleeding body parts were placed in a
heap in the inner courtyard of the Kadhimiyah shrine.
Zarqawi's bombing campaign had been sectarian from the
start, but earlier attacks, such as those on Shia police recruits
and the killing of Muhammad Baqir al-Hakim along with
125 worshippers in Najaf in August 2003, had some military

or political motivation. The Ashura bombings were aimed at killing as many Shia civilians as possible simply because they were Shia. They bloodily demonstrated that the US and the nascent Iraqi government security forces could not provide protection for the Shia masses, enabling the Mehdi Army to justify its existence and rapid expansion as a Shia self-defence force.

Bremer and the CPA could scarcely have chosen a worse moment than March 2004 for a confrontation with Muqtada. His newspaper *al-Hawza* had a circulation of only about 15,000 (Bremer seems to have been one of its few assiduous readers), but within days there were demonstrations by as many as 20,000 people in Baghdad demanding its reopening. Muqtada deliberately decided to make an issue of its temporary closure. The inflammatory tone of his speeches and those of his lieutenants give the impression that he believed this would be a good moment and a good issue on which to confront the occupation authorities. 'We fought Saddam and now we're fighting the Americans,' said Sayyid Hazim al-Araqi, Muqtada's representative in Baghdad. 'Listen, America, Britain and Israel, there's a man named Muqtada al-Sadr and he gives resistance fighters their courage.' Al-Araqi's denunciation of the occupiers was an interesting mixture of Iraqi patriotism, Islamic fervour, a defence of tribal mores, anti-Baathism and anger at the failure of the US to improve living standards. He accused the US and its Iraqi proxies of creating 'streets full of thieves, carjackers and rubbish'. By cracking down on honour killings they had encouraged adultery, and by dismissing only top-level Baathists they were preparing the ground treacherously to reconcile with the Baath party.[10]

What happened in the next few days was as much a sign of the CPA's weakness and poor judgement as of Muqtada's strength. On 31 March a convoy carrying security guards from the US security firm Blackwater was ambushed in the main street in Fallujah, a stronghold of the Sunni resistance.

After killing four guards the insurgents ran off, but day-labourers who normally stood beside the road waiting for work dragged the bodies of the dead Americans out of the burning vehicles and savagely hacked at them with their hoes and shovels, before hanging the charred remains of two of them from steel girders of the bridge over the Euphrates. It was the sort of public humiliation shown on US television, akin to the notorious pictures of the body of a dead American helicopter pilot being dragged through the streets of Mogadishu in 1993, to which Washington was bound to respond. The Sadrists were sharp enough to see that US resources and attention would be largely focused on the spreading Sunni insurrection in Fallujah and the Sunni heartlands. Astonishingly, even after the killings in Fallujah, Bremer went ahead and escalated his confrontation with Muqtada by arresting his senior aide Mustafa al-Yaqubi, a Sadrist militant from Sadr II's time, on 3 April.

The Sadrist response to the arrest was swift and exceeded in scope and violence anything that US officials in the Green Zone imagined. At midday on 4 April Bremer was just congratulating himself on the arrest of Yaqubi when he received an urgent and alarming phone call from the US commander General Ricardo Sanchez. 'All hell is breaking loose with Muqtada,' he said. 'We're getting reports from a lot of different sectors, Sadr City, Najaf . . . al-Kut. Demonstrators flooding the streets. A lot of them carrying AKs and RPGs.'[11] To the horror of the CPA the Mehdi Army swept into cities and towns across southern Iraq without meeting much resistance. The fledgling Iraqi police had no intention of stopping them. The security in important cities in southern Iraq was in the hands of Italian, Polish, Ukrainian, Salvadoran and Spanish troops who had been sent there at the high tide of US success in 2003 and whose governments had never expected them to fight. I had been in Kut, the fly-blown city on the Tigris which was the site of the great British defeat at the hands of the Turks in 1916, a few weeks earlier. Local people did not have a high opinion of the Ukrainian contingent who provided the only armed representatives of the coalition. 'They are even poorer than we are,' said a friend in the city. 'You can bribe them to let your car through a checkpoint by handing them a few cigarettes.' Sadrist gunmen were briefly able to occupy Kut and announced that the Ukrainians held nothing except the bridge in front of their headquarters. In Nasiriyah the Sadrists seized part of the city from the Italians, though the latter swiftly regained control amid accusations from the Sadrists that they had reneged on an agreement to withdraw. Meanwhile, the lethal anarchy that was spreading across Iraq had an important political advantage for the CPA and Washington. Rory Stewart, the adventurous former British diplomat who was senior adviser in Dhi Qar province, the capital of which was Nasiriyah, makes a significant point in his memoir that the situation had become too dangerous for the media to turn up to find out what was happening. 'Then and later,' he writes, 'the world press were unaware that we were losing control of a city of 600,000.'[12]

The spectacular Sadrist gains on the ground during the first week of April far exceeded what they could hold and, in most areas, they were soon on the retreat. There were, in fact, just three cities that the Sadrists needed to occupy permanently. These were Sadr City, their main political and military base; Kufa, where Muqtada delivered his Friday sermons; and Najaf, the spiritual capital of the Shia in Iraq and around the world, which the Sadrists knew the US army would be reluctant to assault because of the danger that they would damage the holy shrines and thus provoke a wider Shia uprising. The Sadrists were not particularly popular in Najaf, the seat of the *hawza* whom Muqtada so often criticised. The 500,000 population of the city were loyal to al-Sistani and also feared that their city would be turned into a battle zone, but with the Mehdi Army in control there was nothing, for the moment, that they could do about it.

Muqtada chose this moment to start a religious retreat in the mosque in Kufa, also very difficult for US troops to storm, but, before doing so, issued a direct call to arms. 'Make your enemy afraid, for it is impossible to remain quiet about their moral offences,' he said. 'I beg you not to resort to demonstrations, for they have become nothing but burned paper. It is necessary to resort to other measures, which you take in your own provinces. As for me, I am with you, and I hope I will be able to join you and then we shall ascend into exalted heavens. I will go into inviolable retreat in Kufa. Help me by whatever you are pleased to do in your provinces.' For a man on religious retreat Muqtada was surprisingly voluble and seemed to relish the confrontation with the US. He issued a statement saying: 'The US-led forces have the money, weapons and huge numbers, but these things are not going to weaken our will because God is with us.' On 5 April Dan Senor, the spokesman for the CPA, announced that a warrant had been issued for Muqtada's arrest several months earlier and implied that it might now be implemented. When Bremer subsequently called Muqtada an 'outlaw' he responded: 'If Bremer means that I am an outlaw according to the American legal code, then I take pride in it.'[13]

Mehdi Army reinforcements from Sadr City poured into Kufa and Najaf. They were untrained, violent but highly committed young men who, as described at the beginning of this book, came near to shooting me, Haider al-Safi and Bassim Abdul-Rahman at their checkpoint outside Kufa on 19 April. One of the militiamen who came to Najaf from Sadr city was a twenty-three-year-old labourer called Ali Ahmed. 'Frankly, the Mehdi Army wasn't prepared for such an uprising,' he says. 'It wasn't even divided into companies and battalions, but was in the form of groups who heeded the call for the coming battle against the Americans, the defence of the holy sites and to ensure that the Sadrist current survived. The biggest concentration of our forces was in Najaf. People either had their own weapons or ones they had taken from the old regime. Some people were selling what they owned in order to buy weapons so they could fight with the Mehdi Army. Very few weapons and ammunition were supplied to us.' Ali Ahmed noticed that one advantage in the first stages of the fighting was that 'there were US troops in Diwaniyah and Hilla provinces but we mostly faced Spanish soldiers'. These Spanish troops were in the process of being withdrawn by the newly elected Spanish socialist government that disapproved of their deployment. Overall, he says, 'We didn't fight because of the closure of the newspaper or the arrest of al-Yaqubi, but because we thought our religion was in danger.'[14]

It was the strength of Muqtada that he could mobilise the Shia masses, the millions of angry and very poor young men whom nobody else in Iraq represented. His weakness was that he could not control them and he knew the risk of being denigrated as a dangerous and destructive troublemaker. As the uprising began to run out of steam he called on his followers to follow the instructions of Grand Ayatollah Ali al-Sistani who had called for a political solution and negotiations. The Americans were sending emissaries to al-Sistani to persuade him to give them permission to enter Najaf in pursuit of Muqtada (his exact location was unclear and it was easy for him to move between Kufa and Najaf which are only a few miles apart). On 7 April Muqtada issued an interesting statement to his followers justifying the uprising but also admitting that 'a rebellions faction has infiltrated your [Mehdi Army] ranks and deliberately attempted to fan the flames of turmoil by plundering and looting government offices and money changers. They shut the doors of the universities and seminaries in such a way as to distort the image of Islam and of Muslims and of the Mehdi Army.' He said that he was heeding the call of religious, tribal and political leaders for a ceasefire and ordered an end to military operations and demonstrations.[15] His intention was to portray Bremer and the US as the aggressors in the eyes of the Shia community. The last thing the CPA wanted to do was to negotiate with Muqtada because its aim was to eliminate him. Bremer, once again overplaying his hand, said that there were just three choices facing Muqtada: surrender, arrest or death.

Militarily the Mehdi Army was increasingly restricted to central Najaf. US troops had replaced the Spanish forces in the middle of April. Ali Ahmed and the militiamen he was with moved into the vast cemetery of Wadi al-Salaam, where millions of Shia lie buried 'because it is large, difficult for the enemy to enter and we knew its layout'. The cemetery was a good place for guerrillas to hide and fight because it is a labyrinth of narrow lanes between earth walls, partitioning off compounds where the dead are interred. 'The number of fighters in each group was between fifteen and seventeen. We moved cautiously at night by the light of torches because we were afraid to reveal our positions. We used snipers, mortars and Katyusha rockets; we were not able to sleep at night and our food, when we could get it, was very simple.' For all their bravery there was little the black-clad militiamen could do against American airpower and armoured vehicles. 'They destroyed the shops and buildings so Najaf became like a city of ghosts. The street fighting was very intense with the American troops staying inside their tanks while we tried to hit them from all directions.' These fights were very uneven, with heavy losses among the militiamen and few US soldiers killed or wounded. On 26 April, for instance, the militiamen outside Najaf attacked an M1 tank with rocket-propelled grenades. During the battle that followed AC-130 gunships, capable of hosing the ground with machine-gun fire, were used against the Mehdi Army. The US said it had killed fifty-seven gunmen and local Najaf hospitals confirmed that they had received the dead bodies of thirty-seven young men of military age.

Muqtada, dressed in his usual dark robes and turban, moved secretly through Najaf to inspect his militiamen. Ali Ahmed recalls how careful he was in making sure his enemies never knew where he was. 'No one knew where he was going in the dark alleyways of the city,' he says. 'He used to give misleading hints about his movements to confuse the enemy, who unfortunately were not only Americans.' As the weeks passed the Mehdi Army's military situation grew weaker, but Muqtada's political position was becoming stronger. Shia politicians in Baghdad and the *marji'iya* wanted to bring the siege of Najaf to an end by negotiations and were desperate to avoid an American assault on the shrine. The CPA abandoned its earlier demand for the arrest of Muqtada and, crucially, the disarmament and dissolution of the Mehdi Army. Muqtada, for his part, agreed to withdraw his men from the shrine and from Najaf.

Another development deeply alarmed the CPA and the US military commanders at this time: cooperation was growing between Shia fighters in Najaf and Sunni fighters in Fallujah. Military supplies came to the beleaguered Mehdi Army men from Fallujah through Kerbala. 'Fighters came from Fallujah though there were not many of them and it was towards the end of battle,' says Ali Ahmed. 'They were useful because they had also fought the Americans and were experienced in street fighting tactics.'[16] The cooperation was brief, but was an important motive for the US to bring the long-running crisis in Najaf to an end. Losses among his men were heavy, but Muqtada had emerged the winner because he had challenged the US-led occupation, held off their greatly superior army for weeks, and survived without making concessions that would weaken him permanently.

CHAPTER THIRTEEN

The Fall of Najaf

On 6 August 2004 Abbas Fadhil, a twenty-four-year-old member of a Mehdi Army company, volunteered with a group of other fighters in Sadr City to go to Najaf to take part in the second battle for the city. It had started three days earlier and shells and bombs were beginning to destroy much of central Najaf as US Marines fought their way towards the Imam Ali shrine. Abbas had some military training because 'when the Mehdi Army was set up we used to train in the open agricultural countryside on the eastern outskirts of Baghdad and pretend that we were hunting'. In addition he had once fought in the resistance against Saddam Hussein some years earlier in Amara and Nasiriyah provinces 'so I knew how to use a Kalashnikov and a PKC [Russian-made light machine gun]'.

Abbas and his companions, who belonged to Mehdi Army's Ahmed al-Shaibani company, named after the imprisoned representative of Muqtada in Basra, drove in a car on what is normally a two-hour drive from Baghdad. They could see US aircraft bombing groups of young men travelling in the same direction as themselves on the assumption that they were going to join Muqtada's forces. The crashes of the explosions unnerved the young men in the car. 'Some got out and disappeared into nearby farms or took lifts in passing cars going back to Baghdad,' says Abbas. As they arrived at Aoun, a village surrounded by date palms just north of Najaf where Shia insurgents had briefly fought

Saddam Hussein's Republican Guard to a standstill in the uprising of 1991, the driver of the car finally lost his nerve. Though he was a follower of Muqtada, he suddenly announced that he was going no further and was returning to Baghdad. His fear infected others among Abbas's remaining companions who took their last chance to avoid fighting in a battle in which they knew they were very likely to die. (These defections are striking because they show that the militiamen in Sadr City were not all fanatical fighters carelessly willing to become martyrs for Muqtada and Islam.)

The flight of the driver left the four remaining members of the party that had set out from Baghdad a few hours earlier standing disconsolately beside the road. 'We four walked on foot to the Haidaria region using an unpaved dirt track because we were frightened of the American bombardment,' recalls Abbas. 'We came across a small saloon car whose driver said, "Get in and I will drive you to Najaf." I do not think he was entirely in his right mind, though he was not completely crazy either. As he drove he kept yelling at people beside the road, saying "You are cowards and agents of the occupier." We stayed silent and did not speak to him. The situation was very dangerous because we were twice targeted by American snipers and we were very exposed because there were no other cars moving on the roads. He drove us by streets he knew until we were close to the Imam Ali shrine and would not take any money when he dropped us off, saying, "This is my work." Najaf was a ghost city, with all the shops closed and there was nobody to be seen apart from Sadrist fighters.' During a bombardment Abbas, by now reduced to a single companion, took refuge inside the shrine.

When the shelling stopped, the two young men left the city again to rendezvous with a company of Mehdi Army fighters near the so-called Sea of Najaf, a lake just to the west of the city. 'They trusted us when we showed them our identity cards, which were given to us in Baghdad, proving that we belonged to the Ahmed al-Shaibani company. We began shooting from long distance at an American convoy. We never saw American soldiers on foot. They were always in tanks or armoured vehicles, even inside the city, and also there were strikes by helicopters.' The Mehdi Army militiamen were very conscious of their military inferiority compared to the far better-equipped US Marines who could kill them without suffering any equivalent losses. They did what they could to combat American armour. Abbas says that a man named Karim Dra'am, who repaired cars in Sadr City, came to Najaf and modified Katyusha rockets and mortar bombs so they would destroy an American tank, but he was killed in action.

Suffering heavy losses and under continual bombardment, the militiamen were ordered to retreat to the Wadi al-Salaam, the Valley of Peace, the largest cemetery in the world, some six miles by two in size, where at least two million Shia are buried, eager to have their final resting place close to the shrine of Imam Ali, a huge necropolis or a 'city of the dead' spreading out in a great semi-circle around Najaf. A few of its streets are wide enough to drive a car down, but most are winding lanes, the layout of which is only known accurately to the gravediggers. Even under Saddam Hussein when the Iran–Iraq border was officially closed, pious Shia in Iran and elsewhere would pay border tribes to smuggle the bodies of deceased relatives across the frontier to be buried in Wadi al-Salaam. It is a good place for guerrillas to use as a refuge because it is a labyrinth, mostly of small tombs above ground that provide plenty of cover. There are also larger ones belonging to rich families which look like small mosques or shrines, their walls painted a vivid pink or green. On the tombs there are sometimes photographs of the dead: ageing sheikhs in Arab headdresses and young men in jackets and ties. Many members of the Mehdi Army who had been killed in the April battles were interred in the Wadi al-Salaam in plots bought by Muqtada, and they were soon to be joined by more of his militiamen.

The Wadi al-Salaam is perfect terrain for guerrillas. 'We fled to the cemetery and stayed in the crypts and fought from there,' relates Abbas, who is very open about his terrifying experience. 'The bombing continued day and night. We saw the graves being demolished and our companions killed. We buried the martyrs without washing them because they were martyrs and the weather was hot [Muslims traditionally wash their dead before burying them but in Wadi al-Salaam there was little water and bodies rapidly decomposed in the heat].' At night the surviving fighters received water and food from people in Najaf. 'The water came in bottles and our food was biscuits twice a day, though in that situation we did not have much appetite. I saw two cars come from Fallujah with humanitarian aid and Muqtada thanked them. We found that there was food on top and weapons underneath, so I don't know how they were able to get past American checkpoints. One morning a rumour spread that Sayyid Muqtada had been killed and some fighters retreated, but others fought even harder. But in the afternoon Muqtada came and visited the fighters, his hand wrapped in a white bandage. He fought with us and we saw him hold an RPG (rocket-propelled grenade-launcher) and fire it at the American tanks. He was always turning up during the battle, though he kept his movements secret.'[1]

A second round in the battle for Najaf was always predictable. In the April crisis Muqtada had, surprisingly, emerged as the outright winner in the confrontation which Paul Bremer and his Coalition Provisional Authority had half provoked and half tumbled into in their clumsy and counter-productive attempt to eliminate him as a political force. They achieved the exact opposite of what they wanted and had elevated Muqtada into a major player, as the world watched the Mehdi Army stand up to the US assault for almost a month. Muqtada had been extremely lucky, or had chosen his moment superbly well, in that his uprising coincided precisely with the crisis in Fallujah. Thanks to extraordinary bungling by the CPA, the Sunni insurgents had acquired their own semi-independent capital half an hour's drive west of

Baghdad. This diverted US attention and made the US army nervous about fighting a two-front war against both Sunni and Shia. The CPA made a humiliating retreat from its threat to arrest Muqtada and disarm and disband the Mehdi Army. In the event many of the militiamen did not even leave Najaf as its leaders had pledged. 'Muqtada gave an order saying everybody had to go back to his family,' recalls Ali Ahmed who took part in the April uprising. 'But many of our men stayed inside Najaf saying that the truce was just a lie, and they also moved into nearby regions such as Mashkab, Haidaria and Abbasia.'[2]

By August the authorities in Baghdad were stronger than they had been in April. An interim Iraqi government had been installed with Iyad Allawi as prime minister on 28 June 2004 and sovereignty had in theory been transferred back to Iraq. There was a great deal less in this than met the eye. The US had total control over security policy. Freshly raised Iraqi military units were incapable of fighting anybody. The new regime resembled many existing authoritarian regimes in the Middle East, but unlike them did not even have its own security service or control of its own army. The Iraqi National Intelligence Service under General Muhammad al-Shahwani was openly funded by the CIA. Iyad Allawi had long been close to the British intelligence service MI6 and the CIA. His defence minister Hazem al-Shalaan had a personal interest in getting rid of Muqtada since he had been one of Sayyid Majid al-Khoei's party who had made the fatal journey to Najaf in April 2003. But he had not been prominent in the opposition to Saddam Hussein and, along with the new interior minister, Falah al-Naqib, was a long-term exile with very limited experience of Iraqi life. Both these security ministers vehemently denounced Muqtada and the Mehdi Army as cat's paws of Iran during the coming crisis. Such declarations were a joy to the ears of the administration in Washington, but they were untrue or grossly exaggerated. Despite the lessons that should have been learned in the April crisis, the US and its Iraqi allies still underestimated Shia solidarity and the mass support for Muqtada. This was a serious weakness because the key to destroying Muqtada and his movement was to isolate him from the *hawza*, the Shia political parties and the Shia community as a whole.

Muqtada's position was both stronger and weaker than four months earlier. He had solidified his grip on Sadr City and he still substantially controlled Kufa and Najaf. The Mehdi Army could, in areas like Sadr City, deliver on security in a way that the police could not, by telling gangs of criminals and dealers to get out or be killed. In Kut Sadrist militiamen provided back-up for the local police. Class division within the Shia community usually determined attitudes towards the Sadrists. The labouring poor and unemployed revered him and the middle class of shopkeepers and merchants regarded him with fear and contempt. 'The Mehdi Army was created to maintain security and give Iraqis their freedom, so the duty of each of its fighters is to work alongside the police and the civil defence corps,' claimed a Sadrist cleric in Kut called Sheikh Muhammad Fadhil al-Musawi piously. But the shopkeepers in Kut felt like Muneer Ahmed, a follower of Grand Ayatollah Ali al-Sistani, who declared himself sceptical, saying: 'The fighters of the Mehdi Army were the cause of the riots that happened a few months ago – and now they are acting like good people?'³

Militarily, the Sadrist militiamen were better trained and equipped in August than a few months earlier when they were no more than bands of religiously inspired gunmen. By now they were organised into companies and battalions with specialised crews for mortars and machine guns. 'We tried to avoid the mistakes we had made in the first battle by studying their causes and finding solutions for the problems we faced,' says Abbas Fadhil. He reckoned the army had '4,000 to 4,500 very well-trained fighters'.⁴ Opponents of the Mehdi Army have a simple explanation as to why this happened. Writing towards the end of the 2004 one well-informed commentator wrote that Muqtada 'commands not a ragtag militia of dispossessed Shiites, but increasingly, a

well-armed, well-trained force of insurgents. The trans-
formation of the Jaysh al-Mahdi [Mehdi Army] lies not in
Iraq, but across the border in Iran.' He goes on to repeat the
claim of the London-based newspaper *Asharq al-Awsat* that
the Qods force of the Iranian Revolutionary Guards had
established three military training camps at Qasr-e-Shirin,
Ilam and Hamid on the Iranian side of the Iran–Iraq border
and were training between 800 and 1,200 of Muqtada's
militiamen.[5] Such claims of Iranian involvement by newspapers
and governments in the Sunni world should be treated with
caution. Saddam Hussein had denounced the Shia insurgents
in 1991 as pawns of Iran though the Iraqi Shia opposition to
Saddam was bitter that Tehran, for all the bellicose rhetoric,
had not helped them. The US and British governments soon
joined the chorus of attacks on Iran, claiming it was the
hidden hand behind the Mehdi Army.

On the battlefield there was never much evidence that
training and better equipment were transforming the Mehdi
Army. Its militiamen were no more able to take on the US
Marines in August 2004 than they had been able to do in
April. They did not have missiles capable of destroying
American armoured vehicles, as the Hezbollah guerrillas in
Lebanon (whom Iran was also accused of arming) were able
to do when they were attacked by Israeli tanks in the summer
of 2006. The most striking feature of the Mehdi Army was
its ability to take massive punishment without disintegrating,
but it never attained the military proficiency of the Sunni
guerrillas fighting the US in Iraq, who were led by
experienced professional soldiers. The Mehdi Army also had
the disadvantage that, in Najaf and Sadr City, it was
defending fixed positions which the US could locate and
destroy with its massive fire power.

Muqtada had told his men to react quickly to any
provocation.[6] There were signs in the first days of August
2004 that the expected crisis was imminent. Muqtada's
representative in Kerbala, Sheikh Mithal al-Hassnawi, was

arrested and demonstrators in Najaf demanded his release. US Marines passed close to Muqtada's house in Najaf and the Sadrists alleged that they planned to arrest him. When eighteen policemen were kidnapped by Sadrists, the US-appointed governor of Najaf, Adnan al-Zurufi, accused the Mehdi Army of working for Iran and called for US military support. Heavy fighting started with US forces in Najaf and Sadr City, and with the Italians in Nasiriyah. This did not at first look very different from previous clashes over the summer, but suddenly the political situation was transformed by a dramatic and unexpected event. It was well known that Grand Ayatollah al-Sistani, like other grand ayatollahs, only rarely left his house. But on 6 August, after secretly leaving Najaf, he arrived in London seeking treatment for a heart ailment. It was evidently not a medical emergency since he visited friends in Beirut on his way to London where he did not immediately enter hospital; and when he did, no surgery was required. Iraqi observers interpreted his swift and secret departure from Najaf as tacit permission for the US to advance into the city: al-Sistani was no longer prepared to allow Muqtada to use his presence to shield the Sadrists from American attack.

As news spread that al-Sistani was in London, Muqtada issued a number of defiant statements. But he was cautious enough to have somebody else read out his sermon in his father's mosque in Kufa. His absence underlined his fear that his enemies intended to kill him at the first opportunity. 'America is the greatest of Satans,' he told worshippers, and accused the US of being responsible for the collapse of law and order. 'I blame the occupier for all the attacks going on in Iraq, such as the attacks on the churches and the kidnapping,' he said. As in the past he foreshadowed his own death: 'Heaven does not come without a price. Don't wait for me to get up in the pulpit and give you directions. I, certainly, will be gone because the enemy is looking for me everywhere. Don't let my death divide you.'[7]

Muqtada's words were accompanied by the rattle of

gunfire in the background. As in so many other US military actions in Iraq, the Marines deployed immense firepower and underestimated the anger felt by Iraqis at the destruction and number of dead. When the Marines claimed that they had killed 300 Mehdi Army militiamen on the first Thursday and Friday of the battle, Iraqi television viewers noticed that some of the bodies scattered in the street were those of women. The slaughter appalled the Iraqi Vice President and leader of the Dawa party, Ibrahim al-Jaafari, who said: 'I think that killing Iraqi civilians is not a civilised way of building the new Iraq, which is based on protecting people and promoting dialogue, not bullets.'[8] The attempt by the US and Iyad Allawi to isolate Muqtada from the Shia community was already beginning to fray. A sign that the Iraqi government was nervous came when Allawi suddenly announced that he invited 'Muqtada al-Sadr to take part in the elections next year'.

People streamed out of Najaf to escape the fighting. The main market had already been pulverised and reduced to rubble. The scene is vividly described by my friend Ghaith Abdul-Ahad: 'The wholesale food market, the size of a football pitch, had been reduced to a pile of warped metal. Everything had been incinerated, and each part of the market reeked with its own stench. The smell of burnt potatoes, figs and grapes marked the vegetables section. The cereals were still burning, giving off a faint smell of overcooked rice, and all round was an overwhelming odour of burnt plastic and the crackle of exploding Pepsi cans. Dozens of men, merchants and workers, were trying to rescue what they could. From the carnage appeared a militiaman wrapped in the Iraqi flag followed by two of his comrades. The trio were trying to stop looters digging into the incinerated merchandise.'[9] Much of the fighting was in the Wadi al-Salaam cemetery. Muqtada's position looked more and more desperate as the Marines closed in on the shrine and cut off Najaf from the outside world. In the other Shia cities the Mehdi Army kept up pinprick attacks.

On 13 August Muqtada himself was wounded in three places by shrapnel from a bomb according to his spokesman. This must have been when rumours of his death briefly circulated among the militiamen. They were swiftly quashed by his appearance. The following day he gave a press conference declaring that 'Najaf has triumphed over imperialism and the imperial hubris'. The press conference was run in full by al-Jazeera satellite television and his words echoed around the Middle East. He added acidly that calling Iyad Allawi a 'Shiite' was like calling Saddam Hussein 'a Muslim'.[10] Once again, as in April, the US forces, though militarily dominant, hesitated to launch the final attack on the shrine. Its capture, particularly if it was damaged or destroyed in a last stand by the Mehdi Army, would do the US nothing but harm, unless they could also kill or capture Muqtada.

There is strong evidence that the US tried to do just that. All sides had a lot to lose if the assault on the shrine went ahead. The Shia Islamists in particular wanted to prevent an assault. Dr Mowaffaq al-Rubai'e, the Iraqi National Security Adviser and an independent Shia Islamist, led a mediation effort supported by the Americans which at the time he thought was close to success. However, in retrospect he is convinced that the Americans' willingness to negotiate was actually a cover for an attempt to lure Muqtada to a place where he could be killed or captured. 'I believe that particular incident made Muqtada lose any confidence or trust in the [US-led] coalition and made him really wild,' says Dr Rubai'e. As he recounts it, what happened was that he obtained the backing of Allawi, the US embassy and the US military command, and then met with Muqtada, giving him a list of conditions to end the fighting. 'He actually signed the agreement with his own handwriting,' says Dr Rubai'e. 'He wanted inner Najaf, the old city around the shrine, to be treated like the Vatican.' Dr Rubai'e returned to Baghdad to show the draft agreement to Allawi, who approved it, and then went back to Najaf for Muqtada to sign an agreement at a final meeting. This was to take place in Muqtada's father's old house in Najaf. As Dr Rubai'e and the other mediators approached the house, the US Marines targeted it with an intense bombardment. They then saw US Special Forces racing to surround it. They were a few vital minutes too early and missed Muqtada who had not yet arrived.

Both Muqtada and Dr Rubai'e, who was considered to be very close to the Americans, believed they were victims of a set-up. 'When I came back to Baghdad I was really infuriated, I can tell you,' said Dr Rubai'e. 'I went berserk with both [the US commander General George] Casey and the ambassador [John Negroponte].' They denied they knew of a trap and said they would investigate, but he heard nothing more from them.

The impact of what he deemed was a failed attempt to kill or arrest him under the guise of peace talks made Muqtada even more wary than he had been before. 'I know him very well and I think his suspicion and distrust of the coalition and any foreigner is really deep-rooted,' says Dr Rubai'e. After it had happened Muqtada retreated to the Imam Ali shrine itself as the safest place for him to be in Najaf.[11] Back in Baghdad, Dr Rubai'e found that the Interim Government, and the western intelligence services that seemed to direct many of its actions, had backed away from any idea of compromise. He found himself suspected of working for the Iranians – a permanent obsession on the part of the Allawi government when dealing with the Shia Islamists.

The Mehdi Army militiamen holding out in the Wadi al-Salaam suffered serious losses, but did not stop fighting. Their morale, however, was beginning to wilt. Abbas Kodeiri, a thirty-three-year-old militiaman, is frank about the difficulties they were in. 'At the beginning of the battle, which went on for about a month, we had plenty of weapons and supplies,' he says. 'But with the passage of time and because of the blockade, these had started to run out. Especially serious was when they cut off the supply of water to the Imam Ali shrine and the buildings nearby. Frankly, we went through very difficult times, but we remained steadfast and we were hearing Muqtada's orders which encouraged and strengthened us. When there were periods of calm we fighters would talk about what would happen at the end of the battle and some of us were hesitant and fearful. When somebody talked like that we would always shut him up before he had finished in case what he said reached Muqtada. We began to feel that we were weak and the Americans were so strong.'[12]

In the face of vastly superior US military equipment, the pious and naïve young men fighting in Najaf believed they were receiving divine aid. 'My brother returned from Najaf and told us there was a huge bird which cried out in a loud voice,' said a teenager in Baghdad. 'It appeared when the Americans began bombing Mehdi Army positions.' The bird would brush falling bombs with its wings so they would not explode. 'It's a sign from God – that he has soldiers of all kinds,' he added. 'That bird was a soldier of God.' Other militiamen said they had seen mysterious shadows flitting around American tanks which they believed were angels intervening to disable the guns or tracks of the tanks. 'Those tanks could not move – something had fixed them to the ground,' claimed one fighter. Sayf Adnan, a twenty-five-year-old fighting near the Imam Ali shrine with a group of Mehdi Army militiamen, was heavily bombed. 'It went on for half an hour,' he said. 'Bombs struck every metre, but 80 per cent of them did not blow up. Not one of us was hurt. We knew we were under the protection of Imam Ali . . . and nothing would happen to us.'[13]

In the event it was Grand Ayatollah Ali al-Sistani and not angels or other emissaries of divine assistance which saved Muqtada and the Mehdi Army fighters. Al-Sistani and the *marji'iya* wanted the Sadrists out of Najaf, but did not want to see them or the city destroyed, permanently dividing the Shia community. They were also very careful – as Iyad Allawi, the defence minister Hazem al-Shalaan and the interior minister Falah al-Naqib were not – to avoid being seen as American pawns. Al-Sistani had not left Iraq through the US-controlled Baghdad airport, but made the arduous journey by car through southern Iraq to get a plane from Kuwait. The US and its favoured ministers in the government behaved as if their propaganda about the Sadrists being 'foreign fighters', Iranian puppets or 'anti-Iraq forces' (the latter term was dreamed up by an American PR company) was true. As late as 25 August Hazem al-Shalaan, speaking from the safety of a US army base outside Najaf, boasted: 'This evening, Iraqi forces will reach the doors of the shrine and control it and I appeal to the Mehdi Army to throw down their weapons. If they do not, we will wipe them out.'[14] He spoke as if Iraqi security forces were leading the assault, but most Iraqis were aware that they were only playing a cosmetic role in the fighting. Mainstream Shia clergy were often far more realistic about what was happening on the ground than Allawi or his American mentors. Ayatollah Muhammad Bahr al-Ulum, long an exiled opponent of Saddam Hussein, said bluntly: 'The government has lost control of the Middle Euphrates region and the south, even if it manages to calm down these areas, temporarily, by using brute force.'[15]

Muqtada was also looking for a compromise, despite all his predictions of his own imminent martyrdom. His abortive negotiations with Dr Rubai'e in early August showed he was agreeable to a deal including leaving Najaf, but not to an admission of defeat. As in April, his men had stood up to the US war machine and defied the US occupation, which solidified his support among poor and young Shia. For youthful fighters in Sadr City his legitimacy exceeded that of the four Grand Ayatollahs in Najaf, all very old, three of whom were Iranians. 'Sayyid Muqtada: Don't pay attention to the elderly clerics, they are spies,' shouted an unemployed young man carrying a rocket-propelled grenade-launcher in Sadr City as he celebrated an attack that had destroyed a US Humvee. A Shia policeman in Baghdad added: 'We will remain behind Muqtada. He is still a holy warrior even if he leaves the shrine and becomes less visible.'[16]

But this support was by no means universal. Muqtada was feared and despised by the Shia shopkeepers, businessmen and professionals just as the *sans culottes* who manned the barricades during the French Revolution were regarded with visceral terror by the Paris bourgeois. The Sadrists were particularly unpopular in Najaf where many blamed them and not the Americans for the destruction of part of their city. Dr Ahmed, a firm supporter of al-Sistani in Najaf and an opponent of Muqtada, says: 'In the centre of Najaf shopkeepers whose businesses had been devastated hated the followers of al-Sadr. People asked, "Why did they have to choose Najaf for their battle? Why don't they fight in Kufa instead? We hoped that American forces would eliminate all those who took part in the battle." '[17] For Dr Ahmed the Sadrists were an arm of the criminal classes.

Among the Shia leadership there was also a belief that Muqtada's confrontation with the US was ill-advised. The broad strategy approved by the Shia political parties and the *marji'iya* was to cooperate with the US occupation in order to compel the holding of elections in 2005, which the Shia as the majority of the population would inevitably win. Armed resistance by the Mehdi Army and anti-American nationalism, however popular on the street, might have the disastrous effect of alienating the US at the very moment when the Shia community in Iraq was within touching distance of winning the greatest victory in its history.

Until quite late in the day, the hawks in the Iraqi government and the Anglo-American intelligence agencies seemed to think they were winning. On 19 August Qassim Dawood, the minister of state for military affairs, demanded that Muqtada publicly announce that he would disband the Mehdi Army, hand over weapons in all provinces, leave the shrine in Najaf and confirm in writing that he would not undertake any armed action in future. But Muqtada categorically refused to disband the Mehdi Army.[18] Furthermore, on the same day as Dawood was making his demands, al-Sistani left his hospital in London and his spokesman indicated that the Grand Ayatollah would accept the symbolic key to the shrine and control of the shrine complex. There was no mention of the Mehdi Army being disbanded. Al-Sistani's action pre-empted the Interim Government's plan to storm the shrine in order to eliminate Muqtada. The government's first reaction was to indulge in fanciful wish fulfilment similar to that of the Mehdi Army militiamen who saw angels disabling American tanks. A government spokes-man announced, wholly falsely, that Iraqi security forces had captured the shrine of Imam Ali without a fight, the Mehdi Army militiamen had thrown down their arms, and Muqtada himself had escaped 'under the cover of darkness'. All this was fantasy, as journalists in the shrine swiftly reported. On 25 August al-Sistani returned to Basra and, after meeting the governor of the city, it was announced that he would lead a peace march to Najaf to save the shrine of Imam Ali. The Sadrist spokesmen accepted a ceasefire and said they would do whatever al-Sistani ordered. The Sadrists inside the shrine were particularly joyful. 'The situation is getting worse day by day and only God's intervention can save us,' Muhammad al-Battat was quoted as saying. 'I think this march is a gift from God.' Though the peace march was shot at by police and national guards, al-Sistani's presence in Najaf check-mated the hawks who could no longer storm the shrine. On 26 August the US military declared a ceasefire and Muqtada visited al-Sistani. They agreed a five-point peace plan under which Najaf and Kufa were to be demilitarised and the Mehdi Army would withdraw from them. The Iraqi police would take over control. There was a call for the withdrawal of foreign forces from both cities and for compensation for those whose property had been damaged. In the margin of the agreement Muqtada wrote the significant words: 'These are not requests, but the instructions of the *Marji'iyya* and I am prepared to implement whatever is in them in response to the *Marji'iyya's* instructions.'[19] A few days later he ordered the Mehdi Army to cease fighting in the rest of the country.

*

The main losers in the second battle of Najaf were Iyad
Allawi and the Interim Government. They had intended to
isolate Muqtada from the rest of the Shia political and
religious leadership, and had ended up by isolating
themselves. Allawi was blind to the consequences of appearing as a US proxy in Iraq and relying on US military might.
On 4 December 2005, while campaigning in the second of
two parliamentary elections held in that year, Allawi
unwisely visited the shrine of Imam Ali in Najaf. Worshippers reacted furiously at the sight of him, shouting abuse
and hurling their shoes in his direction. One of the few
television news reports to cause general amusement in Iraq in
recent years was one showing the portly figure of Allawi
running speedily through the gates of the shrine followed by
a hail of shoes, a traditional method of showing contempt.
He later claimed there had been an attempt to assassinate
him by 'about 60 people dressed in black carrying machetes
and pistols', though nobody else saw them or heard shots.[20]

The US had also lost because for the second time it had
deployed its full might against Muqtada, only to see him and
his movement live to fight another day. As so often happened
to the US in Iraq, its military strength failed to produce
political gains. The outright winner of the August battle in
Najaf was Grand Ayatollah al-Sistani, who showed his
immense authority over the Iraqi Shia, which neither the
Interim Government in Baghdad nor the US Administration
in Washington dared confront. Al-Sistani had broken
Muqtada's grip on Najaf and shown that the Sadrists could
not survive without heeding the wishes of the Grand
Ayatollahs. Muqtada could not credibly go on denouncing
and disregarding the 'passive' *marji'iya* which had just saved
him from possible extinction. His militiamen had suffered
dreadful losses but these could be replaced. He had survived,
but he had come close enough to defeat to be wary of
fighting the US army for a third time.

CHAPTER FOURTEEN

Muqtada Turns to Politics

Muqtada and his surviving militiamen were at first depressed by what they saw as a serious defeat in the second battle for Najaf. After losing many dead and injured they had been forced to withdraw from the city for which they had fought for so long. 'At the end of the battle we felt a sense of disappointment and failure,' says Abbas Kodeiri, the Mehdi Army militiaman who had been fighting near the shrine. 'We believed we had moved away from what the people wanted. Even Muqtada retired from daily life and issued no statement for a long time, while we avoided letting people know we were Sadrists.'[1] It was not until 16 May 2005, over eight months later, that Muqtada was to re-emerge in public. By then it was clear that his defeat at Najaf was more military than political.

This was not initially obvious to either the Sadrists or their enemies. 'I knew we had beaten Muqtada when I saw him walking on his own in Najaf without anybody beside him,' recalls Sabah Khadim, a senior official at the Iraqi Interior Ministry.[2] In agreeing to leave Najaf the Mehdi Army lost its grip on the religious capital of Iraqi Shiism. The immediate winners in the three-week war were all Muqtada's rivals or opponents: Grand Ayatollah al-Sistani, the *hawza*, the al-Hakim family and the Supreme Council for Islamic Revolution in Iraq (SCIRI). 'After having resolved the Najaf crisis,' said a student close to the Sadrists, 'Sistani directed that religious schools belonging to the Sadr family be placed

under the *hawza's* control and the Sadr family headquarters
be moved outside the old city. The al-Hakim family, which
leads SCIRI, thus recovered control of the city with al-
Sistani's blessing. It bought several plots of land and
buildings and deployed its Badr militia to protect the holy
shrines. While SCIRI offices mushroomed in Najaf, the
Sadrist movement virtually disappeared from sight. Even
Muqtada's pictures could not be found in Najaf's old city.'[3]
Against these setbacks could be weighed the achievement of
Muqtada and the Mehdi Army in surviving the onslaught of
the US Marines and the Interim Government. They no longer
spoke of arresting him for the murder of Sayyid Majid al-
Khoei (two of his senior advisers, Mustafa al-Yaqubi and
Riyadh al-Nuri, detained for involvement in the crime, were
released in August 2005). There was a further change in
Muqtada's status: he had stopped even purporting to act
under the auspices of Ayatollah Khadhim al-Haeri in Qom
whom Sadr II had nominated as his official successor. 'Al-
Haeri criticised Muqtada secretly during the first battle for
Najaf and never supported him,' says Sheikh Ali, the Sadrist
leader. 'During the second battle he attacked him publicly
and Muqtada later blamed him in his sermons.'[4]

Most important, however, in ensuring the Sadrists'
continued significance was that the political tide in Iraq was
still running strongly in their favour on two crucial issues.
First, the unpopularity of the US occupation increased by the
year with the proportion saying that armed resistance was
acceptable rising from 17 per cent in 2004 to 51 per cent in
2007.[5] Second, the state remained weak, unable to provide
ordinary Iraqis with security against sectarian killers and
criminals, and this favoured the growth of self-defence
forces. As suicide bombers slaughtered people while they
shopped in their markets or formed long queues to join the
police or army, Shia with no sympathy for the militias
nonetheless welcomed the protection of themselves and their
families by men with guns. This naturally made the Mehdi
Army more acceptable as a defence force in Shia districts. 'If

you don't have a militia you're not in politics in Iraq,' remarked a veteran Iraqi observer of the political scene.

Having lost control of the old city of Najaf, Muqtada could no longer live in his father's house near the Imam Ali shrine down a narrow lane in the Hanana district of Najaf. It was here that Sayyid Majid al-Khoei had been brought by a furious mob in April 2003, and reputedly denied refuge by Muqtada minutes before he was murdered. It had been a convenient house as a family headquarters because, although the entrance was small, it was otherwise spacious and, like many older Najaf houses, had cavernous cellars extending far under ground. Used for storage and keeping cool in summer, the cellars made excellent bomb shelters and places of concealment. In the coming years Muqtada moved, for obvious security reasons, from house to house in Najaf outside the old city and in Kufa, though he lived mainly in a modern blue-painted house in the middle-class Ashtraki district of Najaf.[6] His disappearance after the battle of Najaf was prolonged, but scarcely out of character. Ever since 2003 he had intermittently vanished from view when his political fortunes had been at a low ebb. These absences excited controversy among the foreign media which routinely speculated on whether he had fled the country. But they are not out of the ordinary in Iraq where ayatollahs are frequently secluded in their houses for years and where the Imam al-Mahdi, the Messiah whose return is longed for by the faithful, disappeared in Samarra over a thousand years ago.

It was during this period of seclusion that Muqtada adopted a new political approach. He replaced military with political action, though his opposition to the US occupation remained unchanged. He explained that his strategy had evolved through three stages: 'The Sadrist movement first resorted to peaceful resistance, then to armed resistance and finally to political resistance. This does not present any problem: every situation requires its own response.'[7] He admitted that the military option had failed, but said he was right to try it.[8] His new strategy was intelligent and in keeping with the times. It recognised that al-Sistani's policy of conditional cooperation with the US occupation had worked. The Grand Ayatollah had compelled Washington to agree to two elections and one referendum in 2005, all of which would inevitably be won by the Shia majority. Iraqis would vote for a transitional government on 30 January, for or against a new constitution on 15 October and, finally, for a four-year parliament on 15 December. Muqtada expressed doubts about the validity of polls that were taking place under the auspices of the occupation, but even so they would mean a radical transfer of power to the Shia. The Shia parties agreed to form an electoral coalition called the United Iraqi Alliance (UIA) on 16 December 2004, which, since it was backed by al-Sistani and the *marji'iya,* was to prove unbeatable at the polls. Once the Sadrists had publicly forsworn armed resistance to the occupation, the main difference between their approach and that of al-Sistani disappeared (though Muqtada has not seen al-Sistani since 2004). Inevitably they became part of the UIA, winning 32 out of 275 seats in the December election. Essentially, Muqtada intended to have his cake and eat it: he wanted to control service ministries in the government such as Health and Transport, both big employers, but he also sought to distance himself from the government's blunders, failures and corruption. Iyad Allawi, high up in the Sadrists' demonology, was replaced as prime minister in May 2005 by Ibrahim al-Jaafari, the Dawa leader who had denounced the attack on Najaf. It was going to be very difficult in future to form an Iraqi government without Muqtada's agreement.

Did Muqtada have any alternative to joining the Shia coalition? Could he have ever united with the Sunni insurgents to form a common front against the occupation? The Sadrists had always been anti-sectarian and Iraqi nationalist. Sadr II had called on Shia to go and pray in Sunni mosques. Muqtada enjoyed brief popularity among some Sunni up to the end of 2005 because of his vocal opposition to the US. His first act on his re-emergence in April 2005 had been to seek to arbitrate between Shia and Sunni. An important reason why the US had been eager to bring the first battle for Najaf to an end in April 2004 was fear that the Shia and Sunni insurgencies might combine. I had watched outside the main blood bank in Baghdad as Shia as well as Sunni gave blood for the wounded of Fallujah when it was being shelled by the US Marines. But six months later, after merciless suicide bombings over the summer, the Shia of Baghdad wanted the rebellion in Fallujah crushed as soon as possible. The followers of Abu Musab al-Zarqawi, the founder of al-Qaida in Iraq, issued bloodcurdling denunciations of the Shia as heretics deserving death. The supposedly more nationalist insurgent groups were also increasingly *salafi* and *jihadi,* born-again Sunni fanatics waging holy war on the Shia as well as Americans. The romantic vision of a popular front of Shia and Sunni was never really feasible. Muqtada very reasonably demanded that Sunni constitutional politicians who wanted to cooperate with him on an anti-occupation platform must first unconditionally condemn the murderous bomb attacks on Shia civilians, but this they refused to do. Both communities frequently claimed to be Iraqi nationalists, but in reality their definition of Iraqi nationalism differed radically. Shia friends complained to me that foreign journalists such as myself always exaggerated the extent of Sunni–Shia divisions in Iraq. They would say they had Sunni friends and relatives married to Sunni, but then they would add all-important exclusion clauses to this supposed amity, such as saying that all former Baathists should be arrested. Sunni friends would likewise claim that sectarian strife was less than I supposed, but would then go on to dismiss al-Sistani, Muqtada and the Shia religious parties as all mere creatures of Iran.

People in the Middle East are notoriously prone to believe in conspiracy theories, but the most poisonous myth in the region is surely this conviction that the Shia of Iraq are puppets manipulated by Iran. The long struggle of the Iraqi

Shia against Saddam Hussein, in which Iran had played a minimal role, is ignored. The former regime had denounced Shia political activists and the insurgents of 1991 as Iranian proxies and it had found willing, if not very well-informed, listeners in Washington. Sunni leaders in the Arab world, notably in Saudi Arabia, Jordan and Egypt, spoke nervously of the election victories of the Shia in Iraq in 2005 as presaging an Iranian drive to the west. Saudi envoys in Washington repeatedly denounced, to anybody who would listen, the Shia-dominated governments of Ibrahim al-Jaafari and Nouri al-Maliki. Much of the vituperation was ill-disguised sectarianism, but the White House progressively adopted a similar view by which the machinations of Iran were detected behind many of America's disasters in Iraq. The Bush administration had always been happiest with its 'axis of evil' rhetoric demonising Iran, obvious though it was that Saudi Arabia and the Sunni states were the main support for the Sunni insurgents when it came to providing money and suicide bombers. 'Shia extremists are just as hostile to America [as al-Qaida],' said Bush in his State of the Union address on 23 January 2007, 'and are also determined to dominate the Middle East.' These were dangerous, absurdly exaggerated beliefs. The Shia Hezbollah movement in Lebanon and Muqtada's Mehdi Army in Iraq might be effective on their home territory, but had no chance of making headway in Sunni states where Shia were usually a small and persecuted minority.

The Sadrist movement was historically anti-Iranian as described above. But the US accusations of Iranian complicity with Muqtada were to a degree self-fulfilling. 'Iran can afford to compromise in Iraq, but it cannot afford for the US to be victorious,' a veteran Kurdish observer of Iraqi politics told me. 'If the Americans threaten Iran then the Iranians would prefer to fight the Americans in Baghdad than in Tehran.' In many ways Iranian policy was simple and openly declared. In 2001 and 2003 the Iranian government had been overjoyed to see the overthrow by the US of two of its inveterate enemies, the Taliban in Afghanistan and Saddam Hussein's regime in Iraq. It might have worried about the potential threat posed by the US military forces in both countries, but these were soon tied down by Sunni insurgencies that had nothing to do with Iran. In Iraq, the only large Arab state with a Shia majority, fair elections inevitably meant a Shia-dominated government led by men with long links to Iran. The Iranian leaders wanted Iraq to stay together, but as a weak state under Shia leadership that would never threaten them again.

The US had entirely played into Tehran's hands in 2003 and 2004. Despite frequent accusations of Iranian involvement there was little sign of it. But the Iranians could not always expect events in Iraq to develop in their favour. They wanted to have influence within every Iraqi Shia organisation, religious or political. Tehran could also see the immense advantage to itself of having 160,000 US soldiers stuck in the Iraqi quagmire and who were therefore vulnerable to Iranian-backed forces if the US attacked Iranian nuclear facilities.

In the course of 2005, Iranian intelligence did start to increase its influence in the Sadrist movement and the Mehdi Army. According to a leading anti-Iranian Sadrist militant, whose *nom de guerre* is Hussein Ali, and who was proposing to flee Iraq in the fall of 2007, Muqtada strongly opposed this surge in Iranian material support and influence within his movement, but he was unable to oppose it effectively. 'In 2005 the situation changed with the Sadrists,' says Hussein Ali, 'as the Iranians became more involved [in the Sadr movement] with the help of important advisers to Muqtada. Iranian policy was to offer aid in the shape of financial support, modern weapons and good communications systems. Once lured into accepting them the recipient cannot do without them.' The loose organisation of the Sadrists made it easy for Iranian intelligence to penetrate it and bring certain of its units under their control, though they remained formally loyal to Muqtada. 'They [Iranian intelligence] started giving $800 to anyone who would attack the Americans or assassinate some Iraqi figures,' says Hussein Ali. 'People were given lists of names of former Baathists, present-day political figures or ordinary people to be killed because they were meant to be working against society. If they refuse to do what they are told then they face death.' Two of Ali's fellow critics of Iranian influence within the Sadrist movement were mysteriously assassinated. In one case the killers took advantage of the surprise success of Iraq's football team over South Korea in the Asia Games in 2007 to murder their victim as Baghdad erupted with celebratory gunfire.

There was another reason why it was easy to infiltrate or suborn Mehdi Army units. Most of its men were not paid. 'Iranian intelligence secretly recruited young people to train in Iran,' continues Hussein Ali. 'They give volunteers $300–400 a month, train them to use weapons and to fight the Americans. Of course this is an indirect way of controlling Iraq. It is easy enough for Iranian intelligence to persuade a man to join the groups it controls through money and good weapons if he is unemployed and the Mehdi Army pays no wages.'[9]

The Mehdi Army was hardly the sole Shia organisation to be penetrated and influenced by Iran. Muqtada's main rival in organising the Shia, SCIRI, had carefully cultivated its connections with Washington, but there was never any real evidence that it had severed its traditional connection with Iran. Its leader, Abdul Aziz al-Hakim, now ailing with cancer, made visits to Tehran before announcing any fresh policy initiative. The Iranians had a particular reason for cultivating the Mehdi Army in that they had always found it frustratingly difficult to turn SCIRI's militia arm, the Badr Organization, into an effective military ally. They concluded that the Mehdi Army and the Sadrists had more grass-roots support and would be easier to expand. The Iranian moves seem to have been precautionary because Iran did not want to overthrow the Iraqi government. Paradoxically, while abusing each other, Tehran and Washington both supported the Shia–Kurdish coalition government that ruled in Baghdad after 2005. But Iran also wanted to make sure that it had assets in Iraq which could help ignite an anti-American explosion in Iraq if the US ever made good its oft-repeated threats to attack Iran.

There was endless speculation and numerous newspaper articles were published after Muqtada was first identified as a threat to the US which discussed how far the Mehdi Army was trained and armed by the Revolutionary Guards in Iran. There was also some debate on the Mehdi Army's links to the Hezbollah movement in Lebanon. The focus on the supply of IEDs (Improvised Explosive Devices) as a sign of Iran's secret involvement in Iraq was always misconceived. Roadside bombs have been common guerrilla weapons since the IRA were fighting the British Army in Ireland in 1920–1. Lethal devices can be made out of weed killer. Shaped charges could be made in Iraqi workshops as well as Iran. Obtaining military equipment has never been a problem anywhere in Iraq so long as there is money to pay for it. As for training, which Iran and Hezbollah were supposedly providing, it is noticeable that all the Shia militias are extremely badly trained. Muqtada may have aspired to lead a movement modelled on Hezbollah in Lebanon. His distant cousin Musa al-Sadr had been the inspirational leader of the Lebanese Shia until he disappeared in Libya in 1978. But the Sadrists were never able to emulate the discipline and unity of the Lebanese guerrillas.

Many in the Mehdi Army were unhappy about Muqtada's turn towards constitutional politics in 2005. Hatred for the US occupation ran deep among the militiamen and there was a wholly justified disbelief that the new Iraqi administration was truly independent. 'The American strategy was clever in drawing the Sadrists into the government,' laments Abbas Fadhil, the battle-hardened militiaman who had fought in August amid the tombs in the Wadi al-Salaam cemetery in

Najaf. 'At the beginning our movement was revolutionary because it was the only political trend for the poorest members of society. But this changed when we entered mainstream political life. Parliament didn't do anything for us. The Americans just wanted to make us believe that we were in power and at the same time to end our confrontation with them.'[10] This explanation probably credits US officials in Baghdad with more political imagination than they ever showed signs of possessing. It might have been in their interests to keep the Sadrists inside the government, but instead they regarded their presence there with deep suspicion and agitated to get rid of them.

Taking part in constitutional politics brought material benefits to the core areas of Sadrist support like Sadr City where unemployment had been around 70 per cent. There was a desperate hunger for jobs of any kind. While Muqtada was confronting the government in 2003–4 he was, notes Sadrist veteran Sheikh Ali, 'preventing anyone from joining the army and police, so many young people lost opportunities to get work'. The government has always been the main source of employment in Iraq because it controlled the oil revenues which were the country's only wealth (Iraq's next biggest export used to be dates). For the first time the Shia underclass began to get a share of the cake. 'There were no jobs immediately after the fall of Saddam Hussein, but things got better two years later in 2005,' says Sheikh Ali. 'Many of the jobs were for cleaning and garbage collection. If anything happens to Sadr City, Baghdad will sink into the dirt because the majority of the city's cleaning staff comes from Sadr City.' (Given the prevailing filth in the rest of Baghdad it is not clear that Sadr City's garbage collection is as effective as he claims.) The provision of jobs at a more senior level became easier once the Sadrists had taken control of ministries from 2006. 'Instead of writing to ministries asking them to give jobs, we appointed people wholesale as minor officials.' Hospitals became Sadrist strongholds which Sunni were afraid to enter and medical orderlies who did not have the correct Sadrist connections lost their jobs. 'The economic situation in Sadr City became much better,' says Sheikh Ali. 'Before people were using donkey carts, while now they have cars and good-quality televisions. The Ministry of Labour and Social Affairs provides loans of $10,000 for projects for which people apply with fake documents to get the money which they later refuse to return. Many poor people who could only dream of education under Saddam started doing intensive night study, even old people who want to catch up.'[11] There were other practical benefits that people in Shia districts of Baghdad drew from Sadrist control: everybody else was frightened of them and with reason. Once, when electricity cuts were more than usually prolonged in Baghdad's Jadidah district neighbouring Sadr City, the Mehdi Army went to the house of the official responsible. 'The Mehdi Army militiamen put him in the boot of their car and threatened to punish him,' says Salim Shehab, a twenty-three-year-old student. 'After that the electricity remained on permanently for many days, the streets were cleaned and fuel and gas were more available to people.'[12]

Some of this sounds a little too good to be true, but the Shia poor of Baghdad were increasingly a power in the land. Despite murderous suicide-bombing attacks, their districts were peaceful compared to Sunni neighbourhoods. The Shia middle class in the centre of the capital were often worse affected than the poor living in shanty towns in the east of the city. Immediately after the fall of Saddam, Sadrist militiamen had sold their mobile phones to buy weapons, but the movement now increasingly had access to money and jobs. Both were important in order to secure political allegiance and to compete with SCIRI which controlled local government in most of southern Iraq. Many Mehdi Army members might not be paid directly, but they were given sinecures in the government where the Sadrists were in control. Jobs, handouts and political loyalty went together as in US cities controlled by Irish-American political machines a

century ago. In each neighbourhood in Sadr City there was a
Sadrist office, with a social supervisor in charge of giving
monthly salaries to the very poor. 'I saw a family,' says one
visitor, 'consisting of nine members, the father disabled
because of a car accident and without a breadwinner. All
their money came from Sadr's office, which even paid their
rent. They love Muqtada because he keeps them alive.'

The role of Mehdi Army gunmen is usually emphasised in
explaining the strength of the Sadrists in Baghdad, but
control of ministries was also very important. Manale
Youssif, a thirty-two-year-old woman working in the
Ministry of Health, gives a graphic description of what
Sadrist control had meant at her ministry. 'The main ministry
building is close to Fadel, a Sunni district in central Baghdad,
so all the security guards are from the Sadrist movement,
although Muqtada gave orders from the beginning that jobs
should not only go to his people. But what really happened
was the precise opposite of his instructions. The head of the
Sadr office in Sadr City would send lists of names of people
to be employed to the ministry. There was no place for any
Sunni.' Manale says this is true of other ministries such as
transport, where every Baathist employee was dismissed and
the first jobs available go to a Shia who can claim a martyr in
the family: 'Good jobs go to those with education certificates
and jobs as guards go to those without.' All employees carry
guns and when they are asked by the police if their weapons
are licensed they simply reply: 'It is on the orders of the
Office of the Martyr (Sadr's office).'

Nobody is in doubt who is in control from the moment
they enter the Health Ministry building. 'Before you reach
the reception hall there is a room for searching women,' says
Manale. 'All the women in this room wear the veil, a cloak
and gloves and their perfume is the same that you smell
inside holy shrines. The women doing the searching treat
people who are not from their [Shia] districts with a sort of
arrogance, as if to have revenge for the lack of respect shown
to them in past decades. The same thing happens to men.'[13]

Sunni doctors and medical staff are squeezed out. 'I cannot go to the ministry,' says Mahmoud Qassim, thirty-eight, a Sunni doctor. 'All the Sunni doctors are now working in Sunni districts just as I do now, practising in the Amariya district.'[14] Many Sunnis believe that there is a room in the basement of the health ministry used for torturing Sunni and known as the 'cellar of the guillotine'.

The Iraqi state never recovered from its collapse in 2003. Ministries became rackets for those who controlled them. What looked like much-needed reforms to Iraqi and US embassy officials were often only a new form of corruption in disguise. When new vehicle number plates were introduced the only way to obtain them was by bribery. The same was true of new passports, known as 'G' passports, which were supposedly more secure than the old, but could only be obtained by paying between $500 and $1,000 to a range of officials. Overall the Sadrists were disappointed by their own ministers such as Dr Ali al-Samari, Muqtada's personal doctor, who, on becoming minister of health, stated: 'Our work is professional and I do not want anybody who wears a turban interfering in my work.' This did not go down well with the other Sadrists who, in addition, complained that health services in Sadr City were no better than before. Salim al-Maliki, who was transport minister, attracted criticism of a different sort. He was seen as only 'willing to help those who were close to him' and was much criticised for commandeering a whole plane to take his extended family on pilgrimage.[15]

The Sadrists' brand of Islamic puritanism spread rapidly on the fall of Saddam. 'Before the fall women in Sadr City were both veiled and unveiled,' recalls one woman in Baghdad, 'but on the second day after the fall all women started wearing the veil. I had a friend who was wearing the veil, but not the black cloak until a threatening note was thrown into her house. Her brothers rushed out into the street screaming that whoever had written the note was a coward. Now she is forced to wear a cloak inside Sadr City, though she takes it off when she leaves.'[16] All music and video shops in Sadr City were closed in 2003 and shop owners who insisted on reopening them had their premises burned. It used to be common to hear popular songs blaring from shops and houses in Sadr City, but today the only songs that can be heard are those praising Muqtada. Alcohol stores were closed, though these had already been limited in number during Saddam Hussein's 'Faith' campaign in the 1990s and ownership was confined to Christians.

The Sadrists stood for the separation of men and women rather than the total subjection of women like the Taliban in Afghanistan. Most of the women students in Mustansariyah University were from Sadr City. The Sadrists had their own courts up to 2005 when they were closed because of Muqtada's more conciliatory attitude to the government. While they operated, Manale Youssif, who worked in the Health Ministry, reports they 'heard women's complaints and asserted their rights, particularly in matters of divorce and child custody'. Muqtada's insistence on women wearing the veil was in keeping with the attitude of his father, but did not make much difference in most of southern Iraq where women traditionally wore the veil anyway. 'The Sadrist current,' says Manale, 'gave women the freedom to work, but on one condition – that every woman who wants to work should not mix with men.' Of three Shia religious parties – SCIRI, the Sadrists and Fadhila – she thought SCIRI was the most bigoted against women and Fadhila, which controlled Basra, was the best because many of its leaders were well educated.[17]

It was not only state authority that collapsed after the fall of the old regime. In the universities the staff wholly lost authority over students and did not dare give them low marks or fail their exam papers. 'The professors have no control over the students who openly cheat in front of them,' says Muhammad Tariq, a twenty-five-year-old Sadrist student activist at Mustansariyah University. When one female professor asked a student not to cheat in an exam, he replied chillingly: 'Do you know that the price of a bullet is less than a dinar?' Mustansariyah University on Palestine Street is close to Sadr City and Sunni students and teachers moved from there to Baghdad University. Muhammad Tariq says that the Sadrists tried to stop attacks on Sunni students, but they failed: 'The students who were controlling the situation and the Mehdi Army in the university held religious celebrations like Ashura with black banners and black clothes and threatened to kill anybody who objected.'[18]

The Sadrists had never been social revolutionaries, but their supporters were the millions of impoverished Iraqis whose lives had been destroyed by the disasters of war, insurrection and sanctions that had shattered Iraqi society after 1980. This vast and dangerous underclass had little time for the Iraqi government or its American protectors, but Muqtada felt he had no choice after Najaf but to pursue a political rather than a military strategy. This essentially meant that he did not intend to confront the US military again if he could help it, though the Mehdi Army did not disappear or even contract in size. Its checkpoints were still everywhere in Shia Baghdad and it was a potent weapon in intra-Shia feuding. One event in particular showed the Mehdi Army's continued strength. In August 2005 the Badr Organization in Najaf held a demonstration claiming that Muqtada's staff at one of the few offices he still maintained in the city were secret Baathists. None of the staff was armed under the agreement of a year earlier and they, along with other Sadrists praying near the shrine, were beaten up by Badr militiamen. Muqtada had a habit of either not retaliating at all to a provocation, because he considered the moment inopportune, or retaliating with far more vigour than expected. In this case he chose the latter option and, within hours, some 350 SCIRI offices in Baghdad and across southern Iraq were ablaze. This ability of the Sadrists to mobilise thousands of militiamen was of great importance as Baghdad and central Iraq hurtled, with ever increasing speed, towards a civil war between Shia and Sunni.

CHAPTER FIFTEEN

The Battle of Baghdad

I kept in touch with Bassim Abdul-Rahman, my driver, and Haider al-Safi, my translator and guide, who had nearly been killed with me by the Mehdi Army outside Kufa on 19 April 2004. Bassim continued driving for me occasionally, while Haider left Iraq for London to do a university course, though his family stayed in Baghdad. What happened to both men and the districts they came from vividly illustrates the differing fates of Shia and Sunni in Baghdad as the struggle for control of the city escalated. On 22 February 2006 men in police uniforms tied up the guards at the al-Askari Shia shrine in Samarra and blew it up. This turned the sectarian conflict in the capital into a raging civil war of extraordinary cruelty and bloodiness. I had always admired Bassim for his quiet competence and cool nerve, but after Samarra it had become too dangerous for him as a Sunni to drive in much of Baghdad. The Mehdi Army, by now the generic term used for all Shia militias, was winning the battle for the city. When Bassim picked me up at the airport in the summer of 2006 our journey back to the al-Hamra hotel, where I was staying, took three times as long as usual because he had to take a serpentine route to avoid checkpoints that might be manned by police commandos doubling as Shia death squads. Sometimes it was too dangerous for Bassim and other Sunni working for my newspaper to go home so they had to stay in the hotel overnight. When I went in 2007 to visit Hussein al-Shahristani, the oil minister, his towering ministry building was too deep in Shia-held territory in east Baghdad for a Sunni to go there and I had to find Shia drivers and bodyguards.

For Bassim, as for many Sunni in Baghdad, life had turned into a nightmare. 'I remember very well what happened to all of us when we were in Kufa in April 2004,' recalled Bassim three-and-a-half years later. 'I thought we were dead men at the time and it is a terrible thing to think about.' At the time he was living in a house in part of the Jihad district in south-west Baghdad which was largely Shia, but with some Sunni. Though there was intense fighting in the rest of Baghdad, Jihad was relatively quiet until the Samarra bombing. Afterwards the Mehdi Army began to attack Sunni mosques and houses and many people fled. 'I was thinking of leaving,' says Bassim, 'but I did not have another house to stay in. Frankly, I was confused and decided to stay and I thought that the government would be able to control the situation very soon, but it could not. I decided to go for a short period to Syria with my family and we stayed there from the end of July until the middle of September 2006. When we returned I went to our district and found pictures of Muqtada pasted to the gate of our house. The people who put them there knew that I am a Sunni from Adhamiyah and they asked my neighbours if they knew my new address. I asked my Shia brother-in-law to go to my house in order to gather some stuff like electrical goods and some important identity cards and other documents. He had only managed to pack up the television and some blankets when our neighbours came and warned him to be as quick as he could because if the [Shia] militia came they would stop him or even kill him.'

The house in Jihad was locked and for a time remained empty. Bassim was forced to go to live in one small room in the house of his friend Muhammad, another driver, who lived in Khadra, a wholly Sunni district from which Shia had fled in south-west Baghdad. In this single cramped room Bassim lived with his wife Maha, thirty-nine, and his children Sarah, fourteen, Noor, nine, and Sama, four. 'We used to have information about our house from time to time from my Shia neighbour who told me on 5 June 2007 that it had been taken by the militia. They accused me of being a high-rank officer in the former intelligence service and because of that they got a permit [from al-Sadr's office] to take it over.' Two Shia families moved into Bassim's house for two months and when they left it they took all of his remaining belongings. They left the house unlocked and available for another Shia family to stay in. The permanent loss of his home, his only valuable possession, was a terrible blow to Bassim and Maha. 'I have nothing else to lose aside from my house,' he says, 'and because of what happened I had a heart attack and so did my wife. I worked as a taxi driver for a few days, but I couldn't do it for any longer because of the dangerous situation and I had no other way to make a living. Finally I sold my car and my wife's few gold things and I will try to go to Sweden even if I have to go illegally. It has been a hard decision, but it is the best solution for a family who lost their home through threats.'[1]

Losing his house and his ability to make a living as a driver, the twin disasters which devastated Bassim's life, were common enough occurrences in Baghdad by the fourth year of the war. Both communities were affected, but the Sunni were outnumbered and had more to lose. By the end of 2006 it was obvious that the Shia had won the battle for Baghdad. 'The Mehdi Army dominates 50 per cent of Baghdad and 80 per cent of Shia regions in it,' estimated Hussein Ali, the former commander.[2] At least ten neighbourhoods, which had been mixed a year earlier, were entirely Shia according to residents and Iraqi and American military commanders.[3] The push by the Mehdi Army continued during the so-called surge and by the summer of 2007 the US military estimated that the proportion of Baghdad's population that was Shia had risen from 65 per cent to 75 per cent.[4]

Haider had never much cared for the Sadrists or the Mehdi Army, even before our nerve-racking encounter with them in Kufa. At that time they had little influence in

Kadhimiyah, the predominantly Shia district centred on the shrine of Musa al-Kazim and his grandson Muhammad al-Jawad, the Seventh and Ninth Imams, in north-west Baghdad where he and his family lived. 'They only had one small *husseiniyah* and nobody took them seriously at the beginning,' says Haider. In the first year of the occupation the most influential person in Kadhimiyah was a cleric, Hussein al-Sadr, a distant cousin of Muqtada and a beneficiary of the al-Sadr name, but in every other way the opposite of his revolutionary relatives. Claiming to be only interested in religion and not in politics, he had echoed the regime's pronouncements under Saddam Hussein, but 'he spoke in such a way that implied he was speaking under compulsion. There was also a desperate need for religious leadership in Kadhimiyah at the time.' Al-Sadr's influence was strong enough to prevent looting in the district during the anarchy when Saddam Hussein fell, but afterwards he made a mistake. 'Like most of the political parties, he thought the best way to gain political power was to be close to the Americans,' says Haider. 'His house was fully protected by his followers and he received many of his new American friends there. Like many others he was cultivating the American ruler Paul Bremer and invited him to his home. What really broke the back of his credibility was that he was shown on television stamping his hot kisses on Bremer's cheeks and handing Bremer a holy Koran.' Al-Sadr's influence waned and was replaced by that of the followers of his cousin Muqtada and the Mehdi Army. The other two religious parties, SCIRI and Dawa, had never been very strong in Kadhimiyah. SCIRI tried to take over the shrine and the area around it, but failed. Dawa, though it once had many followers in the area during Sadr I, was always a small party of the highly religious and well-educated elite.

Kadhimiyah was not natural Sadrist territory, even though Muqtada's family came from there. It is surprising but instructive to see how the Mehdi Army was able to take over in the following years. More prosperous than Sadr City, it had never been the home of the impoverished underclass which was the main constituency of the Sadrists. Its people were generally well educated and famous for their solidarity against outsiders. 'But during the high point of Hussein al-Sadr's power,' recalls Haider, 'the Sadrists succeeded in attracting young guys by opposing the occupation. Their influence increased day by day and they started to control Kadhimiyah with checkpoints everywhere and militants in black clothes searching people's cars. The Mehdi Army started opening Sadrist offices, called after Muqtada's father, using the houses of Baath party members or just empty houses all over Kadhimiyah. They made patrols everywhere and recruited unemployed guys. In order to finance the huge number of people they had on their payroll they started to collect fees for protection from every house, particularly from those with the better houses.' Many people locally were dubious about the presence of the Mehdi Army and many of those coming into Kadhimiyah were from two neighbouring strongholds of the Sadrists in the districts of Shuala and Hurriya. As savage sectarian warfare spread through Baghdad people in Kadhimiyah felt that 'if they had to choose between the *salafi* and the Mehdi Army, then they would choose the Mehdi Army'.

When the US 'surge' started in February 2007 it was partly directed at breaking the grip of the Mehdi Army over much of Baghdad. What happened in Kadhimiyah is an example of why it did not entirely succeed. Muqtada, as we have seen, was particularly good at dodging a punch and, ever since the second battle of Najaf, was determined to avoid an outright military confrontation with the US army. The Mehdi Army, far larger, better trained and better equipped than in 2004, was stood down and its commanders sent out of Baghdad. Militants blended back into the civilian population. Haider described the events that followed: 'After the "surge" began, most of the Sadrist militants left Kadhimiyah and took down signs outside the Sadrist offices, but the Americans started raiding these houses anyway and arresting anybody there. They checked every single house in our area and gave my mother a phone number to call if she had any information about the Mehdi Army. Essentially Kadhimiyah remained under the control of the Mehdi militia, but Hussein al-Sadr still had some influence there [By another account he did a deal whereby the Mehdi Army came in as a protection force on condition they did not harm local Sunnis.] He has his own protection force which is a battalion from the Iraqi army. The Sadrists kept a very low profile during the whole period of the "surge" and didn't resist the Americans. The Mehdi Army seemed determined to avoid any confrontation with them.'[5]

Haider believed that the retreat of the Sadrists was temporary and deceptive, and beneath the surface they were still in command. One sign of this came in August 2007 when there were serious clashes in Kerbala during the Shaaban pilgrimage when the Mehdi Army fought SCIRI (now renamed the Supreme Islamic Iraqi Council – SIIC). 'What happened showed the power of the Sadrists, not only in the government, but also in controlling the streets. When the fighting started in Kerbala they immediately burned three offices of SCIRI in Kadhimiyah. Car loads of militants came from different directions, took over the offices and arrested everybody who was there.'

President Bush was later to speak as if Sunni–Shia warfare started with the bombing of the Samarra shrine in 2006. In reality suicide bombings clearly targeting Shia because they were Shia had begun at least as early as March 2004 when 270 Shia pilgrims were killed during religious celebrations in Kadhimiyah and Kerbala. Grand Ayatollah Ali al-Sistani counselled against retaliation as a matter of principle and because the Shia leaders saw the suicide bombings as an attempt to torpedo their plan to take power legally through elections in 2005. When organised Shia retaliation did occur it came after the first Shia government was formed in May 2005 and was carried out by the Shia-dominated police and police commandos. They dragged former Baathists from their houses in broad daylight and left their tortured corpses beside the road a few days later. Seldom have death squads operated so openly. The relentless suicide bombings and assassinations carried out by al-Qaida in Iraq progressively infuriated the Shia community as a whole. Mixed districts in Baghdad were becoming less mixed. Excluded from power, the Sunni felt they had no choice but to fight. The Shia, for their part, believed they had been patient for far too long against a merciless assault on their community. By early 2006 it only needed a particularly spectacular bombing or assassination against a Shia target to trigger massive and bloody retaliation.

Many people expected an explosion of Shia rage but it was shocking when it came in the hours after the attack on the shrine in Samarra in February 2006. Mehdi Army commanders say they tried and failed to calm their people down. 'As news spread of the Samarra bombing there was an explosion of rage among the people,' says Sheikh Ali, a militia leader. 'I was in the market at the time and I saw one young man who was so angry that he began to smash things inside his own shop. A group of youths ran towards a *husseiniyah* which opened its doors and began to distribute light weapons so they could march on Samarra to fight. But a group of older men came, closed the *husseiniyah* doors and screamed at the youths to go away and not to act individually. One of them shouted at the angry crowd: 'Wait for orders from Muqtada.' Al-Sadr was in Saudi Arabia en route from Lebanon and had to cut short his visit to come back to Baghdad. We were under orders to stay calm, but we couldn't control the angry crowds of young men who went to the *husseiniyahs* shouting: 'Do something! We want to go to Samarra! Give us guns!' Even women were marching and screaming. Youths started advancing on Sunni mosques and killing people just because they were Sunni. They were dragging people out of cars in Palestine Street and slaughtering them.' Sheikh Ali says that the Mehdi Army did not have the kind of organisation that could restore order.

'We could not control the situation because we are a popular movement without a salaried staff. When people went to the Sadrist leader in a district and he did not agree with an attack on Sunni mosques they would leave him saying he was a coward and feeling let down.'[6]

Some 1,300 people, mostly Sunni, were killed in the next few days and this was only the beginning of the butchery that was to increase every month up to December. 'Armed men of the Mehdi Army took over the al-Neda'a mosque in al-Adhamiyah near Palestine Street, but it was empty because the Imam and [Sunni] worshippers had fled,' says one commander. 'They gave orders to burn cars and take away Sunnis in cars to the Sada region on the edge of Sadr City, where they were killed and their bodies thrown into the street. Muqtada gave orders for this to stop but nobody responded.'[7] All communities in Baghdad and central Iraq began to organise themselves for self-defence, which was not difficult in a city where everybody is armed. In the mixed Hamraa district in west Baghdad Sunni families prepared themselves for an assault from the Shia Hi Ameel district and the call to arms came from the mosques at 11 p.m. as the Shia militiamen began to enter the area in their cars. People shot from the roofs of the houses for ten minutes. The police arrived, saying they were there to protect Hamraa and asking for a ceasefire, but nobody obeyed them because they believed the police were cooperating with the Mehdi Army. The shooting went on until the mosques said the militiamen had retreated. Soon afterwards Sunni gunmen attacked a big Shia *husseiniyah* in Hamraa but were driven off by its armed guards. One of the attackers accidentally dropped his mobile phone which was later found by the Mehdi Army. 'The phone rang and one of their men answered it,' says an eyewitness. 'The caller was the attacker's wife who was asking for him and mentioned his name, which was that of a former army officer and a Sunni living in the neighbouring Yarmouk district. Several days later we heard that the Mehdi Army killed him.'[8]

Each community saw itself as a victim, its own acts of violence understandable retaliation for atrocities committed against it. There was little pity for the other side, and Shia as well as Sunni saw themselves as fighting for survival. Salim Shehab, the Shia student from the Jadidah district in east Baghdad, had a Sunni woman friend called Bida'a who was compelled to flee her house in the Hurriya district after the Samarra bombing. 'She was forced to leave her home but she was allowed to take her furniture,' he says. 'The Sunni were expelling Shia from their homes without letting them take anything with them.' He believes that Sunni families had often left their homes before they were threatened and later falsely claimed, 'We have been expelled from our houses.' Of course, there were many people who sensibly ran away before they were threatened or killed without any prior warning. A pervasive sense of terror settled over Baghdad and central Iraq as people who had lived together for decades began to kill each other or identify targets for the death squads.

The Mehdi Army and all other militias, including the Sunni insurgents, were strengthened because everybody wanted security and the state could not provide it. Baghdad broke up into dozens of warring townships that began to exchange mortar and rocket fire. People in flight often looked to the militias for help and protection. Given that by the summer of 2007 there were some 2.2 million Iraqis internally displaced within the country, the growth of this refugee population helped the militias expand their authority. People became deeply suspicious of any strange face or car in their district. For instance Salim Shehab describes a Shia man, who, after being shot at in the street by two Sunni gunmen, fled with his wife and four children to the Shia part of Hai al-Jihad (from which Bassim had fled intimidated). Having rented a house from an expelled Sunni family, he contacted one of the leaders of the Mehdi Army in his district who was called Abu Aya. He told him he was a Shia, described what had happened to him and asked for permission to stay in al-

Jihad. Abu Aya listened and told him reassuringly: 'If anybody asks what you are doing here just say you know Abu Aya.' Several days later some Mehdi Army militiamen picked up his fourteen-year-old son Alaa in the street. He was dark-skinned enough to be from the south and therefore a Shia, but they were suspicious of him because they did not know him and beat him up. He mentioned that he knew Abu Aya, but the beating continued until they finally decided he was telling the truth and released him. When he returned home his father complained to Abu Aya who sent the young militiamen to a local building called 'the House of Happiness'. 'Inside this house,' reports Shehab with grim approval, 'Abu Aya punishes Mehdi Army young men who do not obey his orders. You could hear screams of pain from it because they were tortured. For more serious offences he would sometimes send them to Najaf.'[9]

Each community had isolated enclaves that were too small to be defended. The Shia majority controlled the police, the police commandos and part of the army. The majority of the dreadful harvest of bodies found dumped in the streets every morning in Baghdad were Sunni, often people picked up at police or Mehdi Army checkpoints. The main form of Sunni retaliation was vehicle-borne suicide bombs exploded in crowded Shia markets or in places where labourers would gather early in the morning to look for work. On the outskirts of Baghdad it was usually the Sunni who were in the ascendancy because their gunmen controlled all the roads radiating out of Baghdad. Shia workers on their way to work in the capital were regularly slaughtered there.

How far did the Mehdi Army foster the Shia death squads? Muqtada decried sectarian killings and declared that the priority was to end the US occupation of Iraq, but did he covertly allow his movement to take the lead in sectarian cleansing as all Sunni were convinced he did? Iraq had become such an extraordinarily dangerous place for any reporter that it was impossible to get a clear picture. While

Bush and Blair were absurdly denying that a civil war was
taking place there, hundreds of local civil wars were erupting
in central Iraq, turning every village, town and city district
into a battlefield. These bloody conflicts were difficult to
follow because of the paucity of information and the
complexity of Iraq's sectarian mosaic. I was in touch by email
and phone with Shia leaders in the isolated town of Balad
north of Baghdad, which was one of the few Shia outposts in
this predominantly Sunni region. My informants sent me
highly detailed accounts of what was happening which,
though sometimes difficult to follow because they assumed
encyclopaedic knowledge on my part of the local sectarian
and tribal geography, conveyed the flavour of this time of
atrocity and counter-atrocity.

The killings in this area had started with Shia labourers
from Balad who were working in the Sunni town of
Dhulu'iya a few miles away on the other side of the Tigris
river. Elsewhere in the nearby towns of Taji and Sabaa al-
Bour individual Shia were also being picked up, their heads
cut off and their bodies thrown into the Tigris river. 'After
the beheadings,' said my informant, who was a tribal leader
in Balad, 'a local militia was formed to counter the increasing
attacks. The people involved were mostly those families
whose members had been killed.' The nearest large Shia
community which might aid those besieged in Balad was in
Kadhimiyah. The leaders in Balad 'contacted Sayyid Hazem
and Ba'haa al-Arrajy in Kadhimiyah, both clerics linked to
[Muqtada] al-Sadr's movement. The clerics had expressed
sympathy for armed groups, but had declined to join the
Mehdi Army or give any support for reprisals against
innocent Sunni civilians. This was part of an agreement with
Ayatollah Hussein al-Sadr in Kadhimiyah whereby the Mehdi
Army was allowed to guard the shrine area on the condition
that no innocent person was targeted.'[10]

Between the besieged town of Balad and north Baghdad
was the Taji area which was mostly Sunni, but with some
Shia who had set up their own militia. 'The militiamen were

known to be the sons of locals with no connection to the Mehdi Army. One day they stopped a minivan full of Sunni civilians and slaughtered them. As an act of reprisal the Sunni decided to attack Balad, despite the fact that those who had killed the Sunni were from Taji. The Sunni put Balad under siege, sabotaging the water, sewage and electricity systems and stopping food getting in.' The Shia in the town were by now becoming hysterical with fear and my contact in Balad was worried that the systematic sabotage of the utilities in his town and the overall sophistication of the Sunni strategy meant that 'we may witness the first sectarian cleansing of a town as big as Balad'. He accused the Americans in their enormous airbase at Balad of doing nothing. 'When the Mehdi Army and local volunteers tried to break the siege by attacking north from Kadhimiyah and Taji, they were bombed by US helicopter gunships which inflicted heavy losses on them in the outskirts of northern Baghdad.' The Shia fled to northern Baghdad where they were given food and water. Then in October 2006 the refugees learned they could go home because the Mehdi Army had now taken over Sabaa al-Bour.[11] Anger at American attacks on what the Shia saw as purely defensive measures by their local militiamen reveals a fear on the Shia side – this was long before the Sunni tribes in Anbar started allying themselves with American forces to fight al-Qaida in Iraq in 2007 – that the Americans were changing sides and starting to back the Sunni against them.[12]

The Sunni population of Iraq almost universally blamed Muqtada and the Mehdi Army for any sectarian attack on them. The Mehdi Army was used as a generic term to refer to any Shia militia. Yet many of the militiamen who formally acknowledged Muqtada's leadership had no intention of accepting his orders. The Mehdi Army had always had a loose structure and its fighters were largely unpaid. Units often had their origin in locally raised vigilante groups which were never amenable to discipline from the centre. And as the sectarian war got bloodier, local commanders became more independent and more powerful. Muqtada himself stoutly denied that the Mehdi Army, as he conceived it, was involved in sectarian killings and that his name was being misused to give the killers an alibi. He complained that 'death squads that say they kill on behalf of the Mehdi Army are trying to destroy us and divide us and prevent us from raising arms against the forces of occupation. Criminals are using my name as cover for their actions.' He added that the Mehdi Army had been dragged into sectarian fighting when trying to defend Shia pilgrims from Sunni gunmen on the road between Baghdad and Kerbala. 'They were killing anyone called Haider or Hussein or Karrar, [in fact] anyone with a Shia name,' he said. 'The Mehdi Army wanted to defend these innocent people.'[13]

A convincing account of the relationship between the death squads, the Mehdi Army, Muqtada and the Sadrist movement as a whole was given by a Mehdi Army member and self-confessed death-squad leader called Abu Kamael in Jordan at the end of 2006. A lawyer by training, he said he had fled to Amman earlier in the year after being threatened by other death-squad members because he had objected to one proposed killing. On the overall objective of the campaign he admits: 'It was very simple, we were ethnically cleansing. Anyone Sunni was guilty: if you were called Omar, Uthman, Zayed, Sufian or something like that, then you would be killed. These are Sunni names and you are killed according to identity.' Sometimes the killings were in retaliation to Sunni attacks and sometimes they were in implementation of a death sentence by a Sadrist religious court. 'The Mehdi Army is supposed to kill only Baathists, Takfiris [Sunni fanatics who do not regard Shia as Muslims], those who cooperate with the occupation and the occupation troops,' says Abu Kamael. 'It does not always happen like that though and it can turn into a mafia gang.' As with the confiscation of the house of Bassim Abdul-Rahman, my former driver, it was easy enough to label a Sunni whose property somebody else wanted as a Baathist official and take it. At the time Abu Kamael estimated that the Mehdi Army was killing thirty Sunni a day. In September 2006 alone 3,539 Iraqi security forces and civilians were killed.[14]

Abu Kamael did not believe that Muqtada personally agreed with the murder campaign being carried out in his name. 'Sadr was sometimes surprised by the actions of his soldiers. He had banned the killing of any Baathist or Iraqi unless there was evidence that they had blood on their hands. There are hundreds of thousand of fighters and office workers, how can he possibly know what they are doing all day? Sadr is trying to impose control, he is trying to imbue religious values in the soldiers, make them learn the Quran and the Hadiths. Only God knows if this will be successful. In my opinion, the political wing of the Sadr line is being weakened by the worsening security situation. Those who refused the political way are saying, "We were right". The arrests of Sadr figures and the [US military] missions against Sadr City are seen as evidence that politics are failing.'[15]

Other Mehdi Army leaders of death squads had no qualms over what they were doing. Abu Rusil, previously a taxi driver in the Hai al-Salaam district which was formerly mixed, would leave a note on the bodies of dead Sunni saying 'best regards'. 'There is no innocent Sunni,' he said, claiming that his brother had been shot dead at a Sunni checkpoint. Abu Rusil's victims are found with drill holes in their bodies, their bones smashed by being pounded with gas canisters and their hands and feet pierced by nails. Once a poor man, the death-squad leader preyed on his victims, confiscating their goods. He now has a house and three sports utility vehicles, and consequently an incentive for the killing to go on. It would only end, Abu Rusil said, when every Sunni had left the country and Muqtada al-Sadr was ruler of Iraq. 'The Mehdi Army will lead the revolution in Iraq as Imam Khomeini did in Iran,' he predicted. He candidly admitted going to Iran eight times for training and said all the Mehdi Army's weapons aside from their AK-47s were supplied by the Iranians. Other arms, such as rocket-propelled grenade-launchers and improvised explosives devices, came from the Iraqi security forces, he said. On occasion his men wore army and police uniforms. Overall Abu Rusil was typical of the district warlords thrown up by the sectarian warfare after Samarra. Pledging loyalty to the distant figure of Muqtada his gunmen were wholly controlled by himself and killed any Shia who criticised his actions.[16] But the revolution he had in mind would be a purely sectarian one. Iraq was breaking up. Sunni, Shia and Kurds could no longer live in the same street.

CHAPTER SIXTEEN

Muqtada and the Surge

Muqtada was feeling under attack from all sides. 'I am being described as Azrael, the angel of death, as if I was the cause of all the killing in Iraq,' he complained to a group of supporters who visited him.[1] To other Iraqis and the outside world he might have looked like the kingmaker of Iraq with a powerful militia at his command. But Muqtada saw himself as surrounded by enemies. 'I have transferred my family to a safe place,' he told an interviewer in January 2007. 'I have even made my will, and I move around constantly, acting in such a way that only a very few people know exactly where I am.' Others might see the Mehdi Army as infiltrating the Iraqi police and army and thereby knowing every move of the US army before it was made, but Muqtada took a far gloomier view. 'The exact opposite is true,' he said. 'It is our militia group that is crawling with spies. Of course, it does not take much to infiltrate a grass-roots army.' He said there were no less than four armies ready to move against his movement: the US army, the Kurdish *peshmerga*, the private army of Iyad Allawi, the former Iraqi prime minister, and a 'shadow army', Iraqi troops trained by the US military in the Jordanian desert. The reference to Allawi, who had no militia, is mysterious, but, if by the 'shadow army' Muqtada meant Iraqi army units wholly under the control of the US, these certainly existed. The US criticised the Iraqi prime minister Nouri al-Maliki for not acting firmly enough against the Sadrists because his majority in parliament depended on them, but Muqtada suspected treachery from his ally. 'Between myself and [Maliki] there has never been much sympathy,' he admitted frankly. 'I have always suspected that he was being manipulated, and I have never trusted him. We have met only on a couple of occasions. At our last meeting he told me: "You are the country's backbone," and then he confessed that he was "obliged" to fight us. Obliged! Can you believe it?' The crackdown had already begun: 'They arrested over 400 of my people last night. We will not put up any resistance for the time being.' He repeated vigorously that there was just one long-term solution to the crisis in Iraq: 'An immediate American withdrawal.'[2]

Muqtada's outrage at Maliki's two-faced attitude to his movement was understandable. It was the Sadrists who had, in effect, made him prime minister in May 2006 after the Americans had turned decisively against his predecessor Ibrahim al-Jaafari, the leader of the Dawa party. While outwardly treating the Iraqi administration as sovereign, Washington was brutal in asserting its authority in private. It threw its weight against Jaafari, partly because of his good relationship with the Sadrists, and in favour of Adel Abdul Mehdi, the chosen candidate of SCIRI. The US ambassador Zalmay Khalilzad was told to inform SCIRI's leader Abdul Aziz al-Hakim that Bush 'doesn't want, doesn't support, and doesn't accept' that Jaafari should lead the next government.[3] It was Muqtada's influence which had kept Abdul Mehdi out of the prime minister's office and led the Shia coalition, the United Iraqi Alliance, to select Maliki, for many years Dawa's representative in Damascus, as a compromise candidate. At the time Maliki was chosen, he was so obscure that the US embassy was not even sure of his real name (like many opponents of Saddam Hussein he had operated under a pseudonym). But, from the moment he was appointed, he was under constant pressure from Washington to clamp down on Muqtada and his movement. This was justified by the pretence that all militias in Iraq were to be dissolved, though this was not going to affect the powerful armed wings of the

Kurdish parties and SCIRI, friendly to the US, which operated under the guise of being part of the Iraqi security services.

Maliki was squeezed between the US and the Sadrists and, though he had responsibility, he had limited real power. The Iraqi government was far less independent than it looked and its authority over security was seriously curtailed. Its intelligence service, the Iraqi National Intelligence Service (INIS) under General Muhammad al-Shahwani, was still openly funded and controlled by the CIA ('What! Are all our secret agents volunteers?' exclaimed an Iraqi member of parliament on discovering that funding for INIS does not appear in the Iraqi budget).[4] Al-Maliki declared ruefully that he could not move a company of troops without American permission. One Iraqi army commander who obeyed an order from the prime minister, without getting approval from the Americans first, was promptly dismissed and imprisoned by the US military.[5] Ultimately dependent on the US, Maliki was always likely to come out against Muqtada though he tried to avoid making a choice between them as long as possible.

Washington never deviated from its deep hostility to Muqtada, though the battles for Najaf in April and August 2004 made the US wary of confronting him again. But on 10 January 2007 President Bush surprised the world by announcing that he was going to escalate American involvement in Iraq by sending over 20,000 US soldiers as reinforcements. Spelling out the new direction of US policy in the State of the Union Address on 23 January, Bush gave priority to regaining control of Baghdad. It was a move which was bound to affect the Mehdi Army who were now emerging as the winners in the battle for the city. Ominously for the Sadrists, Bush spoke of 'an escalating danger from Shia extremists', who, he claimed, were just as hostile to the US as Osama bin Laden. He also targeted Iran which was 'funding and arming terrorists' and asserted that 'Shia and Sunni extremists are different faces of the same totalitarian threat'.[6] The Sadrists were evidently going to be one of the targets of the 'surge', though the US military in Iraq was more chary than the White

House of taking on a new enemy in Iraq. Muqtada thought the US was trying to provoke him into armed confrontation. Predictably, he announced that his militiamen would not resist US forces and he even supported negotiations aimed at easing US deployment in Sadrist strongholds.

Muqtada's followers admit that they came under intense pressure. They might control most of the Baghdad police, but there were also Iraqi military units that obeyed the US military and were known in Sadr City as 'the dirty squad'. 'Many arrests have occurred as a result of the dirty squad,' says Hussein Ali, the Mehdi Army leader who was planning to leave the country because he believed he was in danger of assassination by a pro-Iranian faction of the militia. 'It consists of Iraqi army soldiers supervised and under the orders of the Americans. They understand Iraqi society and know how to deal with people. They come to Sadr City, or any other Shia district, moving from house to house, sometimes shooting innocent people and supported by US helicopters.' When the Mehdi Army returned fire it was in response to raids and arrests by US forces. 'Most young people do not stay in their homes at night because if the Americans arrest one of us they will never release him.'

Mehdi Army commanders were ordered to go deep under cover or leave Baghdad. Media attention was focused on their departure, but in reality Muqtada was most interested in preserving his political lieutenants, the militant clerics often referred to collectively as the 'sheikhs', who were the cadres for his movement. These were usually clerics of his own age, some of whom had worked with his father, who were influential in different parts of Iraq. Their importance often determined the extent to which the Sadrists controlled the local Shia community. 'Muqtada had sent an order to the Sheikhs to "save themselves" because he greatly depended on them and did not want to lose them,' says Hussein Ali. This happened not only in Baghdad, but in Shia cities like Diwaniyah in the south. The most important Sheikhs acting on his behalf at this period were Saheb Ismail Hwade,

Baquer al-Moubarqa, Ali Smaism, Ahmed al-Sheibani and Abdel Hadi al-Daraji. Daraji was arrested on 19 January and accused of being involved in death-squad activity, as was Ali Smaism, though both men were released later in the year. 'These Sheikhs are very important because they were the main operational leaders of the movement and sometimes took Muqtada's place in issuing instructions,' says Hussein Ali.[7] He often moved them around but they were central to ensuring that the movement would be able to regenerate itself however many of its militants were arrested or killed.

Muqtada believed that the US government wanted to eliminate him if it could do so without provoking a political explosion from the Shia. His suspicions are scarcely surprising given that most of his close family had been killed by Saddam Hussein and he was conviced that the Americans had deliberately set him up to be killed or arrested in Najaf in August 2004. Just as he did after the second battle of Najaf, Muqtada now disappeared from view and was not seen again in public until four months later.

Exactly where he was concealed during this period became a topic of rancorous dispute. American sources swiftly claimed he had fled to Iran, a story which fitted in with Washington's scenario that the Sadrists were creatures of Tehran. The aim was to puncture Muqtada's credibility as an Iraqi nationalist. Obvious though the propaganda was behind these allegations, this does not necessarily mean they were untrue. But his closest lieutenants, including some who later left the movement, say they are certain that Muqtada stayed in his house in Najaf all this time. 'He did not go anywhere,' says Hussein Ali. 'But the Americans spread the rumour he had left the country because they feared a big reaction from Sadr's offices after there were so many arrests. Their aim was to reduce his authority so people would not obey his instructions, though in fact he was in Najaf all the time.'[8] On the street supporters of Muqtada stridently denied he was in Iran and sang songs about how he was still in Iraq. At the entrance to the Valley of Peace cemetery in Najaf, where so many Mehdi Army volunteers had fought and died in 2004, some small kiosks had been set up selling cassette tapes of religious songs. One of the most popular of these, which was widely played during the months of his disappearance, spoke of how he would never leave Iraq.

There was a further reason why Muqtada may have wanted to go underground at this time. After vastly expanding in the previous two years, the Mehdi Army was riven by factions and had become the label attached to every Shia vigilante or criminal gang or units controlled by Iran. 'Muqtada did not disappear,' says Hussein Ali, 'but since his orders weren't implemented by his followers who began to co-operate with Iran he stayed in his house and did not meet anyone. Muqtada gave the prime minister Nouri al-Maliki a list of 450 names to arrest because they were criminals.'[9] If Muqtada was allowing the Iraqi government forces backed by the US to purge the Mehdi Army of gangsters and sectarian killers, this alone would be a reason for him to hide. There were those who believed that differences between Muqtada and Maliki were publicly exaggerated by the former to conceal from the Americans the extent of their covert co-operation. Maliki himself, after all, belonged to the Damascus wing of Dawa which had been founded by Muqtada's father-in-law, Muhammad Baqir al-Sadr. One of Maliki's senior government officials in Baghdad said Maliki 'emulated Muhammad [Baqir] al-Sadr as a father figure and he is loyal to the movement and his memory'. He added that three months earlier, on 14 February 2007, when the Americans began to implement their 'Baghdad Security Plan', 'the prime minister urged Muqtada to make sure that his ten most vulnerable security people could not be found' or arrested. The official was contemptuous of reports that Muqtada had left Iraq. 'We heard these reports on CNN and Fox News that Muqtada had 'fled' to Tehran and we laughed. They are gullible, for they have received this from the White House. Muqtada going to Iran! He would do no such thing. Do you believe we are afraid of the Americans? Are they worse than

Saddam? If Muqtada went into exile it would be a repud-
iation of his family. This he would not do.' The official said
that the Americans did not understand the Iraqi prime
minister's loyalties or political background. 'We are con-
tinuously asked, "Do we support Muqtada al-Sadr?" ' said the
official. 'It is as if the Americans had never looked at our website. His [father-in-law and cousin Muhammad Baqir al-Sadr's]
picture is right there. His sermons are right there. Do you think
that we would forget this part of our glorious history?'[10]

The question was rhetorical but many Sadrists were,
indeed, convinced that Maliki and his supporters had
forgotten their Iraqi roots and were now puppets of the
Americans. This was why in December 2006 Muqtada had
'frozen' his ministers' participation in the government, giving
as his reason that Maliki had met President Bush in Jordan
without demanding an American withdrawal. It was a
pattern that was to continue through 2007 with the Sadrists
pulling out of government, announcing their return, withdrawing from the United Iraqi Alliance Shia coalition, but
somehow not voting the government out of office in parliament. Even to the most cynical Iraqi political observers it was
never clear who was two-timing whom. Contradictory
allegiances were not just the outcome of the byzantine and
treacherous nature of Iraqi politics, but of the muddled and
contradictory nature of American policy in Iraq. Washington
was trying to create a strong Iraqi government to replace
Saddam, but was also trying to marginalise the Sadrists who
provided the government with its popular base in so far as it
had one. A so-called 'moderate' Iraqi government shorn of its
Sadrist wing, consisting of the Kurds, SCIRI, Dawa, the
Sunni Iraqi Islamic Party and Iyad Allawi, a scenario which
was the dream of some US officials, would have had even less
legitimacy in the eyes of Iraqi Arabs than its predecessors.

There was a second contradictory element in US policy to
which Iraqi politicians had to accommodate themselves. In
the course of 2007 the US became increasingly confrontational with Iran and edged towards air strikes against

Iranian nuclear facilities. Iran was demonised, as Saddam Hussein had once been, as the dark and secret force behind every act of hostility towards the US. This was a more peculiar policy than the American public ever realised. Paradoxically, Iran – in contrast to Saudi Arabia, Egypt, Jordan and the Sunni Arab states – supported the Shia–Kurdish government in Baghdad. 'This government is as good as it is going to get for them,' Hoshyar Zebari, the Iraqi Foreign Minister, told me.[11] The US confrontation with Iran and accusations that it was funding and arming anti-American insurgents was self-fulfilling. The more Tehran feared an American attack, the more it had an incentive to prepare a potential counter-stroke in Iraq. On a visit to Washington in October 2007 Mowaffaq al-Rubai'e, the Iraqi National Security Adviser, pleaded with his audience not to attack Iran, saying there should be 'absolutely no – big fat no, N–O – bombing of Iran. They will react against us. They will not come to New York. They will not come to Washington. They will come to us, I can tell you that, and we will be in big, big trouble.' He said that there were already signs in late 2007, as US–Iranian relations became even frostier, that more modern weapons – such as upgraded grenade launchers and roadside bombs – were being supplied by Iran to Shia militiamen.[12]

Muqtada had a further important reason for keeping his distance from the Iraqi government while at the same time not severing his links to it. Isolated in the Green Zone in Baghdad, the Iraqi administration was almost universally loathed by Iraqis because of its failure to provide security or the basics of life such as rations, electricity and clean water. American politicians and the foreign media focused too exclusively on war and the number killed as the sole indicators of what was wrong in Iraq. Too little attention was paid to other failures, such as the collapse of the food rationing system, which reduced the millions of Iraqis to a life of malnutrition and near starvation. By the end of 2007 food rations were half what they had been under Saddam

Hussein four years earlier. Some five million Iraqis depended on the state-subsidised ration to survive, but two million of these people were no longer being fed because they had been forced to flee their homes. 'It is rare to find items such as baby formula among rationed food,' said Muhammad Ala'a Jabber, director of the west Baghdad office responsible for the delivery of food rations. 'This never happened under Saddam Hussein's regime when it was common to see an abundance of baby formula. The rice which is available is of bad quality and the beans might require hours to cook. The quantity of flour and tea given to each family has decreased and at least 20 per cent of families in search of food rations return home empty-handed.' Iraq was filled with more and more utterly desperate people. 'I've had a delay in my food ration for more than two months,' said Abu Akram, a father of four in Baghdad. 'My children are sick, suffering from malnutrition and I'm unemployed. I don't know where to go to get money to feed them.'[13]

Outside the fortifications of the Green Zone, Iraqi society was dissolving. Three-quarters of doctors, pharmacists and nurses had left their jobs and half had fled abroad. It was becoming impossible to find even simple medicines in Baghdad. A cholera epidemic had started in Sulaimaniyah and was spreading to the rest of the country. The misery of people living in central Iraq – and the 4.2 million people who had fled within Iraq, or to Syria and Jordan, mostly came from this area – began to equal that of sub-Saharan Africa. The difference was that Iraq was still a rich country in terms of oil revenue, much of which was unspent. (This was why foreign aid donors were unwilling to fund programmes in Iraq because they did not see why the Iraqi finance ministry should not provide the money.) Not surprisingly, the political class that had flourished in the post-Saddam era was regarded with general hatred. One of the most spirited denunciations of this governing elite came from Ayatollah Sheikh Muhammad al-Yaqubi, the lieutenant of Sadr II who had refused to follow Muqtada in 2003 and had set up the

Fadhila party which was the main authority in Basra and had fifteen members of parliament. Given his reputation for moderation, al-Yaqubi's scathing attack on the failings of the returned exiles who had taken power in Iraq was particularly telling. It is worth quoting at length because it shows Iraqis' true attitude to politicians who were treated with respect by presidents and prime ministers abroad during their frequent foreign trips. Speaking from Najaf, al-Yaqubi said the returned exiles 'set out to plunder and greedily fill their pockets and [bank] accounts and those of their followers with no efforts to serve people and rebuild the country; they have cocooned themselves inside the Green Zone and have not mingled with the people or experienced their hardships'.[14]

Muqtada reappeared on 25 May 2007 travelling in a long motorcade from Najaf to Kufa to deliver his Friday sermon to 6,000 worshippers. He began with an elaboration on his father's traditional chant: 'No, no to Satan! No, no to America! No, no to the occupation! No, no to Israel!' He repeated his demand for the US to leave Iraq. 'We demand the withdrawal of the occupation forces, or the creation of a timetable for such a withdrawal,' he said.' I call upon the Iraqi government not to extend the occupation by even a single day.' He also denounced sectarianism saying he was ready to cooperate with Sunni Arabs 'on all issues', adding, 'It is prohibited to spill the blood of Sunnis and Christians. They are our brothers, either in religion or in the homeland.'[15]

There were signs during the summer of 2007 that Muqtada was regaining control over the Mehdi Army. It had largely, but not entirely, obeyed his instructions not to put up armed resistance to 'the surge'. There were other signs of a centralised authority in command. When on 13 June 2007 two minarets that remained standing after the earlier attack by Sunni on the al-Askari shrine in Samarra were toppled by twin bomb blasts, Baghdad braced itself for a furious reaction from the Mehdi Army. Muqtada called for restraint and ordered that there must be no attacks on Sunni mosques. This time he was obeyed. 'Muqtada's full control of the

Mehdi Army was shown after the second bombing of Samarra in June,' claims a Sadrist militant. 'First, he called for a peaceful march on Samarra and all his followers prepared to go. But when the Sadrist offices called it off, everybody followed his order. No one went and nobody even discussed the change in our instructions.'[16] His followers may exaggerate the degree of his success in asserting control over his militiamen, but it was certainly greater than a year earlier. 'Muqtada al-Sadr's recent move to control and centralize his Mahdi Army appears to be working,' wrote Babak Rahimi, an academic specialist on the Iraqi Shia, 'and his immediate call for restraint after the second attack indicates the extent to which he has successfully gained control over his militia since his reappearance in May – or perhaps earlier this spring.'[17] The split in the Sunni insurgency between al-Qaida in Iraq and the Sunni tribes, along with other more nationalist anti-American groups, encouraged Muqtada to stress his nationalist programme. Shia hatred of the Sunni was no longer being reinforced every few days in Baghdad by car bombs in the middle of crowds. 'The enemy of all Islam has become the Takfir [Sunni extremists who declare Shia to be infidels],' Muqtada told Iraqi television. 'Before they were killing Shiites with their car bombs. Now they are killing Sunni with their car bombs. They have become a common enemy.' He rejected any negotiations with the Americans as had been proposed by Lieutenant General Raymond Odierno, the American second-in-command in Iraq. 'I refuse any sit-down with the occupation, whether in Iraq or outside.'[18] His aides said Muqtada wanted a nationalist front of Sunni and Shia against all 'foreign elements' in Iraq with al-Qaida being considered equally as enemies.[19]

At the beginning of the year Muqtada had spoken of four armies preparing to attack him: the Americans, the Kurds, Iyad Allawi's forces and a 'shadow army' of Iraqis under US control. Strangely, he did not mention a fifth army that posed far more of a threat to him than any of the others. This was the Badr Organization, the military wing of SIIC, previously SCIRI, the party which was the traditional rival of the Sadrists as the political voice of the Shia of Iraq. There had been clashes between the two movements since 2004 and by 2007 the conflict was turning into all-out war. SIIC had many political and military assets: it was a dominant force in the Interior Ministry in Baghdad and controlled most of the provincial councils in southern Iraq. Its supporters also made up much of the police forces in the south. Ever since the second battle of Najaf in 2004, the Badr-led forces had held Najaf and Kerbala, the Shia Vatican, though not nearby Kufa where Muqtada was in control. Politically, SIIC was very powerful as the mainstay of prime minister Maliki's government and the preferred party of Grand Ayatollah Ali al-Sistani and the *marji'iya*. Remarkably, SIIC even had good relations with the US, though many Iraqis believed the party was still effectively controlled from Tehran. It had the resources to buy political and military support. For instance, when the Mehdi Army, far stronger in Baghdad than Badr, started burning SIIC offices in August 2007 Badr responded by hiring a thousand tough tribal mercenaries from Amara province and bussing them to Baghdad.[20]

There were intra-Shia clashes all over southern Iraq between Badr-controlled government forces and the Mehdi Army. These were essentially turf battles over control of political and economic resources and had nothing to do with the US occupation or the Shia–Sunni conflict. American forces generally supported SIIC and Badr, claiming hypocritically that they were simply backing up the Iraqi government, while knowing full well that the police and army were effectively militiamen in uniform. In Basra, from which the British were withdrawing, there was a complex three-cornered fight between SIIC, Fadhila and the Sadrists. Muqtada had no illusions about what the battle in Basra, which sits on top of some of the largest oil reserves in the world, was really about. When two of his commanders from Basra came to see him, he reputedly sniffed sourly and said:

'I smell gasoline.' But in Basra, unlike Baghdad, he was prepared to claim credit for armed resistance to the occupying force, which in this case was the British Army. His different attitude is probably explained by the fact that in Basra he knew the British were going. 'The British have given up and they know they will be leaving Iraq soon,' Muqtada said. 'They are retreating because of the resistance they have faced. Without that, they would have stayed much longer . . . The Mehdi Army has played an important role.'[21]

Muqtada's strategy towards the US was shaped by his assessment that, sooner or later, they would follow the British by drawing down their forces. It therefore made sense to avoid a military confrontation with them whatever the short-term provocations or losses through US raids. But SIIC, Badr and the al-Hakim family were not going to leave Iraq. The battle with them, which had started twenty-five years earlier, was for the future of Iraq and would have be fought to the finish. The Mehdi Army might lie low during US operations, but against the Badr militiamen they had to come out and fight. There were bloody clashes in Nasiriyah, Diwaniyah, Kut, Najaf and many other Shia cities and towns. Senior officials from all groups and parties were mysteriously and very professionally assassinated. They included two SIIC-affiliated governors of Diwaniyah and Muthanna, Sadrist officials in Hilla, and several senior aides of al-Sistani in Najaf.

The Sadrist–SIIC violence culminated at the end of August during the Shabaniyah festival in Kerbala marking the birth of Muhammad al-Mahdi, the Twelfth and last Shia Imam. Up to one million pilgrims were in the city, many of them Mehdi Army from Baghdad, who were highly identifiable since they were wearing their white martyr's shrouds over their black shirts. Some were carrying weapons to protect themselves from attack in Sunni towns along the road. Since the police and shrine guards in Kerbala were drawn from SIIC and Badr the situation was tailor-made for the clashes which predictably broke out around the shrines of Hussein and Abbas on 28 August. By the time the fighting ended fifty-one people had been killed and hundreds injured. A government committee later accused the Mehdi Army of starting the violence, but the claim relied on dubious evidence from the SIIC-controlled Kerbala police and a confession extracted by them from a single Sadrist prisoner.[22] The account of one Mehdi Army pilgrim from Baghdad may better explain the origins of the violence and chaos of that day. 'We left our cars in the outskirts of Kerbala and then walked,' he said. 'We asked the policemen what was going on and they said nothing. We entered the city in groups, all of us from the Mehdi Army, and we were clapping and singing religious songs or chants, though we had been forbidden from holding the "Tajeel prayer" which would have identified us as Sadrists. [The al-Tajeel prayer is only used by Sadrists. It begins with the words: 'I ask Allah to send Imam Mehdi to us soon and spread peace upon all mankind.'] The shrine guards came and asked us to stop our celebration and there was a quarrel with them, which led to a nine-year-old child being killed. Things escalated very fast after that. We were near the Imam al-Abbas shrine and we saw bullets being fired at us from the Imam al-Hussein shrine [400 yards away]. I was unexpectedly hit in my back and fell on the ground, but my friends pulled me away. I saw many people killed and wounded. The shrine guards opened heavy fire and others retaliated against them until they fled inside the shrine and closed the gates.'[23]

Muqtada responded to the violence by freezing all actions of the Mehdi Army for six months. All Sadrist offices were closed. He said he felt that the Mehdi Army's proclivity for violence was discrediting his movement and took further measures to assert central control by ordering that all Friday sermons should be centrally vetted to prevent calls for retaliation or vengeance. If Muqtada was to confront the US, the Iraqi government or his Shia rivals for power, he intended the battle to come at a moment of his own choosing.

CHAPTER SEVENTEEN

Muqtada

Muqtada al-Sadr is the most important and surprising figure to emerge in Iraq since the US invasion. He is the messianic leader of the religious and political movement of the impoverished Shia underclass whose lives were ruined by a quarter of a century of war, repression and sanctions. From the moment he unexpectedly appeared in the dying days of Saddam Hussein's regime, US emissaries and Iraqi politicians underestimated him. So far from being the 'firebrand cleric' as the western media often described him, he frequently proved astute and cautious in leading his followers. During the battle for Najaf with US Marines in 2004, the US 'surge' of 2007, and the escalating war with the Supreme Islamic Iraqi Council, he generally sought compromise rather than confrontation. So far from being the inexperienced young man whom his critics portrayed – when he first appeared they denigrated him as a *zatut* (an ignorant child in Iraqi dialect) – he was a highly experienced political operator who had worked in his father's office in Najaf since he was a teenager. He also had around him activist clerics of his own age or younger who had hands-on experience under Saddam of street politics within the Shia community. His grasp of what ordinary Iraqis felt was to prove far more sure than that of the politicians isolated in the 'Green Zone' in Baghdad.

Mass movements led by messianic leaders have a history of flaring up unexpectedly and then subsiding into insignificance. This could have happened to Muqtada and the

Sadrists, but did not because their political and religious platform had a continuous appeal for the Shia masses. From the moment that Saddam was overthrown, Muqtada rarely deviated from his open opposition to the US occupation, even when a majority of the Shia community was prepared to cooperate with the occupiers. As the years passed, however, disillusion with the occupation grew among the Shia until by September 2007 an opinion poll showed that 73 per cent of Shia thought that the presence of US forces in Iraq made the security situation worse and 55 per cent believed their departure would make a Shia–Sunni civil war less likely.[1] The US government, Iraqi politicians and the Western media habitually failed to take on board the extent to which hostility to the occupation drove Iraqi politics and, in the eyes of Iraqis, de-legitimised the leaders associated with it.

All governments in Baghdad failed after 2003. Almost no Iraqis supported Saddam Hussein as US troops advanced on Baghdad. Even his supposedly loyal Special Republican Guard units dissolved and went home. Iraqis were deeply conscious that their country sat on some of the world's largest oil reserves, but Saddam Hussein's Inspector Clouseau-like ability to make catastrophic errors in peace and war had reduced them to a state in which their children were stunted because they did not get enough to eat. The primal rage of the dispossessed in Iraq against the powers-that-be exploded in the looting of Baghdad when the old regime fell and the same fury possessed Muqtada's early supporters. Had life become easier in Shia Iraq in the coming years, this might have undermined the Sadrist movement. Instead, people saw their living standards plummet as provision of food rations, clean water and electricity faltered. Saddam's officials were corrupt enough, but the new government cowering in the Green Zone rapidly turned into a kleptocracy comparable to Nigeria or the Congo. Muqtada sensed the loathing with which the government was regarded and dodged in and out of government, enjoying some of the fruits of power while denouncing those who held it.

Muqtada's political intelligence is undoubted, but the personality of this highly secretive man is difficult to pin down. While his father and elder brothers lived he was in their shadow, and after they were assassinated in 1999 he had every reason to stress his lack of ability or ambition in order to give the *mukhabarat* less reason to kill him. As the son and son-in-law of two of Saddam Hussein's most dangerous opponents he was a prime suspect and his every move was watched. When Saddam fell Muqtada stepped forward to claim his forebears' political inheritance and consciously associated himself with them on every possible occasion. Posters showed Muqtada alongside Sadr I and Sadr II against a background of the Iraqi flag. There was more here than a leader exploiting his connection to a revered or respected parent. Muqtada persistently emphasised the Sadrist ideological legacy: puritanical Shia Islam mixed with anti-imperialism and populism.

The first time I thought seriously about Muqtada was a grim day in April 2003 when I heard that he was being accused of killing a friend of mine, Sayyid Majid al-Khoei, that intelligent and able man, with whom I had often discussed the future of Iraq. Whatever the involvement of Muqtada himself, which as we saw earlier is a matter of dispute, the involvement of the Sadrist supporters in the lynching is proven and was the start of a pattern that was to repeat itself over the years. Muqtada was always a man riding a tiger, sometimes presiding, sometimes controlling the mass movement he nominally led. His words and actions were often far apart. He appealed for Shia unity with the Sunni against the occupation, yet after the bombing of the Shia shrine in Samarra in February 2006, he was seen as an ogre by the Sunni, orchestrating the pogroms against them and failing to restrain the death squads of the Mehdi Army. The excuse that it was 'rogue elements' among his militiamen who were carrying out this slaughter is not convincing because the butchery was too extensive and too well organised to be the work of only marginal groups. But the

Sadrists and the Shia in general could argue that it was not they who had originally taken the offensive against the Sunni, and the Shia community endured massacres at the hands of al-Qaida for several years before their patience ran out. Muqtada had repeatedly demanded that Sunni political and religious leaders unequivocally condemn the horrific attacks by al-Qaida in Iraq on Shia civilians if he was to cooperate with them against the occupation. That they did not do so was a short-sighted failure on their part, since the Shia, who outnumbered the Sunni Arabs by three to one in Iraq, controlled the police and much of the army. Their retaliation, when it came, was bound to be devastating. Muqtada was criticised for not doing more, but neither he nor anybody else could have stopped the killing at the height of the battle for Baghdad in 2006. The Sunni and Shia communities were both terrified, and each mercilessly retaliated against the latest atrocity against their community. 'We try to punish those who carry out evil deeds in the name of the Mehdi Army,' says Hussein Ali, the former Mehdi Army leader. 'But there are a lot of Shia regions that are not easy to control and we ourselves, speaking frankly, are sometimes frightened by these great masses of people.'

US officials and journalists seldom showed much under-standing of Muqtada, even after Paul Bremer's disastrous attempt to crush him. There were persistent attempts to marginalise him or keep him out of government instead of trying to expand the Iraqi government's narrow support base to include the Sadrists. The first two elected Shia prime ministers, Ibrahim al-Jaafari and Nouri al-Maliki, came under intense pressure from Washington to sever or limit their connection with Muqtada. But government officials were not alone in being perplexed by the young cleric. In a lengthy article on him published in its December 2006 edition *Newsweek* admitted that 'Muqtada al-Sadr may end up deciding America's fate in Iraq'. But the best the magazine could do to assist its readers in understanding Muqtada was to suggest that they should 'think of him as a young Mafia don'.[2] Of course Muqtada was the complete opposite to the type of Iraqi leader whom proponents of the war in Washington had suggested would take over from Saddam Hussein. Instead of the smooth, dark-suited, English-speaking exiles, whom the White House had hoped would turn Iraq into a compliant US ally, Muqtada looked too much like a younger version of Ayatollah Khomeini.

Muqtada epitomised the central dilemma of the US in Iraq which it has never resolved. The problem was that the overthrow of Saddam Hussein and his Sunni regime was bound to be followed by elections which would produce a government dominated by the Shia allied to the Kurds. It soon became evident that the Shia parties that were going to triumph in any election would be Islamic parties and some would have close links to Iran. The Arab Sunni states were aghast at the sight of Iran's defeat in the Iran–Iraq war being reversed and spoke of a menacing 'Shia axis' developing in Iran, Iraq and Lebanon. Much of this was ignorance and paranoia on the part of the Arab leaders. Had the Iranians been tempted to make Iraq a client state they would have found the country as prickly a place for Iranians as it was to be for Americans. It was the US attempt to create an anti-Iranian Iraq that was to play into Iranian hands and produce the very situation that Washington was trying to avoid. The more Washington threatened air strikes on Iran because of its nuclear programme, the more the Iranians sought to make sure that it had the potential to strike back at American forces in Iraq. Sadr I believed before he was executed that he had been let down by Iran, Sadr II had bad relations with Tehran and at first Muqtada denounced his Shia opponents in SCIRI and the *marji'iya* as being Iranian stooges. But American pressure meant that the Sadrists had to look for help from Iran and in a military confrontation the Mehdi Army saw Iran as an essential source of weapons and military expertise.

On reappearing after his four months' disappearance in May 2007, Muqtada called for a united front of Sunni and

Shia and identified the US occupation and al-Qaida in Iraq as the enemies of both communities. The call was probably sincere, but it was also too late. Baghdad was now a largely Shia city and people were too frightened to go back to their old homes. The US 'surge' had contributed to the sharp drop in sectarian killings, but another reason was that the Shia had won and there were few mixed areas left. The US commander General David Petraeus could rightly claim that security was improving, but by the beginning of 2008 only 30,000 families out of the two million Iraqis who had fled to Syria and Jordan had returned to Iraq. Muqtada was the one Shia leader capable of uniting with the Sunni on a nationalist platform, but the Sunni Arabs of Iraq had never accepted that their rule was ended. If Sunni and Shia could not live in the same street they could hardly share a common identity.

The political and military landscape of Iraq changed in 2007 as the Sunni population turned on al-Qaida. This started before the 'surge', but it was still an important development. Al-Qaida's massive suicide bombs targeting civilians had been the main fuel for Shia–Sunni sectarian warfare since 2003. The Sunni Arabs and many of the insurgent groups had turned against al-Qaida after it tried to monopolise power within the Sunni community at the end of 2006 by declaring the Islamic State of Iraq. Crucial in the change was al-Qaida's attempt to draft one son from every Sunni family into its ranks. By the autumn of 2007 the US military command in Baghdad were trumpeting successes over al-Qaida, saying it had been largely eliminated in Anbar, Baghdad and Diyala. But the Sunni Arab fighters, by now armed and paid for by the US, did not owe their prime loyalty to the Iraqi government. Muqtada might speak of new opportunities for pan-Iraqi opposition to the US occupation. But many anti-al-Qaida Sunni fighters had quite different ideas. They wanted to reverse the Shia victory in the battle of Baghdad in 2006. A new breed of American-supported Sunni warlords was emerging. One of them, called Abu Abed, formerly a member of the insurgent Islamic Army, operates in the Amariya district in west Baghdad. He is a commander of the US-backed 'Amariya Knights' whom the US calls 'Concerned Citizens'. His aims show that the rise of the new Sunni militias may mark only a new stage in a sectarian civil war. 'Amariya is just the beginning,' says Abu Abed. 'After we finish with al-Qaida here, we will turn towards our main enemy, the Shia militias. I will liberate Jihad [the mixed Sunni–Shia area near Amariya taken over by the Mehdi Army], then Saadiya and the whole of west Baghdad.'³

The al-Sadr family has an extraordinary record of resistance to Saddam Hussein for which they paid a heavy price. One of the grossest of US errors in Iraq was to try to marginalise him and his movement. Had he been part of the political process from the beginning then the chances of creating a peaceful, prosperous Iraq would have been greater. In any real accommodation between Shia and Sunni the Sadrists must play a central part. Muqtada probably represented his constituency of millions of poor Shia better than anybody else could have done, but he never wholly controlled his own movement. He never created as well-disciplined a force as Hezbollah in Lebanon. None of his ambitions for reconciliation for the Sunni would take wing unless the Mehdi Army ceased to be identified with death squads and sectarian cleansing. The war in Iraq has gone on longer than World War I and, while violence diminished in the second half of 2007, nothing was resolved. The differences between Shia and Sunni, the disputes within the Shia and Sunni communities and antagonism against the US occupation were as great as ever. The only way Muqtada, the Sadrists and the Mehdi Army could create confidence among the Sunni that he means what he says would be to take them back voluntarily into areas in Baghdad and elsewhere from which they have been driven, but there is no sign of this happening. The disintegration of Iraq has probably gone too far for the country to exist as more than a loose federation.

Notes

CHAPTER I

1 *The Succession to Muhammad: A study of the early Caliphate* by Wilferd Madelung (Cambridge University Press, Cambridge 1997) p. 308.
2 AP 2 January 2007.
3 I asked Haider al-Safi and Bassim Abdul-Rahman in February 2007 to write separately their own accounts of what had happened to us to cross-check my own recollections.
4 UNHCR press briefing by Jennifer Pagonis, Palais des Nations, Geneva, 5 June 2007.

CHAPTER 2

1 Interview with Sheikh Ali, a veteran Sadrist leader, Baghdad, August 2007.
2 *The Heirs of the Prophet Muhammad and the Roots of the Sunni-Shia schism* by Barnaby Rogerson (Abacus, London 2006) pp. 339–45.
3 *Faith and Power: The politics of Islam* by Edward Mortimer (Faber and Faber, London 1982) pp. 39–55.
4 www.Sistani.org, 3 June 2007. There are four different questions asking if it is permitted to play chess, all of which receive the same negative answer.
5 *The Shi'ite Movement in Iraq* by Faleh A. Jabar (Saqi Books, London 2003) pp. 185–98.
6 *Iraq: Land of Two Rivers* by Gavin Young (Collins, London 1980) pp. 123–4.
7 Jabar, *The Shi'ite Movement in Iraq*, p. 191.
8 *The Shi'is of Iraq* by Yizhak Nakash (Princeton University Press, Princeton NJ 2003) pp 3–9.

9 Nakash, *The Shi'is of Iraq*, p. 14.
10 Jabar, *The Shi'ite Movement in Iraq*, p. 55.

CHAPTER 3

1 *Iraq's Muqtada al-Sadr: Spoiler or Stabiliser?* International Crisis Group report no. 55, 11 July 2006.
2 Interview, Baghdad, May 2007.
3 *The Shi'ite Movement in Iraq* by Faleh A. Jabar (Saqi Books, London 2003) pp. 226–34.
4 Answer to written questions by Jafar al-Sadr, son of Muhammad Baqir, Baghdad, August 2007.
5 *The Old Social Classes and the Revolutionary Movement in Iraq* by Hanna Batatu (Princeton University Press, Princeton NJ 1978) p. 1,141.
6 Interview, Najaf, 6 June 2007
7 Interview with Ghanim Jawad of the al-Khoei Foundation, London, 11 June 2007.
8 Hussein al-Shami interview, Najaf, June 2007.
9 *Saddam Hussein: The Man, the Cause and the Future* by Fu'ad Matar (Third World Centre, London 1981) p. 70.
10 Interview with Kamran Karadaghi, Iraqi journalist, June 1997.
11 Interview with Hussein al-Shami, Najaf, 5 June 2007.
12 Ibid.
13 Transcript of videotape of meeting shown on WGBH, *Frontline*, 26 June 1991.
14 Jabar, *The Shi'ite Movement in Iraq*, pp. 206-7.
15 Interview with student of Baqir, Najaf, June 2007.
16 Interview with Hussein al-Shami, 5 June 2007.
17 Jabar, *The Shi'ite Movement in Iraq*, pp. 208–15.
18 International Crisis Group interview, Baghdad, December 2005.
19 ICG Report, *Iraq's Muqtada al-Sadr: Spoiler or Stabiliser?* 11 July 2006.
20 Jabar, *The Shi'ite Movement in Iraq*, pp. 280–93.
21 Ibid., 227–32.
22 Answer to written questions by Jafar al-Sadr, Baghdad, August 2007.
23 Interview with Ak Shaiek, Najaf, June 2007; also account of Muhammad Reda al-Noumani who was with Baqir in his final days.
24 Matar, *Saddam Hussein*, pp. 130–5.
25 'Iraq's Oppressed Minority' by Andrew Cockburn, *Smithsonian Magazine*, December 2003.
26 Interview with Iraqi intelligence officer, May 2007.

27 Interview with Najem al-Sadi, nephew of the Iraqi intelligence
     officer, June 2007

CHAPTER 4

 1 DIA report obtained under Freedom of Information Act by
     National Security Archive. *Independent*, London, 12 December
     1992.
 2 *Saddam Hussein: The Man, the Cause and the Future* by Fu'ad
     Matar (Third World Centre, London 1981) p. 134.
 3 *The Shi'ite Movement in Iraq* by Faleh A. Jabar (Saqi Books,
     London 2003) p. 346.
 4 *The Great War for Civilisation: The Conquest of the Middle East*
     by Robert Fisk (Fourth Estate, London 2005) p. 217.
 5 Matar, *Saddam Hussein*, 131–48.
 6 Interview, Baghdad, December 1990.
 7 Interview with Jafar Ali, Baghdad, June 2007.
 8 Interview with Muhammad Yasin, Baghdad, June 2007.
 9 Fisk, *The Great War for Civilisation,* p. 222
10 Interview with Jafar Ali, Baghdad, June, 2007.
11 Interview with officer, Baghdad, June 2007.
12 Interview with Rasheed Abdul Gafoor, Baghdad, June 2007.
13 Interview, Najaf, May 2007.
14 *Iraq's Road to War* edited by Amatzia Baram and Barry Rubin (St
     Martin's Press, New York 1993) p. 52.
15 Interview with Ghanim Jawad of the al-Khoei Foundation,
     London, June 2007.
16 Interview with cleric close to Muhammad Baqir al-Sadr, Najaf,
     June 2007.
17 Interview with Ghanim Jawad, 25 June, 2007.
18 *Faith and Power: The politics of Islam* by Edward Mortimer
     (Faber and Faber, London 1982) pp. 370–1.
19 *Dictionary of the Middle East* by Dilip Hiro (MacMillan, London
     1995) p. 164.
20 Interview with Ghanim Jawad, June 2007.
21 *Endless Torment: the 1991 Uprising in Iraq and its Aftermath*,
     report by Human Rights Watch (New York 1992) p. 28.
22 Interview with Sayyid Muhammad al-Musawi, Najaf, 1 June
     2007.
23 Interview with Professor at Najaf University, June 2007.
24 Interview with survivor from Najaf, April 2007.
25 Interview with Ghanim Jawad, London, June 2007.

CHAPTER 5

1   Meeting with Grand Ayatollah al-Khoei, Kufa, April 1991

2   *Endless Torment: the 1991 Uprising in Iraq and its Aftermath*, report by Human Rights Watch (New York 1992) p. 49.

3   Interview with Sayyid Majid al-Khoei, London, 2 June 1998.

4   Interview with Gen Wafiq al-Samarrai, head of Iraqi Military Intelligence, London, 3 October 1998.

5   Interview with Sanaa Muhammad, Baghdad, 27 June 2007.

6   Interview with Hussein al-Shahristani by Andrew Cockburn, Tehran, 10 March 1998.

7   Interview with Colonel Othman, former army officer, Baghdad, 28 June 2007.

8   Interview with Brigadier Ali, London, 13 March 1998.

9   Interview with Captain Azad Shirwan, Salahudin, June 1991.

10 *Why the Intifada Failed* by Faleh 'Abd al-Jabbar in *Iraq Since the Gulf War*, editor Fran Hazelton (Zed Books, London 1993) p. 107.

11 HRW, *Endless Torment* p. 42.

12 Interviews, Basra, 22 April 1991.

13 HRW, *Endless Torment* p. 42.

14 Interview with General Wafiq al-Samarrai, London, 3 October 1998.

15 *Cruelty and Silence* by Kanan Makiya (W. W. Norton, New York 1993) p. 61.

16 Interview with Brigadier Ali, London, 13 March 1998.

17 Makiya, *Cruelty and Silence*, p. 68.

18 Interview with Sanaa Muhammad, Baghdad, 27 June 2007.

19 Makiya, *Cruelty and Silence*, p 74.

20 Interview with Ali Muhammad, Kut, 30 June 2007.

21 Interview with Sayyid Majid al-Khoei, London, 2 June 1998.

22 Interview with Brigadier Ali, London, 13 March 1998.

23 *The General's War* by Michael R. Gordon and General Bernard E. Trainor (Little, Brown and Company, New York 1994) pp. 518–19.

24 The proportion of Shia to Sunni in Baghdad is a vexed question. Sunni often claim that they are equal in numbers to the Shia but the referendum on the constitution in October 2005 and the general election two months later indicated that Shia made up at least 70 per cent of the capital's population and possibly more.

25 Gordon and Trainor, *The Generals' War*, p. 517, cite President Bush writing on 13 June 1994.

26 Gordon and Trainor, *The Generals' War*, p. s 516.

27 HRW, *Endless Torment* p. 37.

28 Ibid.
29 Interview with Sayyid Majid al-Khoei, London, 2 June 1998.
30 Interview with Saad Jabr, London, March 12 1998.
31 Faleh 'Abd al-Jabbar, *Why the Intifada Failed* pp. 108–9.
32 Interview with Sanaa Muhammad, Baghdad, 27 June 2007.
33 Interview with Colonel Othman, Baghdad, 28 June 2007.
34 Interview with Hussein, Baghdad, 3 July 2007.

CHAPTER 6

1 Interview with Sanaa Muhammad, Baghdad, 27 June 2007.
2 HRW, *Endless Torment* p. 51.
3 Interview with Colonel Othman, Baghdad, 28 June 2007.
4 *The Mass Graves of al-Mahawil: the Truth Uncovered*, report by Human Rights Watch (New York, May 2003) pp. 10–11.
5 HRW, *The Mass Graves*, pp. 11–12.
6 HRW, *The Mass Graves*, p. 13.
7 HRW, *Endless Torment* p. 44
8 Interview with Dr al-Rawi, Basra, April 1991.
9 HRW, *Endless Torment* p. 44.
10 Interview with friend of Jassem, Basra, July 2007.

CHAPTER 7

1 *The Occupation of Iraq* by Ali Allawi (New Haven CT, Yale University Press 2007) p. 54.
2 Interview with Ali Hussein Khidr, Baghdad, July 2007.
3 Interview with Sheikh Yassin al-Assadi, June 2007.
4 Interview with Muhammad Hassan Ibrahim, July 2007.
5 Muhammad Sadiq al-Sadr's CD, 1998.
6 Allawi, *The Occupation of Iraq*, p. 57.
7 Answer to written questions by Jafar al-Sadr, Baghdad, September 2007.
8 *Out of the Ashes: The Resurrection of Saddam Hussein*, by Andrew and Patrick Cockburn, (New York, Harper Collins 1999) pp. 132–3. The Baghdad study of children is in the *Lancet*, 346, 2 December 1995.
9 Cockburn and Cockburn, *Out of the Ashes*, p. 290.
10 Allawi, *The Occupation of Iraq* p. 57.
11 *Christian Science Monitor*, 27 April 2004, 'Sadr the agitator: like father, like son' by Dan Murphy.
12 Interview with Sheikh Yassin al-Assadi, June 2007.
13 Conversation with Haider al-Safi, August 2007.
14 Conversation with Ghaith Ahad Awab, June 2007.

15 Answer to written questions by Jafar al-Sadr, Baghdad, September 2007.

16 Interview with Muhammad Hassan Ibrahim, July 2007.

17 Interview with Ali Hussein Khidr, July 2007.

18 *Iraq's Muqtada al-Sadr: Spoiler or Stabiliser?* International Crisis Group report no. 55, 11 July 2006, p. 5, footnote 29.

19 Interview with Yassin Sajad, Sadr City, July 2007.

20 *Iraq's Muqtada al-Sadr: Spoiler or Stabiliser?* p. 5.

21 Interview with Sheikh Yassin al-Assadi, June 2007.

CHAPTER 8

1 Interview with Sheikh Akram al-Assadi, former *hawza* student, 5 July 2007.

2 Ibid.

3 Interview with Muhammad Salem, July 2007.

4 *Tribes and Power: Nationalism and ethnicity in the Middle East* edited by Faleh A. Jabar and Hosham Dawod (Saqi Books, London 2003) pp. 90–6.

5 Jabar and Dawod, *Tribes and Power*, p. 95.

6 'The Sadrist Movement' by Mahan Abedin, *The Middle East Intelligence Bulletin* vol. 5, no 7, July 2003.

7 Interview with Ali Hussein Khidr, 2007.

8 Tape-recording made by Muhammad Sadiq al-Sadr in 1998.

9 Interview with Muhammad Hassan Ibrahim, July 2007

10 Abedin, 'The Sadrist Movement', p. 3.

11 Interview with Ali Hussein Kidr, July 2007.

12 Ibid.

13 *Iraq's Muqtada al-Sadr: Spoiler or Stabiliser?* International Crisis Group report no. 55, 11 July 2006, p. 4, footnote 24.

14 HRW, *World Report*, 1999, p. 2.

15 Interview with Sheikh Yassin al-Assadi, July 2007.

16 Interview with Hassan Mustafa, Najaf, August 2007.

17 Interview with Ali Hussein Khidr, July 2007.

18 Interview with Mustafa al-Khadimi, London, 8 July 2007.

19 *The Times*, February 28, 1999.

20 Interview with Sajad Ali, Baghdad, July 2007.

21 'Ali Hassan al-Majid and the Basra Massacre of 1999', HRW report, February 2005, pp. 9–10.

22 Interview with Jassem, Basra, July 2007.

23 Interview with Tariq Mahmud, Baghdad, July 2007, relating what he was told by an eyewitness in Qom at the time.

24 *Iraq's Muqtada al-Sadr: Spoiler or Stabiliser?*, p. 6, footnote 17.

CHAPTER 9

1 'Understanding Muqtada al-Sadr' by Nimrod Raphaeli, *Middle East Quarterly*, Fall 2004, p. 2.
2 *World Report*, HRW, 1999, p. 2.
3 Interview with Dr Hassan Mustafa, Najaf, July 2007.
4 Interview with Sheikh Ali, Baghdad, August 2007.
5 Raphaeli, 'Understanding Muqtada al-Sadr', p. 2 .
6 *Iraq's Muqtada al-Sadr: Spoiler or Stabiliser?* International Crisis Group report no. 55, 11 July 2006, p. 6.
7 Interview with Sheikh Ali, Baghdad, 2007.
8 Answer to written questions by Jafar al-Sadr, Baghdad, September 2007.
9 Interview with Sheikh Ali, Baghdad, 2007.
10 ICG interview, Najaf, 26 June 2007.
11 Muqtada al-Sadr interviewed on al-Jazeera on 18 February 2006. Translated with a commentary by Juan Cole in *Informed Comment*, www.juancole.com, on 19 February 2006.
12 Interview with a Sadrist militant, Baghdad, August 2007.
13 Interview with Haidar Abdul Hussein and Abdul Hassan Ali, March 2007.
14 Interview with Abu Hatem, Amara, June 2003.
15 'Iraqi Shi'ites under Occupation,' ICG Report, 9 September 2003, pp. 15–20.
16 Interview with Abbas, Baghdad, August 2007.

CHAPTER 10

1 Interview with Ma'ad Fayadh, London, May 2003.
2 Interview with Ma'ad Fayadh, August, 2007.
3 *Sunday Telegraph*, 14 April 2003.
4 Interview with Abdul Hassan al-Khafaji, London, May 2003.
5 Interview with Radwan Hussein al-Rufaie, May 2003.
6 Interview with Sheikh Salah Bilal, London, May 2003.
7 Interview with Sheikh Ali, Baghdad, August 2007.

CHAPTER 11

1 Interview with Abbas, Baghdad, August 2007.
2 Interview with Sadrist militant, Baghdad, August 2007.
3 Interview with Abbas, Baghdad, August 2007.
4 Interview with Sadrist militant, Baghdad, August, 2007.
5 Interview with Dr Ahmed, Najaf, August 2007.
6 'Iraq's oppressed minority,' by Andrew Cockburn, *Smithsonian*,

December 2003.

7 Informed Comment, www.juancole.com, 17 April 2003.
8 'The Sadrist Movement' by Mahan Abedin, *The Middle East Intelligence Bulletin* vol. 5, no 7, July 2003.
9 Interview with Haider al-Safi, August 2007.
10 Abedin, 'The Sadrist Movement'.
11 'Iraq's Shi'ites Under Occupation', ICG report, 9 September 2003, citing interview with Muhammad Fartousi, 21 May 2003.
12 Interview with Sheikh Ali, Baghdad, August 2007.
13 Abedin, 'The Sadrist Movement'.
14 AFP cited by Informed Comment, www.juancole.com, 15 April 2003.
15 'Understanding Muqtada al-Sadr' by Nimrod Raphaeli, *Middle East Quarterly*, Fall 2004, p. 2.
16 Abedin, 'The Sadrist Movement'.
17 Interview with Sheikh Ali, Baghdad, August 2007.
18 *Insurgent Iraq: al Zarqawi and the new generation* by Loretta Napoleoni (Constable, London 2005) p. 157.
19 Raphaeli, 'Understanding Muqtada al-Sadr', p. 2.

CHAPTER 12

1 *My Year in Iraq: The struggle to build a future of hope* by L. Paul Bremer III with Malcolm McConnell, (Simon and Schuster, New York 2006) p. 317.
2 Bremer, *My Year in Iraq*, pp. 121–2.
3 *The Occupation of Iraq* by Ali Allawi (Yale University Press, New Haven CT 2007) p. 211.
4 Bremer, *My Year in Iraq*, pp. 191–2.
5 Allawi, *The Occupation of Iraq*, pp. 267–8.
6 'Iraq Shi'ites Under Occupation', ICG Report, 9 September 2003, p. 17.
7 Interview with Professor Fadhel Muhammad, September 2007.
8 Interview with Munawar Mashelah, Baghdad, August 2007.
9 Institute of War and Peace Reporting, Kerbala, 4 March 2004.
10 Informed Comment, www.juancole.com, 3 April 2004.
11 Bremer, *My Year in Iraq*, p. 318.
12 *Occupational Hazards: My time governing Iraq* by Rory Stewart (Picador, London 2006) pp. 341–2.
13 Informed Comment, www.juancole.com,, 4–7 April 2004.
14 Interview with Ali Ahmed, Baghdad, August 2007.
15 Informed Comment, www.juancole.com, 9 April 2004.
16 Interview with Ali Ahmed, Baghdad, August 2007.

CHAPTER 13

1 Interview with Abbas Fadhil, Baghdad, August 2007.
2 Interview with Ali Ahmed, Baghdad, August 2007.
3 Institute for War and Peace Reporting, 13 July 2004.
4 Interview with Abbas Fadhil, Baghdad, August 2007.
5 'Understanding Muqtada al-Sadr' by Nimrod Raphaeli, *Middle East Quarterly*, Fall 2004.
6 Interview with Abbas Fadhil, Baghdad, August 2007.
7 Associated Press, 6 August 2004.
8 BBC, 7 August 2004.
9 *Guardian*, 9 August 2004.
10 Informed Comment, www.juancole.com, 14 August 2004.
11 Interview with Mowaffaq al-Rubai'e, National Security Adviser, Baghdad, May 2007. The story was first mentioned in *The Occupation of Iraq* by Ali Allawi (Yale University Press, New Haven CT 2007) pp. 324–5.
12 Interview with Abbas Kodeiri, Baghdad, August 2007.
13 Institute for War and Peace Reporting, 6 September 2004.
14 Informed Comment, www.juancole.com, 25 August 2004.
15 Ibid., 15 August 2004.
16 Reuters, 21 August 2004.
17 Interview with Dr Ahmed, Najaf, July 2007.
18 Ali Allawi, *The Occupation of Iraq*, p. 328.
19 Ibid., p. 330.
20 CNN, 4 December 2005.

CHAPTER 14

1 Interview with Abbas Kodeiri, Baghdad, August 2007.
2 Interview with Sabah Khadim, London, September 2007.
3 *Iraq's Muqtada al-Sadr: Spoiler or Stabiliser?* International Crisis Group report no. 55, 11 July 2006.
4 Interview with Sheikh Ali, Baghdad, August 2007.
5 Interview with Sheikh Ali, August 2007.
6 Interview with Abbas Kodeiri, Baghdad, August 2007.
7 Interview with Muqtada al-Sadr, al-Arabiya, 13 January 2006.
8 Interview with Muqtada al-Sadr, al-Jazeera, 18 February 2006.
9 Interview with Hussein Ali, Baghdad, September 2007.
10 Interview with Abbas Fadhil, Baghdad, August 2007.
11 Interview with Sheikh Ali, Baghdad, August 2007.
12 Interview with Salim Shehab, Baghdad, September 2007.
13 Interview with Manale Youssif, Baghdad, September 2007.
14 Interview with Dr Mahmoud Qassim, Baghdad, September 2007.

15   Interview with Abbas Fadhil, Baghdad, August 2007.
16   Interview with Shia woman, Baghdad, September 2007.
17   Interview with Manale Youssif, Baghdad, September 2007.
18   Interview with Muhammad Tariq, September 2007.

CHAPTER 15

 1   Letter from Bassim Abdul-Rahman, September 2007.
 2   Interview with Hussein Ali, Baghdad, September 2007.
 3   *New York Times*, 22 December 2006.
 4   'Security in Iraq still elusive' by Leila Fadel,
     www.mcclatchydc.com, 7 September 2007.
 5   Account by Haider al-Safi, London, September 2007
 6   Interview with Sheikh Ali, Baghdad, August 2007.
 7   Interview with Hussein Ali, former Mehdi Army commander,
     September 2007.
 8   Interview with resident in Hamraa district, Baghdad, September
     2007.
 9   Interview with Salim Shehab, Baghdad, October 2007.
10   Email from sheikh in Balad, August 2006
11   *New York Times*, 22 December 2006.
12   Email from sheikh in Balad, August 2006.
13   'Inside the Mehdi Army death squads' by Phil Sands, *Jane's
     Terrorism and Security Monitor*, 14 February 2007.
14   Iraqi body count citing news reports, iCasualties.org, 2 October
     2007.
15   Sands, 'Inside the Mehdi Army death squads', passim.
16   'Chilling Stories from the Mehdi Army' by Leila Fadel,
     www.mcclatchydc.com, 22 June 2007.

CHAPTER 16

 1   Interview with Hussein Ali, Mehdi Army militant, October 2007.
 2   Interview with *La Repubblica*, 19 January 2007.
 3   *The Occupation of Iraq* by Ali Allawi (Yale University Press, New
     Haven CT, 2007) p. 443, citing *New York Times*, 28 March 2006.
 4   Interview with Ahmed Chalibi, Baghdad, May 2007.
 5   Allawi, *The Occupation of Iraq*, p. 450.
 6   President Bush State of the Union Address, 23 January 2007.
 7   Interview with Hussein Ali, former Mehdi Army leader,
     September 2007.
 8   Ibid.
 9   Ibid.
10   *Financial Times*, 17 May 2007.

11 Interview with Hoshyar Zebari, Baghdad, May 2007.

12 Iraqslogger.com, 5 October 2007.

13 'Iraq: Food rationing system filing as Ramadan approaches' IRIN, UN Office for Coordination of Humanitarian Affairs, September, 2007.

14 'Fadhila leader slams Iraqi politicians' by Zeyad Kasim, Iraqslogger.com, 25 May 2007.

15 Reuters, Kufa, 25 May 2007. *New York Times,* 18 July 2007.

16 Interview with Mehdi Army militant, October 2007.

17 'Second Samarra Bombing Strengthens Status of Moqtada al-Sadr' by Babak Rahimi, *Terrorism Focus,* IV.26, Jamestown Foundation, 26 June 2007.

18 'Al-Sadr Radio Interview decries US presence in Iraq', by Leila Fadel, www.mcclatchydc.com, 28 August 2007.

19 Interview with Muqtada al-Sadr, Kufa, *Independent,* 20 August 2007.

20 'Hired Tribesmen Save SIIC in Sadr Stronghold', Iraqslogger.com, 31 August 2007.

21 Interview with Muqtada al-Sadr, Kufa, *Independent,* 20 August 2007.

22 *Washington Post,* 7 October 2007.

23 Interview with Mehdi Army member, Baghdad, October 2007.

CHAPTER 17

1 ABC/BBC/NTV poll, September, 2007

2 'The Most dangerous Man in Iraq: The Shi'ite cleric Moqtada al-Sadr', *Newsweek,* 4 December 2006.

3 'Meet Abu Abed: The US's new ally against al-Qaida' by Ghaith Abdul Ahad, *Guardian,* 10 November 2007.

Index